Value-Oriented Leadership in Theory and Practice

Jessica Lange
Editors

Value-Oriented Leadership in Theory and Practice

Concepts - Study results - Practical insights

Springer

Editor
Jessica Lange
WERTEmanagement Dr. Jessica Lange
Bokholt-Hanredder, Germany

ISBN 978-3-662-65882-6 ISBN 978-3-662-65883-3 (eBook)
https://doi.org/10.1007/978-3-662-65883-3

This book is a translation of the original German edition „Werteorientierte Führung in Theorie und Praxis" by Lange, Jessica, published by Springer-Verlag GmbH, DE in 2021. The translation was done with the help of artificial intelligence (machine translation by the service DeepL.com). A subsequent human revision was done primarily in terms of content, so that the book will read stylistically differently from a conventional translation. Springer Nature works continuously to further the development of tools for the production of books and on the related technologies to support the authors.

This Springer imprint is published by the registered company Springer-Verlag GmbH, DE, part of Springer Nature.
The registered company address is: Heidelberger Platz 3, 14197 Berlin, Germany

Preface

Good to have you here! Value orientation is an important topic that is receiving more and more attention, and above all depends on the right understanding and awareness. With regard to value-oriented leadership, managers often instinctively do many things right. Nevertheless, it is only from an active awareness of this that even better use of this potential can be made. This book aims to create this awareness with exciting contributions from knowledgeable personalities from theory and practice. In this way, you can put this rather elusive subject on a solid footing. This book goes from deep theory for a comprehensive understanding to real practice in everyday application.

You can choose the topics that interest you and really help you. In addition to many basic principles, you will also receive diverse and proven practical tips. Because only through application can value orientation be lived and the positive effects unfold. Perhaps you are already implementing some of the measures, but the contents of the book will help you to better understand them. Perhaps you can now approach value orientation more holistically and implement it systematically thanks to the information in the book. What used to be just a gut feeling can possibly be confirmed and substantiated with this book. Or you may have had the basics of value orientation in your head for a long time but have not yet managed to bridge the gap to practice, or only partially. No matter in which direction and in which form, we hope to give you useful help with this book. A special feature of this edited book is that the chapters do not simply stand one behind the other, but are actively connected by suitable intermediate texts, thus creating a "large whole" on this major topic.

In doing so, I explicitly ask you to work through this book not in a linear fashion but based on your interests and problems. What do you want to know? What do you need? For this purpose, you will need an introductory article and references to chapters that fit the content always at the beginning. The intermediate texts between the three parts of the book should also help you to find out which chapters are helpful for you right now, and which you might save for later reading. For this reason, I will also present the structure of the book below, clustered by topic rather than linear. Pick out your favorite topics like you would a box of chocolates.

If you are interested in a deep understanding of the fundamentals or also current study results, you will find valuable information in the chapters by Priddat, Becker, Loose, and Preuß (employee loyalty in SMEs) and Preuß (value perceptions of employees of the 50-plus generation). Priddat and Becker provide you with a scientific basis for the concept of values, the social construct of leadership, and the cultural anchoring of value orientation. Here you can deepen your understanding of values and value-oriented leadership and put it on a sound basis. In the chapter by Loose and Preuß, you will find an empirical study on employee loyalty, which is also closely related to value-oriented leadership and is often a desired consequence of value orientation in the company. In the article by Preuß, you will learn more about the scientifically based perception of values of older employees aged 50 and over. An important group in the operational everyday life, which remains however in many considerations of predominantly younger generations and their requirements unnoticed. Value orientation refers to all employees, not only to young professionals.

If the question of the conceptual implementation of value-based leadership in the company is more exciting for you, the topic area of the second part of the book is recommended. Structure-based application of sub-areas of value-based leadership can be found in Ehrenberger et al. and Herold and Schlegel. In the chapter by Ehrenberger, Mäder, and Berna, you can learn more about the possibilities of managing and controlling value-oriented leadership using non-financial internal control systems. Herold and Schlegel, on the other hand, extend prevailing structures of compliance management to include values and integrity. A wonderful mix of structure-based and application-oriented content is offered in the chapter by Lutz and Nummer. Knowledge about organizational behavior helps to understand and actually implement value-based leadership. For the implementation of value-based leadership and why mission statements are far from sufficient for this, you will find a lot of helpful and practical information in Lüthy's contribution. Here, the connection between value-oriented corporate and personal leadership is also well recognizable.

Those who are looking for more practice-oriented texts with a concrete application or even everyday relevance will find what they are looking for in the last part of the book, Practical Thinking, in the chapters by Wagner, Bräuer, and Roth. Wagner provides a topical chapter for reflection on one's own personal values. Then we are really from the practice for the practice in the chapters of Bräuer and Roth. Bräuer tells you in a practical, honest, and authentic way about her experiences in the concrete implementation of value-oriented leadership in everyday business. Roth also reports just as honestly about the problems encountered when introducing value-oriented leadership. You can certainly take away a lot for your own practice from these experiences and obstacles.

Let's start now and put together the big puzzle of value orientation. Have fun!

Hamburg, Germany

Jessica Lange

Contents

Introduction to Value-Oriented Leadership

Jessica Lange

Abstract

The public discussion constantly shows managers and companies that the importance of values is increasing. In the case of comparable products, other differentiating features must be created as incentives to buy. In management relationships, trust and appreciation play a greater role due to changed framework conditions (e.g., new demands of employees, shortage of skilled workers, culture of trust, home office, and virtuality). However, this also gives rise to uncertainty as to how to deal with this growing importance. Do I necessarily need values to be successful in competition? Do values not contradict profit and the market economy? Can I still lead well today without a value orientation? Don't monetary results count more than values? Are values a "nice-to-have" or a "must-have"? These questions and others will be approached in a goal-oriented, understandable, and practical way.

Before we start with the actual topic of value-oriented leadership, we will take a brief look at what values actually are and why they are useful or necessary. In value-based leadership, we will later distinguish between the areas of corporate and personal leadership, each of which has its own content. We will examine all areas of leadership in a practical and application-oriented manner. Finally, there will be some tips for self-reflection as well as small inspirations for practice.

J. Lange (✉)
WERTEmanagement Dr. Jessica Lange, FOM Hochschule für Oekonomie und Management, Hamburg, Germany
e-mail: info@wertemanagement-lange.de

J. Lange (ed.), *Value-Oriented Leadership in Theory and Practice*,
https://doi.org/10.1007/978-3-662-65883-3_1

1 What Are Values?

So, what are values actually? In order to be value-oriented, one must of course first understand this. Values arise from the evaluation of behavior and thus provide a social orientation. What is evaluated as positive is more likely to be repeated than negative evaluations. Thus, values within groups (e.g., family, circle of friends, colleagues, team of co-workers) provide a stabilization of behavior and expectable expectations (Luhmann 1984).

A special feature of values and also of working with them is that they are only partially visible in their presence and effect. The directly communicated corporate values (insofar as they exist at all) are only the "tip of the iceberg." The main part of the values that are lived is informal and invisible (Zimmer 2015, p. 26). If you want to work with these, you must first make them visible through targeted analyses. A good instrument for this is employee surveys. These can be conducted holistically and structurally at the level of the overall organization, but also in the direct day-to-day management with each employee. Ask your employees how they would describe the company or its identity in just three words. If the company were a person, what would that person be like? The more values you make visible, the easier it is to observe them in daily actions and thus to develop the corporate culture positively.

A problem in working with values is also the imprecision of language. Every person interprets their values differently in terms of content and meaning, and this can often only be partially expressed by linguistic terms. This creates a lot of room for misunderstanding and conflict. While "reliability" for one person is also connected with absolute punctuality, for another person, it is only about keeping promises within a larger framework.

Values basically have an effect on different levels of social and also economic life. From a management perspective, two levels in particular need to be considered: the individual and the societal (in relation to the company). On the individual level, the personal values of the manager (self-reflection) must be questioned, and the personal values of the employees managed must be perceived and taken seriously. On the societal level, the question arises as to whether the personal values fit in with the social system in which one works. Do the personal leadership values match the corporate culture and the general corporate values? Do the individual personal values of the managed employees fit with the individual personal values of the manager and also with the corporate culture? As you can see, value orientation as a leader is quite complex. *For more information, read the article by Dr. Hans-Jürgen Lutz and Dr. Daniel Nummer. Here, you will get to know the concept of organizational behavior and can derive a lot from it for the implementation of value-oriented leadership.*

In the understanding so far, we have worked out the status quo of values in their complexity at a certain point in time. Unfortunately, we have not yet finished with this. In addition, there is now the time aspect, the dynamics of values. Without major changes from inside or outside, values are quite stable in the long term. However, as soon as changes occur (e.g., changes in management, corporate strategy, or processes of change from outside, such as changes in legislation or market trends), adjustment processes also take place for values (Zimmer 2015, p. 29). And change is unfortunately becoming more and more the norm, which also entails constant processes of change in values. → *For more information on the dynamics, complexity, and polarity of values, read Günther Wagner's article, which relates value orientation to the global Corona pandemic of 2020.*

Values are formed by the individual in the collective, i.e., by every person in the company. Managers are usually more influential than individual employees. However, there may also be people without management responsibility who exert a particular influence. In change processes, the attitudes and ways of thinking of the people affected often change as well. This means nothing other than that the persons revise their own individual value structure in order to come to terms with the changes. Now perhaps other actions are important, right, and desired. So, the valuations of the actions have to be adjusted. When all people in the company do that – and hopefully in a similar direction, otherwise conflicts arise – the lived company values change. Conflicts are often (not always!) caused by different and incompatible values. A classic example of such a conflict is generational changes in family businesses. The previous generation wants nothing to change in the company, if possible, while the next generation often wants to introduce new ideas (Zimmer 2015, p. 29). → *For a deeper understanding of the concept of values, also read the article by Prof. Dr. Priddat.*

Due to the dynamics, it is recommended to critically review values on a regular basis (e.g., every 5 years). Do the communicated values still match the lived values? Do the values lived match what the company wants to be and where it should develop?

Despite their dynamism, however, values should not be confused with trends similar to fashion (Zimmer 2015, p. 31). Values reflect fundamental behaviors and identity characteristics, and these are not changed as frequently as the winter collection. Values should be defined from within rather than being overly adapted to external trends. If the company adapts to trends, then the values will also follow this path. But this only happens in the long term and not from one day to the next. That would not look very credible. A corporate identity is like a character, and you don't change it too often, do you? Authentic values that are actually lived in the company have the best effect. Permanent changes in the value structure cannot be incorporated into the corporate culture, the "DNA" of the company. Such processes need time. Otherwise, the new values will neither be understood nor accepted by your employees and thus not lived. A clear communication of so-called trend values to the outside would then bring you laughter only or doubters, and both are rather poison for a positive reputation.

One example of such a trend phenomenon that is suddenly found in many descriptions of companies is sustainability (Zimmer 2015, p. 31). Because this concept has a positive connotation in society, many companies now also want to benefit from these effects and present themselves as sustainable companies. It may be critically questioned how many of these companies have actually understood the term sustainability and actually live this concept from their identity and culture. Most business models are at most designed for economic sustainability, which only touches on the actual content of the concept. In addition to fully sustainable products (which are usually already non-existent), this includes, for example, sustainable production processes, sustainable human resources or financial policies, and serious contributions to the community. → *On the value perception of older employees with regard to the three dimensions of sustainability, also read the article by Prof. Dr. Marion Preuß.*

Finally, it remains to be determined what is exactly meant by value orientation. Now that we have discussed the concept of values in detail, we still need to penetrate orientation with regard to these values. It aims in two directions: at oneself and at the other persons with whom one interacts. In relation to oneself, value orientation means knowing one's own values and acting according to them. In common parlance, this is often referred to as being authentic. In relation to other people, value orientation means perceiving, accepting, and considering the values of my counterpart, as a manager, for example, granting employees freedom of action so that they can do their work in their own way. Openness, tolerance, and empathy play a major role here. In relation to the company as a whole, value orientation means recognizing the values of the company (i.e., those that are really lived and not those that you would like to print on your company brochure) and aligning the structures and actions in the company accordingly.

Authenticity is essential for building credibility and trust. An authentic person is stable, credible, and comprehensible in the actions because one always aligns them with the values. If I know the values of this person, I can also anticipate the actions, which gives security and orientation. Trust develops. The situation is similar with an authentic company. This company also aligns its actions, i.e., the actions of its managers and employees, with stable corporate values. This builds trust with customers, employees, business partners, and other people or organizations that come into contact with the company. → *For a deeper understanding of the socio-cultural origins and development of values and leadership, read the article by Prof. Dr. Lutz Becker.*

2 Are Values Necessary?

Let's turn to the questions: Do I necessarily need values to be successful in competition? Do values not contradict profit and the market economy? The economic developments (e.g., financial crisis) of recent years and the ensuing social outrage show us that conventional economics is not enough. The assumption that we all conform to the ideal image of homo economicus has been considered disproved for several decades. Despite this, many business leaders have still adhered to Milton Friedman's "the business of business is business." Yet the economy is not detached from society but is embedded in society in many ways and therefore cannot escape societal demands and values. The economic system is not a natural construct but is socially constructed by people. All actors in this system are human beings, with not only economic but also emotional and moral interests (Müller and Jäger 2015, pp. 7–12).

Can I still lead well today without value orientation? Actually no, but nevertheless, this is often still the way it is taught in companies and universities as educational institutions. Shareholder value and short-term return calculations dominate business education, and moral aspects are often completely or partially ignored. The result is a lack of awareness among managers of the existence and relevance of morality in business. One reason given for this, for example, was that such immoral actions would be expected and also covered by the company (Müller and Jäger 2015, p. 7 f.). Value-based corporate governance can correct these misconceptions and put them on a new moral footing. Marcus Seidel, for example, as managing director of an established medium-sized company, admits in a field report on value-oriented corporate governance: "If I had been asked at the beginning of my professional career what I considered to be the key to building a successful medium-sized company, I would certainly not have named value-oriented corporate governance. [...] Value-oriented leadership is more important to me today than ever before and – I am convinced of this – it is a permanent task that one must by no means neglect as a manager and entrepreneur" (Seidel 2015, p. 50).

In *Hero* magazine, Rainer Krumm even refers to value-oriented leadership as "species-appropriate husbandry" of employees. Without a species-appropriate attitude, animals become sick or aggressive toward themselves and others. This can also be transferred from the animal world to employees. Without proper handling, employees also become sick, aggressive, or depressed. Satisfaction remains absent, but the risk of internal or external resignations increases (Krumm 2015, p. 39). Incorrect or inadequate leadership can lead to low emotional commitment to the company, which in turn can impact absenteeism, quality, customer loyalty, productivity, and profitability. The likelihood of mistakes and risks also increases when mistakes are not voiced. In addition, low retention also increases the likelihood of resignations and turnover, thus increasing personnel costs. → *Read more about employee retention as a central factor related to value-based leadership in the study by Preuß and Loose.*

Performance orientation ("Only what I can measure, I can control") can be seen as the "opposite" of value orientation, if such a comparison makes any sense at all and if integration is not rather to be aimed at. A (too) strong performance orientation and emphasis on measurable, calculable (numerical) values often leaves little room for value orientation, which is then attributed little relevance. Only when this reduces the company's ability to function due to crises, conflicts, and wrong decisions do managers start to look beyond the (performance-oriented) horizon and discover other essential company components (Zimmer 2015, p. 24 f.). Many companies consider value orientation as something they (will) do when the numbers are right. However, value orientation can help improve the numbers in the long run – but only if you do it seriously. If all corporate decisions are geared to short-term performance indicators, important long-term developments (e.g., employee loyalty, employer attractiveness, innovation culture, corporate culture, image) will be missed out.

One cannot lead without values already because these are always formed in social contexts. A company is also a social system (Luhmann) and is therefore no exception. Every cooperation of people, whether in society, in the family, in a circle of friends, or in a company, needs rules as a behavioral orientation. Which behavior is desired and accepted? Otherwise, anarchy and chaos would prevail. The belief that values and value orientation are nice-to-have topics that can be dealt with when there is nothing else important to do (when should this time be?) is wrong. A company does not perform without values. In every company, values are formed, and people act toward values. The only question is whether these values are the right values and whether the values of different levels fit together. If values are not observed, there is a risk of breaking the psychological employment contract.[1] If a value is personally particularly important to an employee, but the manager or employer constantly violates this value, negative consequences such as dissatisfaction, lack of loyalty and commitment, and internal or external resignation can be the result (Schmidt 2013, p. 274). Positively fulfilled values, on the other hand, favor the development of organizational commitment. This refers to an employee's commitment to a company. Precisely fulfilled values can trigger an affective or normative commitment that is independent of monetary factors (Schmidt 2013, pp. 235–237).

The well-known Gallup study, which has been conducted annually since 2000 on key topics such as employee loyalty and satisfaction, has unfortunately shown rather unpleasant results since the beginning, which have hardly changed. Between 60% and 70% of the employees surveyed stated that they had little or no loyalty to their employer (for details, see www.gallup.de). Value orientation can be helpful in turning these results around.

Many companies today see themselves as responsible and also present themselves as such to the outside world. Due to globalization and liberalization, the scope of responsibility for many companies has grown today. Legal and political regulation can increasingly no longer ensure moral action in business and society due to diminishing power. State tasks are being outsourced to private bodies (privatization) and subjected to economic market conditions (liberalization). This is accompanied by a different distribution not only of rights but also of duties. Globalization mainly affects the economy, while law and politics are still often bound to national borders. In this way, companies can evade economic policy and also economic ethics regulations. Their power is growing. The state is less able to fulfill its task of ethically shaping the market order. Legality and legitimacy are increasingly diverging. Companies should fill these gaps in the sense of a comprehensively understood corporate responsibility. Assuming responsibility always means acting according to certain values. Therefore, a value orientation is immanent for this.

[1] A psychological employment contract contains the mutual expectations of employee and employer regarding the employment relationship. The problem is that these are often not communicated directly (Raeder and Grote 2012, p. 2).

3 Value-Oriented Leadership

In general, a distinction must be made between *corporate leadership* and *personal leadership* (Fig. 1). While corporate leadership focuses more on the management of performance targets and the creation of corporate structures, personal leadership is employee-oriented and aims more at organizing the personal leadership relationship with the employee (e.g., with regard to motivation and orientation).

This distinction must also be considered in the context of value-oriented management. Value orientation in the context of objective-oriented management refers to the perception, creation, and change of the value structures of the company as an organization. → *For the management and control of values as non-financial parameters, read further in the article by Ehrenberger, Mäder, and Berna. Here, the area of structural value-oriented corporate management is explored in greater depth.*

Value-oriented corporate management includes, for example, the analysis and further development of the corporate culture or the implementation of a mission statement and code of conduct.

Within value-oriented people management, on the other hand, it is more about understanding one's own (leadership) values and the individual values of the employees. This includes the development of a suitable leadership style based on a consistent leadership culture and the individualization of employee leadership based on values (e.g., recognizing desires and expectations before conflicts arise from them).

3.1 Value-Based Corporate Governance

In corporate management, a distinction is made between three management levels: normative, strategic, and operational (Fig. 2). Corporate values are part of the fundamental

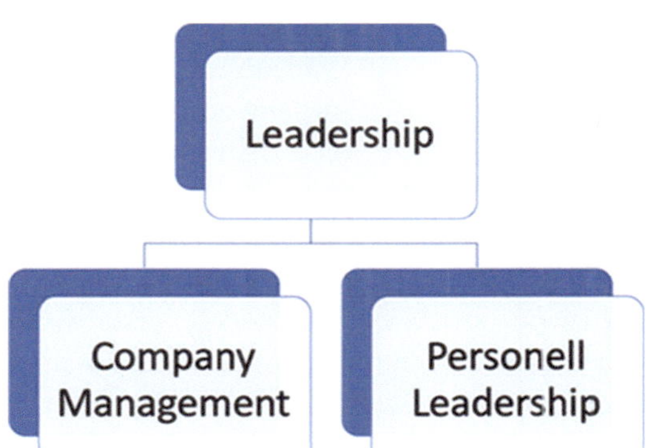

Fig. 1 Corporate and personal management

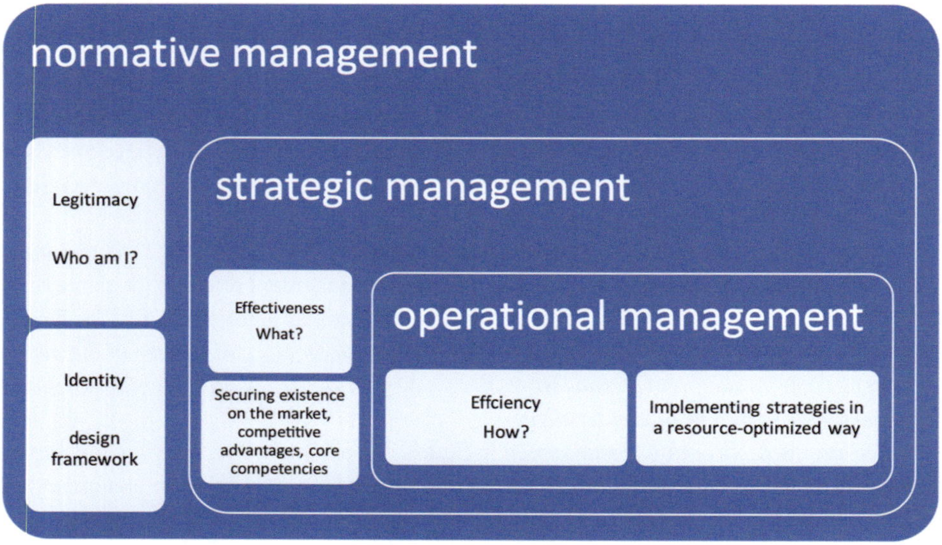

Fig. 2 Management levels

corporate identity that is to be formed within normative corporate management. This level of management should provide the general framework for shaping the company and answer the question: Who is the company (character, identity)? Why is it a meaningful market partner (legitimacy)? This framework provides the freedom of action for the strategic (securing existence on the market) and operational (implementing strategies efficiently) levels.

The relationship between the levels can also be illustrated by means of a house. The normative management level forms the foundation. This decides which form of house (competitive strategy, etc.) can be built stably at all. If you build a big house on a foundation that is too small, sooner or later you will have problems with stability. Therefore, it is important to know what kind of foundation one has (awareness of identity) in order to be able to adjust the actions (house building, furnishing) that are built on it. When building a house, this is almost a matter of course for everyone, while in corporate practice, this understanding is still comparatively rarely really conscious. The general shape of the house (walls, floors, roof) embodies the strategic management level. This determines the possible uses of the house (competitive strategy, appearance on the market). These can only be changed in the long term. The operational level is determined by the furnishing of the individual rooms and the actions within them.

When strategic and operational actions and decisions move outside the normative framework, conflicts and problems arise within the company that are often difficult to understand without conscious awareness of the normative level of the company. So, if you have problems within your management that are difficult to solve or partly incomprehensible, it is a good idea to deal with the normative management level. Value orientation is an essential part of this.

With such an understanding of value orientation or the connection between normative and strategic management levels, the question of the success of value orientation should also be asked differently. Often a proof of success is expected that value orientation is the right corporate strategy or objective. But this is not the right question at all. It is the other way round. Corporate values determine corporate strategy. Values in themselves are not measurable, but measurable objectives can be taken from them (Zimmer 2015, p. 46). Strategic objectives and measures should be derived from the corporate values, which can then be verified by operational success parameters in controlling. Otherwise, you would also have to ask yourself whether your character is promising for you?! Even if we live in the age of personality development, this is of course not arbitrarily malleable. → *In this context, also read the article on value-oriented compliance by Timo Herold and Florentin Schlegel. The entrepreneurial advantage of values becomes even clearer here in the contexts than in this introductory article.*

It is also problematic if values are not systematically anchored in the company, but are attached to individuals (e.g., company founders, charismatic managers). In the event of generational changes, ownership changes, or restructuring, these values can then be lost in day-to-day activities. Therefore, value-oriented personal leadership is not enough. Values must also be internalized in structures that are stable.

Helpful instruments for this are mission statement and the code of conduct. However, the understanding of these two concepts is sometimes confused in practice, so a brief explanation is provided below. The mission statement represents the basic values of the company, which form the identity of the company. It answers the question of what values a company has. These values should be stated and communicated clearly and concisely. The mission statement is the basis to create a code of conduct and is intended to answer the question of how the basic values can be lived out in daily interaction within the company and with stakeholders. It therefore goes into much greater detail and is therefore longer in its formulation. In addition, it is aimed at a specific, purely internal target group, whereas the mission statement is also intended for external communication and should therefore be more abstract and suitable for all – including external – stakeholders. In the case of the code of conduct, it often even makes sense to break it down and specify it for different target groups in the company (departments, product lines, hierarchical levels). For the sales department, the life of the corporate values may look different than for the human resources department. For managers in particular, it is often advisable to have their own code of conduct (leadership code or also called leadership principles). They have a special function in living the values in everyday business because they act as role models. If managers set an example of the values, it is much more likely that employees will also adopt the values and behavioral guidelines, accept them, and apply them themselves. In addition, managers also have a multiplier function, i.e., they can also actively communicate the values in their area. The leadership code also shows how value-oriented corporate and personal leadership interact. For this reason, the selection of personnel among

Table 1 Distinction between mission statement and code of conduct

	Mission statement	Code of conduct
Goal/task	Presentation of the identity of the company	Implementation orientation for desired behaviors in accordance with the corporate values
Content	Basic values of the company	Behavioral requirements related to the corporate values
Recipient/ target group	All internal and external stakeholders	Only for internal recipients (employees, management), specification for individual target groups is recommended
Type/formal form	Concise, not too long	Clear, unambiguous, and sufficiently long
	Graphic presentation (reader-friendliness, arousing interest)	Gladly with case studies as action orientation
	Display often on homepage and in company brochures (digital and analogue)	Presentation in the form of manuals, intranet, video presentation via e-learning
	Modern form is the representation as a film	

managers also has a clear influence on the quality of value-oriented leadership. On the one hand, the manager oneself should stand behind the idea of value-oriented leadership, and on the other hand, one should have a sufficiently strong personality to assert this view even in the face of opposition. Character traits should play just as big a role in the selection decision as technical ones (Zimmer 2015, p. 43 f.). Professional deficits can often still be compensated for through further training, while changes in character tend to be rare from adulthood onward.

Table 1 compares the mission statement and the code of conduct on the basis of various parameters in order to further clarify their distinction.

Table 2 provides some examples of the formulation of mission statements and codes of conduct for further understanding and perhaps also as a starting point for your own application in practice.

3.2 Value-Oriented Personal Management

In contrast to structurally oriented corporate management, people-oriented personnel management has a dual function to fulfill. On the one hand, a manager has a responsibility for success. They should influence the performance and work on the behavior of the employees in such a way that the success goals of the company are achieved. On the other hand, the manager also has a human responsibility. Here, the needs of the employees with regard to working conditions and other work factors are to be considered. Every manager therefore has the task of meeting these responsibilities equally. Within value-based

Table 2 Examples of mission statement/code of conduct

Value	Formulation in the mission statement	Formulation in the code of conduct
Loyalty	We are loyal to our colleagues	Problems should be addressed directly with the person concerned. The supervisor should only be called in if direct clarification has been unsuccessful or if there is a (criminal) danger for the company
Togetherness	We work together and for each other	Conflicts should always be resolved openly and directly. Supervisors should set a good example, identify conflicts quickly, and moderate those involved for clarification. In the event of a mistake, it is not a matter of gloatingly pointing the finger of blame, but of working together to find a solution and learning from it for the future. The strength of the team should compensate for the weaknesses of the individual. Those who are good at something help those who still have problems
Responsibility	We take responsibility for our actions toward customers, employees, and all other stakeholders	It is not about blaming mistakes on others, but about solving them. Each employee should reflect for one's own area what impact the own activity has (positive or negative) on others inside and outside the company. It is also about questioning oneself rather than always pointing the finger at others
Security	We deal consciously with risks and do not risk the existence of the company for short-term profits	Risk management is very important and should be practiced in every department. Managers in particular are required to keep this topic high on the agenda. Above all, long-term thinking should be established. What will happen to the company and its stakeholders in 5 or 10 years with such actions?

leadership, a balance between these two areas can be achieved by the fact that a value-based leadership style usually also positively influences the performance of the employees and thus favors the achievement of the performance targets (Kuhn and Weibler 2003, pp. 375–392).

To really live corporate values, value-based management is not enough. → *Read the article by Prof. Dr. Anja Lüthy. In it, the problem points of mission statements are precisely clarified, and the relevance of value-oriented personal leadership is highlighted in a vivid and practice-oriented manner.*

The living of values only succeeds when managers exemplify these values and employees then apply them as well. The role model function of managers is intrinsic to a consistent value orientation. Here is a brief case study: In the context of corporate management, the goal of reducing hierarchical thinking has been developed and is now to be implemented through various measures. One measure concerns the company car park. Previously, there were parking spaces for managers and parking spaces for ordinary employees, which were marked differently. This marking is now removed, and each parking space is also available for everyone. So, the structure is in place. However, if the managers continue to park in the old parking spaces allocated to them at the time, the parking situation will not change. This is then also emblematic of the fact that hierarchical thinking is likely to persist in other areas as well. Only when managers start parking everywhere will employees dare to park in the former "management parking spaces." Then the new structures can really come to life. So, we see that it is centrally up to the behavior of the managers and thus the personnel management whether values are lived in the company or not. → *If you want to read more about the change from a hierarchical culture to an authentic value-oriented leadership on an absolutely practical level, take a look at the article by Ms. Bräuer.*

One way of "translating" value-oriented corporate management into value-oriented personal management can be through mission statement reviews or value workshops. These should be conducted with all employees or at least representatives from all important areas. Central questions are: What values do we live by? Are these also the desired corporate values? It is very helpful for later understanding and direct applicability to identify concrete stories from the company's everyday life where values have been implemented or unfortunately not implemented (Buchheister and Groß 2018, p. 56 f.). Real stories show that values are not just abstract entities, but actively and constantly influence our daily interactions. In addition to stories, a visualization of values should also be attempted. This stays in our minds better and therefore increases the likelihood that the values are actually lived. → *You are welcome to read more about the problems with such workshops, for example, but also generally with the introduction of value-oriented leadership in Ms. Roth's article.*

A serious implementation of value orientation in people management often succeeds with a change of perspective among managers. Sometimes, it helps to compare it to customers. How about if you as a manager deal with your employees in a similar way as you do with your customers? After all, with the current situation on the job market, many of your employees no longer have to work for you but can choose their employer more and more (Jäger and Müller 2019, p. 159). Where would your company be without your employees? Where would your company be without your customers? As you can see, this perspective makes perfect sense.

At first glance, certain parallels can be drawn between value-oriented personnel management and transformational management. This refers to the active influence on the motives and values of those being led. The employees are to be transformed in the direction of the motives and values of the manager. To this end, the leader acts as a credible role model to the employees. However, this understanding would shorten the value-oriented leadership too much. Value-oriented leadership is not primarily about imposing one's own values on the employees, but about harmonizing the values of the employees with the values of the organization and one's own leadership values. Overlaps can also be seen with authentic leadership. However, this also refers too one-sidedly and abbreviated only to the management of one's own leadership values. Authentic leadership is increasingly about becoming aware of one's own values, goals, strengths, and weaknesses as a leader. This includes the targeted collection of feedback for self-awareness. The values and goals of the leader should be exemplified by the leader, and the leader should always act honestly and openly when dealing with those being led (Gardner et al. 2005, pp. 343–372). These are all sensible elements of a value-oriented leadership, but this leadership approach goes much further. It is not only about the manager's own values and goals but also about recognizing and considering the values of those being managed, as well as integrating the company's values as a framework.

Value-based person leadership has a large overlap space with the ethical leadership approach. This has been well constituted by Trevino et al. (2000) through the positions of moral person and moral manager. The moral person is about the leader's self, the values, and how the leader expresses them in the behavior and especially how the values are considered in decision-making. It is well considered that these values of the leader are also influenced by the values of the organization. As a moral manager, the leader does not act for oneself, but in relation to those one leads. It is a matter of exemplifying one's own values and communicating the company's values. In addition, the moral manager should provide incentives for appropriate, i.e., value-oriented behavior (Trevino et al. 2000, pp. 128–142). However, what is also missing in this approach with regard to a value-oriented people management is the recognition and consideration of the personal values of the employees. Only if their attitudes and needs are also considered can one speak fully of value-oriented personnel management.

Many managers are always looking for ways to positively motivate their employees in the long term. Many company incentive systems are purely materially oriented. Attempts are made to achieve motivation through higher salaries, company cars, or other benefits. Unfortunately, these factors are only suitable for increasing motivation in the short term, and after a certain salary level, this effect even begins to stagnate. Let's face it; do you really get up every morning for your salary? Do you look forward to going to work to change the numbers in your bank account? Or isn't it rather that salary is just a way of recognition and appreciation toward you and your performance? Isn't that actually what we want: recognition and appreciation? To be accepted for who we are and recognized for what we accomplish? And exactly now, we are back to value orientation. Value-oriented leadership can ensure exactly this recognition and appreciation of the employees and this not only materially but also emotionally. Get your employees excited about your idea and your underlying values in it and give them a good reason to get up in the morning and go to work with joy. Inspiring employees and giving them something they can identify with is an important leadership task of value-oriented people management (Seidel 2015, p. 54).

If you want to know why your employees really show up for work every day, you should ask them exactly that, in writing or in person, depending on how you expect the more honest answers according to the culture in your department. If an employee was offered a new job by you that had the exact same financial implications (salary, benefits, hours, cost of travel), what would motivate the employee to switch or what would keep them with you anyway? The given answers are your potential for improvement in (value-oriented) leadership or what is already working well for you in this respect.

Value-based leadership also includes identifying the values and needs of employees and clearly communicating whether and how these can be considered. Employees want, for example, transparency, participation, appreciation, or self-actualization. Sometimes, however, it is not possible or sensible for the company to fulfill all these points immediately or even later. Part of a value-oriented leadership is also to communicate this openly to the corresponding employee. This also creates trust, transparency, and appreciation. As a leader, you need to recognize the values and desires of your employees and see how much overlap there is with the reality of the company. False promises do not help anyone here. Expectations that are perceived but cannot be fulfilled at the moment with a comprehensible justification cause more satisfaction than ignoring such expectations in the hope that they will disappear on their own.

In addition to motivation, another exciting topic of value-oriented personnel management is dealing with mistakes. This clearly shows the values that are lived. Often people try desperately to avoid mistakes or to cover them up, because otherwise they would be a stigma and prevent professional development. In fact, this is simply nonsense. People make mistakes. Everyone does. Really everyone. Even me. Even you. The tabooing of mistakes is even more dangerous. A small mistake that could have been easily corrected can grow into a big problem through cover-up (Jäger and Müller 2019, p. 159 f.).

If you want openness and honesty to prevail in your team, this is especially true when dealing with crises, and every mistake made is basically a small company crisis. If you are open with your mistakes (and yes, you certainly make some), your employees will dare to do so as well. Instead of wasting time and energy pushing the buck around, you can thus rather invest this time in learning from the mistakes and thus a positive future development. Take away your employees' fear of confessing mistakes. In a constructive error culture, mistakes are not a stigma, but a starting point to learn and do better next time. For understanding, sometimes it's helpful to look at sports. How boring and unsuccessful do you think a football match would be if no player shot at goal for fear of not scoring?

Overall, it can be stated that employee motivation and commitment depend on how well an employee's personal values match the company values and the personal values of the direct supervisor. This is fostered by active involvement, consideration of employee welfare and wishes, and a culture of trust based on transparency, openness, and honesty (Barrett 2016, p. 217).

A culture of trust means the dismantling of control structures, as far as possible and reasonable. This is often a necessary concept, especially for the consideration of the values of employees, in order to be able to perceive and implement them. However, if at this point in time there is no or no pronounced culture of trust in your company (and you are not alone in this state), then you must first establish such a culture. This usually takes some time and will not be without conflict. To understand these processes, it can help to compare this development to growing up from a child through the teenage years to young adulthood. Without a culture of trust, employees are treated like children, not trusted, supervised, and controlled at every turn; with a well-developed culture of trust, on the other hand, they are treated like responsible and, above all, responsible adults. In between lies puberty – the American entrepreneur and author Doug Tatum calls this phase "No Man's Land": If a culture of control is to become a culture of trust, you have to walk through a no man's land, comparable to the disorientation and boundary testing of puberty. This means that old structures and procedures no longer fit, but new ones are not yet fully in place or practiced. Just as teenagers need understanding and patient parents, employees who experience such a change in leadership also need a level-headed supervisor – as a manager, I must also constantly question and adapt myself during this time.

Matching the culture of trust is the way you treat your team as a work family. A family environment is always value-oriented in a positive sense. The family is oriented toward individuals and their physical, psychological, and social needs. Communication is specific and primarily oriented toward human issues (Brückner 2019, p. 137 ff.). In companies, on the other hand – and thus also in purely operationally oriented teams – the focus is more on factual problems and purely economic objectives, in which the employees are "only" a solution medium (e.g., selling products, manufacturing products, controlling payments, generating returns). Communication also tends to be more factual goal oriented and less bonding oriented. The work family can form a bridge between these two worlds. Factual problems should be solved in a people-oriented way. It is therefore important not to lose sight of both worlds. Try to transfer family routines (e.g., joint celebrations or weekly rituals) to your everyday life in the team. In addition to the operational problems and solutions, the human needs should also be perceived and taken seriously.

Value-oriented people management also involves making decisions on a daily basis. In the process, there are also conflicting goals that make it difficult to make simple decisions. The matrix in Fig. 3 can provide you with some orientation:

If values in the social context (e.g., between manager and employee or between company and employee) do not match and do not match directly, an adjustment process must take place. There are generally three options for action: leaving the company (separation), attempting to adapt the social values to one's own (rebellion), or adapting oneself to the social conditions (loyalty). Due to high (social) costs of the first two options, especially for employees without a prominent hierarchical position, a certain compulsion for the third option arises, which, however, can be accompanied by inner resistance and dissatisfaction. A real identification with the employer remains, without the possibility to also live own values, mostly missing. This does not lead to stable employee loyalty and, in the worst case, to inner resignation. In addition, according to this understanding, corporate values have a clear influence on employee actions, which is why their ethical content should be well considered (Müller and Jäger 2015, p. 13 f.).

You can avoid this problem in personnel management by hiring suitable employees right away. And by suitable, we do not mean the professional competence, but the personal value structure of the employee. If you hire employees who have a large overlap with your leadership values and your company values, then an adjustment is not necessary at all. The employee can live their own values and the company values at the same time. This creates satisfaction and credibility externally and internally. But how do you find such employees? In general, it is advisable to define the fit of values between the company and the employee as a hiring criterion and to pay particular attention to this in the interview. You should ask the applicant what is particularly important to him or her or how one would act in difficult

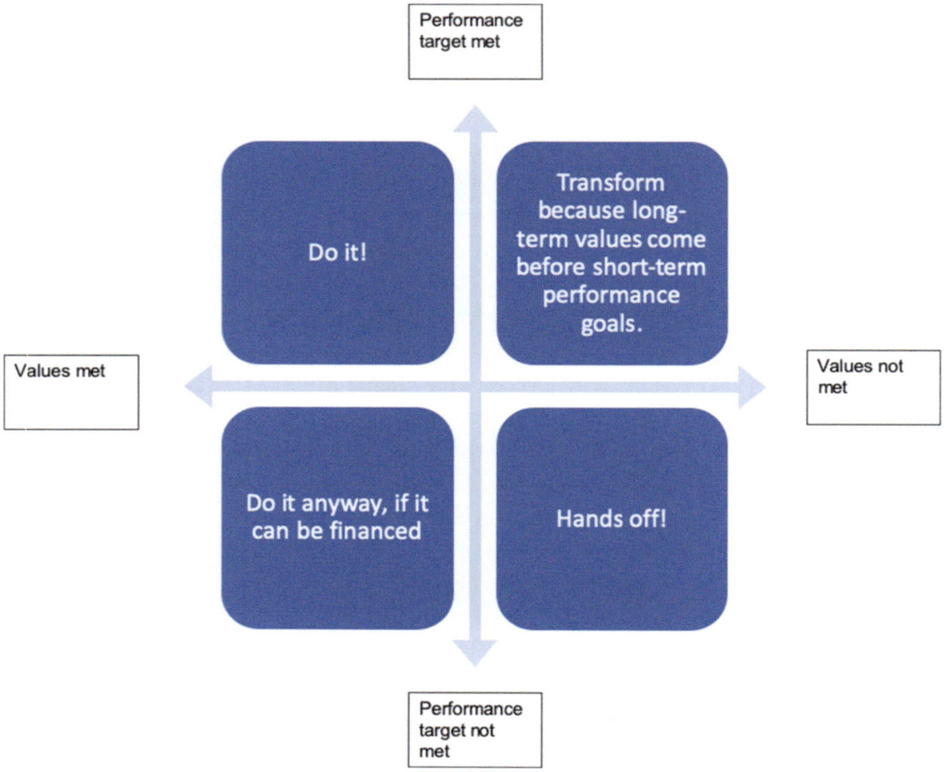

Fig. 3 Decision matrix based on Zimmer 2015, p. 41

decision-making situations. It is precisely in actions in crises or when problems arise that values become apparent. Seidel (2015, p. 60) provides another good tip: Ask good employees for recommendations from their circle of friends and acquaintances. Friends of your employees often have similar value patterns, and your employees can also usually instinctively decide who would fit well into the company and who would not. A positive side effect is that the recommending employee feels responsible and helps the new employee to integrate into the team.

At the end, I would like to give you some questions as orientation for your own (value-oriented) self-reflection:

- Is my action legal?
- Does it make me feel bad/uncomfortable?
- Is it in line with the company's goals and values?
- What if everyone acted like this?
- What if it was in the paper tomorrow?
- Would I tell my kids about it at night?

For value-oriented leadership, especially value-oriented personnel management, the mindset of managers often has to change. Control should gradually be replaced by trust. Giving instructions is gradually replaced by giving support. To do this, leaders need to self-reflect: How do I see my employees? Which prejudices guide me or possibly tempt me to do so? How do I create the conditions for my employees to behave in the desired way? What is perhaps my part in the fact that my employees do not behave as desired?

Finally, I would like to give you a colorful bouquet of ideas for a concrete implementation of value-oriented leadership:

- Act against hierarchical thinking when planning meetings and events, e.g., invite normal employees without management functions to a board event, while their superiors are not invited.
- Introduce Complain Monday, when every employee can constructively say what went wrong last week in 140 characters on the intranet without fear.
- Introduce Joy Friday, when every employee should say in 140 characters on the intranet what went well during the week.
- Introduce Fuckup Nights, where employees and supervisors meet after work in a pleasant atmosphere and report on mistakes – food should be provided by the company.
- Introduce lunch roulette, whereby once a month colleagues are drawn by lots to have lunch together; the meal is paid for by the company.
- Annual task exchange where tasks can be exchanged among employees. Shows whether the tasks are really well distributed (personnel organization).
- It is better to schedule shorter meetings more often (max. 20 min.) and to hold them mainly standing up – ensures that time is used more efficiently.

References

Barrett R (2016) Werteorientierte Unternehmensführung – Cultural Transformation Tools für Performance und Profit. Springer, Berlin/Heidelberg

Brückner A (2019) Familienunternehmen am Scheideweg. In: Dahm und Thode (Hrsg) Strategie und Transformation im digitalen Zeitalter. Springer, Wiesbaden

Buchheister A, Groß J (2018) Mit werteorientierter Führung ein gutes Klima für Veränderungen schaffen. In: DW Die Wohnungswirtschaft, Nr. 8 aus 2018, S 56–59

Gardner WL, Avolio BJ, Luthans F, May DR, Walumbwa FO (2005) Can you see the real me? A self-based model of authentic leader and follower development. Leadersh Q 16(3):343–372

Jäger C, Müller N (2019) Eine (Führung-)Kultur für Veränderungsprozesse. In: Dahm und Thode (Hrsg) Strategie und Transformation im digitalen Zeitalter. Springer, Wiesbaden

Krumm R (2015) Erfolg durch Werteorientierte Führung. Hero Magazine 1(15):38–42

Kuhn T, Weibler J (2003) Führungsethik. Die Unternehmung 57(5):375–392

Luhmann N (1984) Soziale Systeme. Grundriß einer allgemeinen Theorie, Suhrkamp, Frankfurt am Main

Müller N, Jäger C (eds) (2015) WERTEorientierte Führung von Familienunternehmen. Springer, Wiesbaden

Raeder S, Grote G (2012) Der psychologische Vertrag. In: Praxis der Personalpsychologie, Bd 26. Hogrefe, Göttingen

Schmidt A (2013) Organisationales Commitment und Beschäftigungsverhältnisse – Eine Operationalisierung unter dem Aspekt sich verändernder Arbeitsverhältnisse. Peter Lang, Frankfurt am Main

Seidel M (2015) Werteorientierte Unternehmensführung – ein Erfahrungsbericht. In: Müller N, Jäger C (Hrsg) WERTEorientierte Führung von Familienunternehmen. Springer, Wiesbaden, S 50–67

Trevino LK, Hartman LP, Brown M (2000) Moral person and moral manager: how executives develop a reputation for ethical leadership. Calif Manag Rev 42(4):128–142

Zimmer D (2015) Das werteorientierte Unternehmen: Erfolgsgarant oder esoterischer Blödsinn? In: Müller N, Jäger C (Hrsg) WERTEorientierte Führung von Familienunternehmen. Springer, Wiesbaden, S 24–47

Prof. Dr. Jessica Lange has already been combining the theory and practice of value-oriented management for several years: From 2012 to 2016, Mrs. Lange completed her doctorate at the University of Oldenburg (Lower Saxony) on the topic of "Value-oriented management in municipal energy supply." Since 2009, the author has been active in management consulting on a wide range of topics related to corporate culture and value management; since 2013, she has also been self-employed within the framework of her company WERTEmanagement Dr. Jessica Lange. She has been teaching on corporate ethics topics since 2013 and has been a full-time professor of business administration at the FOM University of Applied Sciences in Hamburg since 2018.

Part I

Basic Understanding and Study Results

With the following contributions from this section, you can sharpen your basic understanding of value-based leadership and enrich it with current study results. Theory-based and scientifically sound contributions await you here.

If, after this compact but comprehensive introduction to our topic of value-oriented leadership, you would like to delve deeper into the understanding of the concept of values and the complexity, heterogeneity, complexity, and dynamics of values, we recommend the following article by Prof. Dr. Priddat.

From a complex and well-founded sociological perspective, the concept of value is taken apart here almost literally. Above all, the multifaceted social foundation of the function of values or evaluations becomes visible in this contribution. In the end, it becomes clear that working with values or common beliefs, mental models, or institutions remains complex, which, however, does not diminish their entrepreneurial usefulness, but shows their devaluation as a "nice-to-have" or secondary task, once there is time for it, as a mistake. Above all, it should not be forgotten that a company in Luhmann's sense is always a social system itself and all the problems of the collective handling of evaluations or developments in the collective or network also and especially apply to companies.

We also remain critical in dealing with values, value orientation, or value-oriented leadership with the contribution of Prof. Dr. Lutz Becker. In his contribution, Mr. Becker provides a deep understanding of leadership and culture (cultural evolution of leadership) and relates this to the social integration of values.

In this article, you will find a theory-based socio-cultural anchoring of our topic. It reflects – in depth on the introductory chapter – how values emerge socially and change dynamically. The distinction between economic and philosophical values makes it clear that a purely economic view of values narrows the view too much.

At the end of the paper, it becomes clear that value-based leadership ensures the sustainable survival of groups and organizations under reciprocal resource conditions. Based on this understanding, a comprehensive model of value-based leadership can be derived at the end of the paper.

The article by Preuß and Loose refers to an empirical study conducted as part of a master's thesis at the FOM Hochschule für Oekonomie und Management. The study deals with the crucial factor of employee retention in today's competitive environment, especially related to small- and medium-sized enterprises (SMEs), as they are characterized by more limited resources and opportunities. There is a focus on Generation Y, which is receiving a lot of attention today and which is increasingly playing an essential role in value-oriented management.

Employee retention is also a determining success factor for value-oriented leadership and a hoped-for consequence. For employee retention, just as already mentioned in the book for value-oriented leadership, the wishes and needs of employees must be moved more into the focus of the company. The study examines on a scientific basis which factors promote employee loyalty. These factors are also to be considered for value-oriented leadership in general and concern both direct personal leadership and objective-based corporate leadership.

The article by Prof. Dr. Marion Preuß also refers to current research. Instead of the much-studied Generation Y, Marion Preuß looks at the value perception of employees aged 50 and over. Also, these must not be neglected in the value-oriented leadership, especially the people management. Due to the demographic development, the proportion of older employees is increasing, and the comprehensively demanded innovative ability of companies also depends on the motivation of older employees.

Motivation and value orientation are closely related. Motivation increases if there is the possibility of pursuing the values perceived as personally significant within the professional activity. While many studies have already highlighted a number of expected values as essential for the 50 plus generation (e.g., quality, security, stability, loyalty), Marion Preuß takes a different and exciting approach in her research and structures the investigation on the basis of the three CSR sustainability dimensions (economic, social, and ecological). This shows that for the 50 plus generation, social values have the greatest relevance; furthermore, employee compensation and product responsibility also play an important role.

Are Values Still Modern?

Birger P. Priddat

Abstract

There are many values. The fact of the manifoldness of values has taken us some distance in the use of the concept of the term "value." We now use the word "values" normatively-appellatively: when we wish that everyone should share common values. But we have grown up with the social experience that in society no fundamental values are traded any more, but many small ones.

With the disappearance of the expression of values, an expression of acting from a fundamental conviction also disappears. Our actions are more likely to be carried out in a rule- or institution-opportunistic manner. This does not mean that we become more opportunistic in general, but merely that we adapt our convictions more quickly to what is negotiated in social communications in terms of opinion, validity, and relevance. Translated into the language of values, this would mean that we change the values we share more quickly.

We talk about someone having or holding values. By this, we usually mean that one has convictions which make one's own judge certain aspects of the world in a more or less certain way. One refuses to do anything that contradicts these convictions (as far as circumstances allow).

B. P. Priddat (✉)
Private Universität Witten/Herdecke gGmbH, Witten, Germany
e-mail: birger.priddat@uni-wh.de

J. Lange (ed.), *Value-Oriented Leadership in Theory and Practice*,
https://doi.org/10.1007/978-3-662-65883-3_2

But such a description is not enough, for we are saying nothing more than that one who has values is obstinate and refuses to accept certain aspects of the world. As long as others don't have to worry about the values of individuals, it may pass for *quirk*, attitude, or stubbornness. So, let's distinguish whether the one who has values is satisfied with having them or wants them generalized. Often such a person thinks that if everyone had these values, the world would be better, i.e., would generate appropriate interactions. One then has the value as an attitude to which others should adhere, provided they accept the reasons for these attitudes or beliefs.

Adhering to values, however, is a different process that presupposes a kind of *common belief.* Values are then *shared beliefs*, i.e., commonly shared evaluations.

There are no values, only valuations.

When we talk about values, we usually imagine some kind of communal evaluations that is action oriented. Value is then a kind of consensus – implicit or explicit – about certain attitudes toward the world.

We expect to be able to know the attitudes, beliefs, and intentions of others because they share values with us. We then treat values much like an equilibrium of expectations in which one can rely on others to act in the same way.

That in which all agree to orient their actions is like a spiritual bond that should bind all (coherence of the reasons for action).

This is the ideal representation. We want values because of their normative integration.

We can now say that if someone has a value, we can assign it to a *common belief*, even if no one else currently shares it. The individual value is then a residue of a former common belief that society has already abandoned (this is why values often appear as – sad or aggressive – conservative attitudes of older worlds). More precisely, individual values exist only as residues of older abandoned *common beliefs*, whereas valid values always represent a collective good, because they are valid only if many share them and mutually recognize the belief represented in the value.

Valid values are commonly shared evaluations that are communicable at any time (even if they are not de facto communicated because they are universally valid) and are confirmed and replicated in communication. Now, homogeneously distributed values are rare; we are dealing with diverse and divergent value communities, each of which forms its own networks (identifiable by common validity addressing). As individuals are assigned to different networks, they are assignable to diverse values, without neurotic confusion. Depending on which network one is currently attached to, different values or valuation references apply. Since network communications are not laterally coupled through the diverse networks, one can be fractionally and relatively confusion-free associated.

In fact, however, we are dealing with many different values. I would like to put it like this: We do not have a decline in values, but rather the opposite: more values than before. But in fractions. As a result, their respective binding force is declining or becoming more diverse.

The binding effect of strong, dominant norms in history has not dissolved in today's modernity but has been transformed into weak ties to subdominant norms, especially as ties to manifold-diverse norms that are followed constellatively. Depending on which constellations one finds oneself in, other values are actualized. Instead of a hierarchy of norms, we are dealing with a standard of norm heterarchy (with the only distinction being acute/latent).

Thus, the injunction to hold to common values is a blind injunction since it cannot indicate which values or norms one is supposed to be thinking of at any given moment. One desires common attitudes to the world, but different varieties of oneself have different attitudes. Thus, one can merely state that many people have attitudes, but not universally binding ones.

If we remember the hierarchy of norms as "order," the heterarchy of norms is more pronounced as a "network." One is loosely coupled in diverse connections, but each cohesion in the network generates (temporary) order or norm modalities. If these norm modalities stabilize in the network, they form institutions (or more precisely: temporarily longer-lasting institutional arrangements).

Networks are a social consequence of the heterarchization of norms: One is socially connected, but loose in the normal state, coupling more closely in collaborative constellations that acquire normative force communicatively – but in the network context, i.e., revisable, without strong cohesive force. The normal state is based on individual strategies of action, which, similar to the market, produce constant contacts, but which just as constantly dissolve again. Networks are the media (like resources) of contact potentials (*connectivity*). This coordinative form of sociality focuses locally into collaborative forms that can generate closer network couplings. Norms are then something like temporary action constitutions of collaborative social events.

Unlike markets, in which rational actors meet contingently for transactions whose social structural basis is not defined or left empty, networks form social resources not only of social, loosely coupled relations ("elective affinities") but also of social mediations – as a mode of social communication, if we consider not only the mediation by *brokers* but the communication of elective affinities who open up epistemic fields of world explanation or trade worldviews. Reprojected onto markets, we see that they are also network-based: Networks form the language games (*linguistic communities*) that communicate economic relevancies (goods, qualities, attributions, prices, sense, meanings, etc.).

The fact of the diversity of values has in the meantime made us distance ourselves from the use of the concept of value. We now use the word "values" only in a normative-appealing way: when we wish that everyone should share common values. But we have grown up with the social experience that in society no fundamental values are traded any more, but many small ones.

In the social sciences, we have other names: orders, rules, and institutions. They replace the use of the phrase values when they are interpreted as implicit (or autonomous or emergent) orders, as implicit rules, and as informal institutions (as opposed to their formal or explicit counterparts). Economists talk about incentives generated by specific *governance structures*. Whether we structure the implicit or the explicit, we are dealing with influences that ordain us, rather than beliefs or attitudes that explicate us. To put it more precisely, we are dealing with ordaining structures rather than with attitudes of mind incorporated into individuals.

With the disappearance of the expression of values (they are no longer an analytical concept in the social sciences), an expression of acting from a fundamental conviction also disappears. Our actions are more likely to be carried out in a rule- or institution-opportunistic way. This does not mean that we become more opportunistic in general, but merely that we adapt our convictions more quickly to what is negotiated in social communications in terms of opinion, validity, and relevance. Translated into the language of values, this would mean that we change the values we share more quickly. Values are network-communicated.

Some complete the concept of value with rules, duties, and virtues. I think it is right that value can only be used as a complexion, but I think the nomenclature is outdated because it does not address the contemporary dynamics of value reference. I propose to use the following nexus instead of values: conceptual schemas (*conceptual schemes*) or *mental models*, intentions, institutions (*shared mental models*), and media (of communicative reassurance of institutional arrangements). Values are communicative events at the intersections of these variables of influence. They are stable as long as they are communicated in a high-quality manner.

This is not to forget that we have names of fundamental values in the various *linguistic communities:* human rights, freedom, security, etc. But they are latent social resources, without effective starting points for action. It is only in discrepancies and asymmetries of *mental models*, institutions, and media that attitudes and convictions emerge that address a new constellation of action and reasons for action. However, they then apply primarily to the triggering situation, not in general. And they are figured constellatively, in specific interpretation.

Values as constellated terms of situational action orientation are a different phenomenon; they do not apply to social routines, but to the resolution of differences, as a moment of reflection on what one can or should strive for together. In this respect, they are contingent or temporary consensuses. One decides in difference for "more or less freedom," for the observance of human rights, etc., but always bound to a specific solution.

Since the updating of values happens locally or selectively, it has no binding beyond that; in other differences, other values are updated. The modern self is a web of desires and beliefs (Richard Rorty). Note the plural. Sometimes, beliefs form their own temporary networks with beliefs in other networks: "values" emerge at these account points. But the networks are loosely coupled and always linkable in different ways. Values are social chains of beliefs that last as long as they are communicated. The rest remains in the sleep of cultural memory.

Prof. Dr. Birger P. Priddat is Senior Professor of Economics and Philosophy at the Faculty of Economics at the University of Witten/Herdecke, where he previously held the chair of the same name (since 1991). In between he is co-founder of the Zeppelin University in Friedrichshafen (2003–2007). He has various guest professorships. His main research interests are as follows: philosophy of economics, history of economic theory, future of work, and institutional economics.

Value-Based Leadership: Approaching a Difficult Construct

Lutz Becker

Abstract

Both leadership and values are amorphous in the Weberian sense. From an evolutionary point of view, this chapter describes a leadership that above all ensures the successful survival of groups under changing environmental conditions and sets an orientation framework for this by means of values.

1 Introduction

In 2007, while arresting the Sicilian godfather Salvatore Lo Piccolo, the police found something astonishing in his documents. In addition to the well-known law of silence ("Omertà"), a code of values and conduct contained highly bourgeois values such as punctuality, reliability, and honesty, but also unconditional obedience and references to biblical sexual morality ("Thou shalt not covet thy neighbor's wife"):

1. "No-one can present himself directly to another of our friends. There must be a third person to do it."
2. "Never look at the wives of friends."
3. "Never be seen with cops."
4. "Don't go to pubs and clubs."
5. "Always being available for Cosa Nostra is a duty - even if your wife's about to give birth."

L. Becker (✉)
Hochschule Fresenius, Wirtschaft und Medien, Business School, Köln, Germany
e-mail: lutz.becker@hs-fresenius.de

J. Lange (ed.), *Value-Oriented Leadership in Theory and Practice*,
https://doi.org/10.1007/978-3-662-65883-3_3

6. "Appointments must absolutely be respected."
7. "Wives must be treated with respect."
8. "When asked for any information, the answer must be the truth."
9. "Money cannot be appropriated if it belongs to others or to other families."
10. "People who can't be part of Cosa Nostra: anyone who has a close relative in the police, anyone with a two-timing relative in the family, anyone who behaves badly and doesn't hold to moral values." (BBC 2007; Langer 2007).

What motivates the "honorable society" of all things to establish such canonized behavioral expectations, and what does this have to do with value-oriented leadership? To clarify this, let's go far back into the history of human evolution.

2 How Does Leadership Come into Being?

Humans could well be called an error of evolution. At least when it comes to physical properties and skills, our ancestors who roamed the savannah perhaps 200,000 years ago could barely keep up with their predators and competitors for food. They were neither sufficiently fast nor remarkably strong, nor did they have sharp teeth or armor to protect them. And yet humans have successfully managed to defend themselves against predators, to win resource conflicts with other species, and to reproduce successfully over countless generations. Humans have succeeded in subduing the planet: "(M)ankind will remain a major geological force for many millennia, perhaps millions of years, to come" (Crutzen and Stoermer 2000, p. 18). But how could humankind succeed in rising from a marginal note of evolution to the world-shaper of the Anthropocene (ibid.)?

At the latest when humans began to hunt big game, communication, flexible division of labor, narrative storage of experience, and shared interpretations concerning the conditions became the drivers of a cultural-evolutionary success story (Becker and Montiel Alafont 2015): the humans' collective conquest of the planet. Humans succeeded in replacing their precarious individual fitness by cultural fitness, or as Mad Ridley puts it, "at some point before 100,000 years ago culture itself began to evolve in a way that it never did in other species – that is, to replicate, mutate, compete, select, accumulate – somewhat as genes had been doing for billions of years. Just like cumulatively building an eye bit to bit, so cultural evolution in human beings could cumulatively build a culture or a camera. […] [O]nly human beings have a cumulative culture that goes into the design of a loaf of bread or a concerto" (Ridley 2011, p. 5 f.).

The idea of cultural evolution is based on the assumption that, in analogy to the genetic transmission of genes, cultural practices and ideas are also subject to evolutionary principles such as variation, selection, and retention: more or less successful adaptations to changing environmental or resource conditions. Successful adaptation patterns are transmitted inter- and intra-generationally in narrative form and stabilized in retention processes, which we perceive as culture (Childe 1951; Flannery 1972; Lumsden and Wilson 2005; Witt 2003, 2006; Ridley 2011; McLaughlin 2012).

Furthermore, the cultural evolution of leadership seems to be an important driver for the evolutionary success of the human race. It is not that other species do not have leading babes, leading wolves, or silverbacks. But it seems that in its cultural evolution, the human species has developed a repertoire of leadership practices and competencies that have been beneficial for adapting to changing environmental and resource constellations and helped in developing viable solutions to given problems and thus for the survival and growth of the species (van Vugt and Ahuja 2010).

The society of hunter-gatherers and the early settlements presupposed specific patterns of social coordination, division of labor, and the ability to organize groups in relation to specific environmental constellations and situations. This was a matter not only of efficiency in the sense of making the best possible use of resources but also of building up a repertoire of social coordination practices (alignment). Leadership skills were attributed, for example, to the member who could best credibly demonstrate that he or she knew where there was a shady place to rest, the nearest spring, or the best hunting grounds and who was able to resolve intra-group conflicts and external conflicts in terms of survival and reproduction (van Vugt and Ahuja 2010).

With sedentarization and growing settlement size in the course of the Neolithic Revolution, leadership became institutionalized by means of symbolic artifacts, which could express themselves in tablets, palaces, legions, or ritual popes. A more differentiated division of labor by means of social hierarchies as well as "twin" or "dual leadership" crystallized as a widespread cultural practice: the ritually underpinned separation between spiritual (and financial) and secular-military leadership (Kristiansen 2013).

Interestingly, the concept of leadership was adapted differently by different cultures. While in large Mediterranean settlements (and later the Roman Church) the aforementioned symbolic leadership and hierarchy prevailed as formative concepts, small-scale settling cultures of the North (Vikings, Frisians, Saxons) apparently developed a rather distanced relationship to formal hierarchical leadership structures (Acemoglu and Robinson 2019). This supposed deficit was mainly compensated by democratic elements (thing) or initially orally handed-down forms of jurisprudence (e.g., everyman's law, spade law). The primary concern was to balance the interests between individuals as well as between the individual and the community. However, the lack of a culturally anchored concept of personified leadership in the abovementioned cultures of the North led to the dilemma that these were difficult to reconcile with the need for representation in growing settlements (von Rosen 2008).

So if we want to revisit the historical line of growing group sizes from the small group of gatherers and hunters in the African savannah to growing urban structures of Mesopotamia and their administrative needs to the "global audience" in the mediatized societies of the twenty-first century, it is worthwhile to look at how leadership depends on the cultural context, the respective arena (politics, economy, etc.), and the size of the group of followers.

Overall, it becomes clear that leadership is far older and far more complex endeavor than what we call management today. Leaving aside military and administrative contexts, the roots of management can be traced primarily to the transition from the nineteenth to the twentieth century (Fayol 2018; Taylor 1911). In contrast, literary and scholarly reappraisals of leadership point far back into the pre-Christian era. For example, numerous religious writings contain proto-scientific explorations of leadership issues (e.g., Jesus as "the good shepherd" in John 10:11). The Arthashastra, a scripture attributed to Chanakya (c. 230–283 BC), can already be understood as an early scientific approach to leadership issues (Olivelle 2013).

3 What Is Leadership?

Looking at the long lists of failures and scandals surrounding leaders (Enron, Lehmann Brothers, or Wirecard to mention a few), practice seems to defy any theory of good leadership. But let's have a closer look:

Historically, leadership has been described and explained as a social phenomenon in quite different ways. First, there are the "great-man" theories, dating primarily to the Victorian Scottish writer Thomas Carlyle (1841). A notion that is decisively anchored in Schumpeter's image of the entrepreneur as well as in a zeitgeist that likewise found expression in Goethe's Faust, in Schopenhauer, and above all in Friedrich Nietzsche's notion of the "Übermensch" (hyperanthropos) as a destructive and value-shattering creator (Richter 2012, p. 127). Furthermore, leadership was understood as a trait or skill of leaders (Stogdill 1974).

Similarly, following James MacGregor Burns (1978), leadership is readily understood in a process-related sense as either transactional or transformational, with the transactional perspective being closer to the supposed ratio of the optimizing and efficiency-seeking manager as administrator, while the transformational in turn reflects again the motif of Zarathustra's transformations into perfection into the "hyperanthropos."

Not to forget the perhaps typically German approach, the "purest type of legal rule […] by means of a bureaucratic administrative staff" (Weber 1922, § 4), which ties leadership to the administrative structures embedding it – that is, to a position in the hierarchy – and thus closes the bridge to the twentieth-century concept of management. Today, this administrative perspective is readily reproduced in software: Rights and duties, who has to lead whom and how, are hardwired into the user profiles of managers and their direct reports.

Leadership is a central, but by no means exclusive, element of group coordination. Ultimately, leadership can also be understood as an entity of resource allocation by means of communicating and organizing, evaluating, and deciding. Due to power, this entity has the power to accumulate and redistribute group resources, also including shares of power (and leadership). Among others, this results in the general question of how leadership shares in organizations are distributed (differentiation between leadership and followership, shared and changing leadership roles, etc.). In particular, the latter is becoming increasingly important due to flatter, more globally distributed, and project-driven organizations. However, more powerful technologies – such as ERP and HRM systems as well

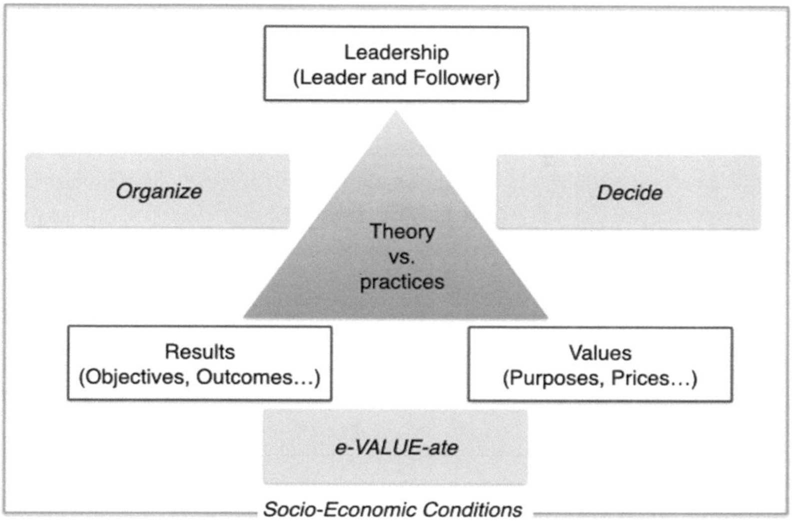

Fig. 1 Contextualizing value-oriented leadership

as social media and artificial intelligence – inevitably question contemporary boundaries between leadership and execution, between leadership and followership being redrawn over and over again (Fig. 1).

One can hardly imagine fire brigade operations beginning with a palaver in a circle of chairs. Equally, a dictatorial order may not make sense when it comes to complex organizational issues, a complex project involving different experts, and the fair balancing of interests. In the latter case, corporate democratic elements will possibly dominate (Zeuch 2015). In the immediate one-to-one management situation, the conversation at the coffee machine or the palaver under a tree, the ping-pong of communications under the conditions of mutual reference or double contingency (Luhmann 1984), as long as this is not broken up by the direct exercise of power, plays the decisive role.

However, the bigger the audience gets, the more significant symbolic leadership becomes. In this case, the spectrum of successful leadership interventions is limited by the fact that they are measured by the group of followers according to whether the leader can make it clear that he or she is able to solve the respective group problems. In the end, it is always about conflicts and balancing mechanisms between individual and community, between efficiency and resilience, between group coherence and individual freedom, between claims to power and community values, between value creation and basic needs under changing environmental conditions and challenges for the community. In order to find the right balance for all social dynamics, suitable mechanisms and good standards are needed.

This encounters a social adjustment loop in which each individual tries to find out (1) whether he or she is a valuable member of the group, (2) whether his or her own contribution is positively endorsed, or (3) whether there is even a threat of exclusion from the group (as a reminder: for our ancestors in the savannah, an exclusion from the group would have been like being sentenced to death). This behavior is in turn mirrored by the behavior of the group toward the leader. How compliant must the individual member be? How loyal does he or she have to be toward the leader? Metaphorically speaking, our prehistoric horde leader could decide who got how much of the prey or whether he possibly put the whole group on a diet right away. The distribution of resources in a group comes along with the power to sanction behavior which should not be underestimated. Therefore, it was important to be a respectable member of the group (1) to be protected by the group and (2) to get access to the resources distributed within the group. Individuals, group, and leaders are thus mutually "leveled" and evaluated permanently. The mechanisms may be symbolic acts – such as the withdrawal of resources, praise, or disregard – or simply gossip (van Vugt and Ahuja 2010).

These perspectives mentioned here should avoid the fallacy of locating the phenomenon of leadership solely in the (apparent) leader. Instead, leadership suggests itself as contingent and an emergent social phenomenon. We also should understand leadership itself as a resource of groups, which ideally has a positive effect on its fitness, i.e., performance and adaptability, coherence as well as problem-solving, and hence the ability to survive in a conceivably hostile environment (van Vugt et al. 2008; van Vugt and Ahuja 2010; Price and van Vugt 2014).

Put simply: if the leadership is good, everyone should do fine. But the reverse is also true: If the members of a group are doing well, this may be an indication of good leadership.

4 How Does Value Emerge?

Economic and non-economic concepts of value intermingle in the discourses around leadership (Fig. 2); furthermore, similar to Weber's concept of power, values, as long as they are not subject to factual economic categories, remain amorphous – or following Max Scheler: Value is not at all. It is as impossible to define as the concept of being (Scheler 1971, p. 98). Any logical consideration of value must necessarily presuppose a standard, which is itself again a value judgment. Thus, a normative circular argument remains unavoidable. Or to put it differently: Any approach to the subject of values requires value judgments a priori.

The question remains, however, what values are oriented toward. Everything that is not necessarily predetermined by natural law or possibly is from divine origin (Harari 2017) is culture and thus contingent. It is shaped by humans and can be changed by humans. This again leads to the question of which maxims can guide value concepts. One possible maxim has already been suggested above, the sustainable survival of the group (community, organization) under changing environmental conditions, or qualitatively upgraded: the sustainable good life of the many. But no one with half open eyes would call this

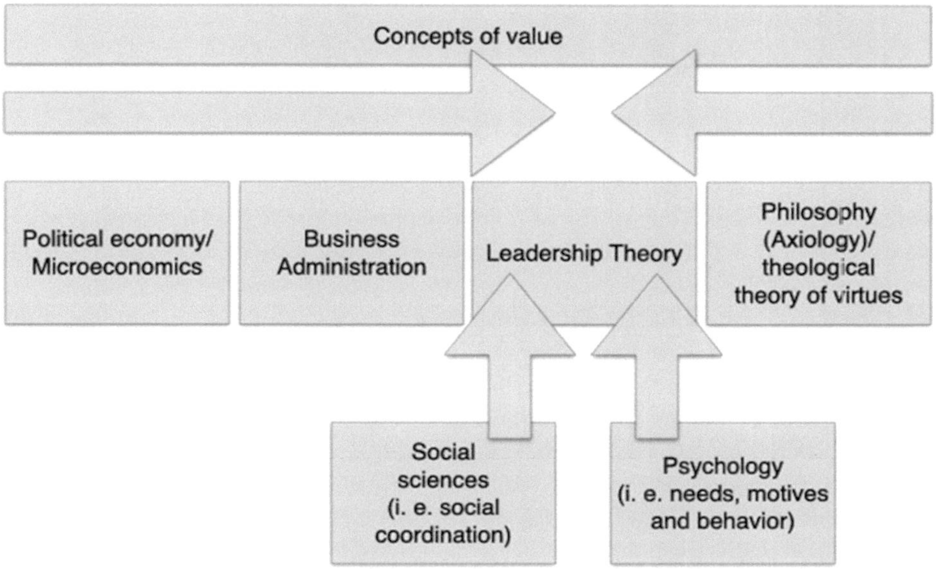

Fig. 2 Plural approach to value-based leadership

factual; bottle collectors and food banks, wars, and famines speak a different language. Values can at best serve as noble ideals, imaginary states, or even transcendent concepts.

Sublime values are one thing, but values, in Scheler's (1971) sense, cannot exist outside of action. Rather, they develop along the contour of factual practices and can only take shape in reflection in relation to these practices. Numerous societies have therefore developed norms of behavior, ideals, commandments, and virtues as sanctionable instructions for human behavior. In this way, amorphous value concepts can be incorporated into a society's repertoire of practices. Cultural artifacts reproduce value concepts in a society through the practices they shape.

The dynamic amorphousness of what we call values thus comes up against the no less amorphous construct of "leadership," which further complicates a structured scientific approach. What are the bearers of value in this context? Is value, in the end, merely an economic quantity? Should we therefore approach it from the perspective of economic value theory? Or should we approach values preferably from a sociological (community) or psychological (individual) perspective? Do we need a philosophical approach or could the banal insights of classical business administration be sufficient? And in the end, another circular argument crystallizes: Who defines value in situations when leadership intervenes? Is leadership possibly only value-oriented because it reflects the value concepts staged by the leader in a self-referential way? Is it the leader who makes the values?

Thus, in the end, there is nothing left but to illuminate the highly multiplex and iridescent term "value-oriented leadership" from a wide spectrum of perspectives, without ever being able to expect anything like a unified theory.

5 The Imagination of Value

Broadly speaking, we can approach the question of how value is created through the notion of two different value doctrines (Fig. 3) it in a first step: first economic, and second a philosophical perspective.

From both perspectives, the question arises as to what constitutes subjective value and whether there is such a thing as objective (or objectifiable) value. In the case of economic value theories, we have first of all two major objective value theories, namely, (1) the question of natural value or (2) the value of and the creation of value by labor, prominently raised by Karl Marx, and (3) the subjective value theories, above all scarcity and utility theories. In contrast, but without always being able to draw a proper line, philosophical value doctrines are primarily devoted to the big question of universal values as well as, in the broadest sense, value relations in the field of tension between subject and practices. Primarily, but not exclusively, economic value doctrines refer to goods, whereas philosophical value doctrines refer to individuals and their actions. However, this does not yet answer the question of whether, for example, the notion of "Ehrbarer Kaufmann" ("honorable merchant") (Becker and Ray 2017) is an economic or a philosophical category or both. In addition to the economic and normative question, there is also the question of the extent to which values and the status of the individual in the group are related. In particular, there is the question of whether an individual is a valuable member of the group, more

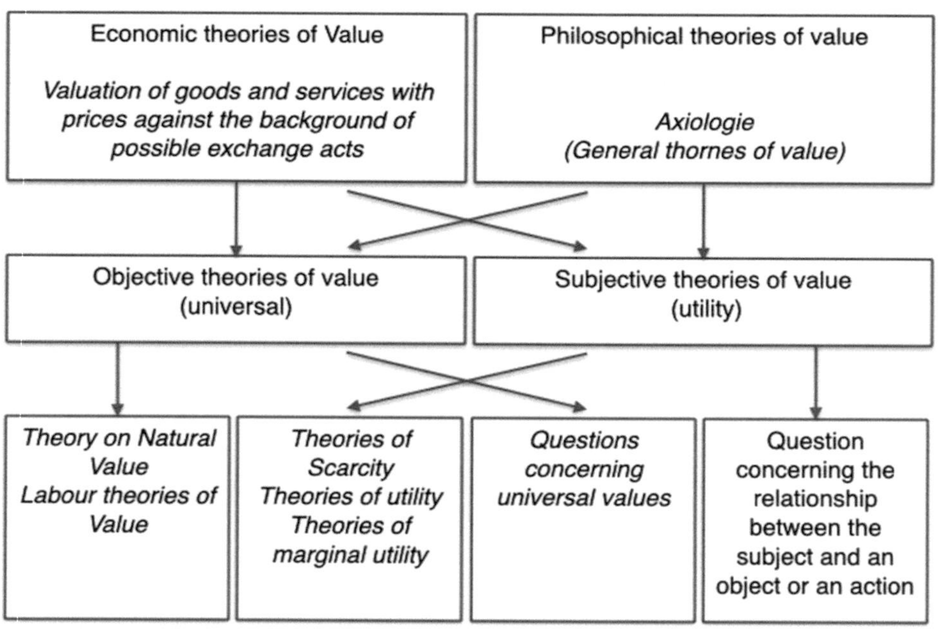

Fig. 3 Theoretical approaches

likely to be at the center or on the margins, or far up or down in the stratification of the group (Beckert 2018). Artifacts, action, or objects sometimes have a high symbolic value; think of going to Canossa, scepter or orb, or the appropriate car in the driveway. Access to such artifacts gives the power to determine what is to be regarded as a value or what is to be considered valuable.

In any case, with the advent of industrialization and the invention of business administration, primacy of value creation and the tightly pre-programmed social coordination according to the "rational principle" (Marx 2018; Gutenberg 1929) evolved. These principles do not only determine the context of leadership; they even themselves become the purpose and legitimation of leadership.

If no alternative value constructs (Fig. 4) are kept present, the economization may lead to a narrowed and opportunistic focus on the accumulation of monetary values. Value-based leadership in this sense will aim to increase a company value that is expressed either in a market price or in a subjective expectation of the future that is backed by prices (Voigt et al. 2005). Value-based management in this sense aims to ensure that management action has the purpose of maintaining or increasing the financial value of the company or fulfilling the value expectations placed on the company by its stakeholders, whereby the rational principle and the realization of payment expectations are means to this end. Often, these go hand in hand with the expectation of a future exit, for example, through sale, IPO, or passing on to a subsequent generation (Becker 2019).

The consequences of a conception of value reduced to economic quantities are the shadowing of the social space and the programmatic narrowing to payment expectations

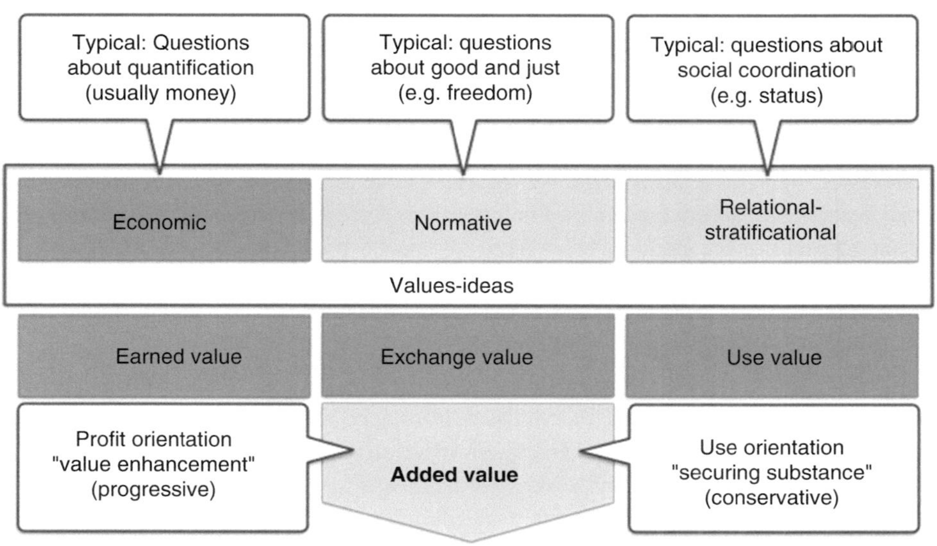

Fig. 4 Value creation

(Witt 1994). In contrast, the socially based value constructions may secure the long-term survival of the group or organization.

A closer approach to the concept of value would be through three basic questions, namely, (1) the quantification of values, (2) the two major normative questions of "good" and "just," and (3) social status ("being a valuable member of a community"). This means looking at the question of value-based leadership from an economic, a normative, and a relational perspective.

Thus, the protein that our ancestors captured while hunting in the savannah could have a higher value to the settler than to the hunter himself. On the other hand, this may have been reversed in the case of crops. This is the condition for a successful exchange. Consequently, the question should be asked about exchange value ("what is the actual market value of a good, service, or action?"), income value ("above all, what is the possible surplus value I can earn from a good, service, or action?"), and utility value ("what benefit do I get and for how long?"). In this context, utility value tends to be conservative in that the use value of, say, a dwelling is generally a function of use over time and, in a sustainable sense, is focused on preservation. In contrast, income value tends to be value enhancing, i.e., progressive and geared toward growth and maximization (and therefore possibly rather incompatible with the principle – or value – of sustainability). Crucial in both cases, however, is the fiction of a future development of value (either through utility or through yield), but also of (subjective) scarcity.

6 Culture – Values – Economy

We can see that the classical concepts of value are only partially suitable for providing a comprehensive answer to the question of value-driven leadership. When we talk about a concept of value in this context, we should firstly distinguish the transcendent and the economic construction of value and secondly acknowledge the fictionality of both.

On the one hand, the (quantitative) attribution of value is indispensable for economic acts of exchange and a prerequisite for the emergence of trade: How many chickens is a camel worth? Since direct attribution is difficult and presupposes a temporal and spatial coming together of the goods to be exchanged, the act of exchange was mediatized early on: Money as a unit of value came into play. It is through the construction of value and the quantifiability of value that goods can be economized in the first place. Nevertheless, value and currency cannot simply be equated.

For example, how does one measure whether an employee is a valuable member of a team? How does one weigh the individual performance in intra-organizational competition where the weakest go to the wall against altruistic services for the success of the whole? Valuing performance and success of actions is sometimes, quite independent of money and economic exchange rationality, a condition of leadership. Could our ancestors measure what was the fair share of the prey? What role did subjective expectation, hierarchies and distribution of power, or disagreement in the group play? Ultimately, ways must be found to level intra-group conflict, so that the resources can be saved for the important challenges of the survival of the group. In the end, reciprocity – that is, a fair and peaceful balance that conserves resources – can only be ensured through group-wide shared or even universal value constructs and established regulatory mechanisms (institutions) derived from them. And here is where culture comes into play. Can it be that the genesis of leadership and value occurred hand in hand within the framework of human cultural evolution?

At the latest with the sedentarization of humans in the Neolithic Revolution, a qualitative aspect was added that we subsume today under the term value. As the story of biblical Babylon tells us, the inhabitants of the growing cities, increasingly organized around the division of labor, could no longer keep distance and thus avoid conflict like the nomadic hunter-gatherers of earlier cultures. Growing and diverse communities had to develop institutional arrangements that allowed them (1) to live together, (2) to create stock an ownership, and (3) to share immobile resources, such as fields and mines. With the emergence of large urban settlements and the invention of writing, shared values and guidelines for action became codified. The ten commandments in each of the Christian and Hebrew Bibles can be cited as evidence of such codification. Insofar as these commandments or laws guiding action are internalized and reproduced intra- and, above all, intergenerationally, they synthesize in the form of further cultural artifacts whose recognition becomes sanctionable.

From this, in turn, institutions developed that regulated the distribution of resources, for example, in a system of sacrifices, levies, and taxes. From religiously charged commandments, such as "Thou shalt not kill" or sacrificial regimes (the religious leaders had the task of accumulating and distributing resources), social value standards institutionalized.

Such transcendent value attributes are thus able to justify sanctionable behavioral norms, group pressure, and power relations, but also cultural practices. At the same time, they relieve leaders from the need of direct leadership interventions – parts of what constitutes leadership become reproducible and virtually automatic. Direct leadership action has thus been replaced by symbolic and institutional forms of leadership supported by value constructs, which in turn makes it possible to lead growing communities and delegate leadership shares. Along with an increasing division of labor, a differentiation took place, in which (1) religious leadership structures (which initially also performed legislative, judicial, and fiscal tasks) and (2) an executive authority with own leadership and structural logics were able to emerge in parallel.

Although cultural practices, values, virtues, and social norms are relatively stable and deeply anchored in collective memory, they are by no means immutable. For example, our mobility – the way we travel, the daily professional commute, etc. – is stably embedded in our culture, but it is also not far more than 100 years old (it all started with Bertha Benz in 1888). Due to changes in technological, economic, social, and ecological conditions, the societal arrangements are under permanent pressure (Becker and Montiel Alafont 2015). Thus, family values or other social norms have changed. To have a morning run instead of going to church on Sundays was hardly conceivable 100 years ago. Especially since the Enlightenment and the invention of printing, counter-narratives and heresies challenge dominant narratives and the cultural mainstream. It begins with heroic worship of characters challenging the dominant value system (think of Robin Hood or the Vitalien Brothers, e.g.) and ends with conspiracy theories on the internet. Technology, scientific, political, media, and social change do not simply bypass supposedly unshakeable values, norms, and virtues; they affect them directly. Boundary shifts are permanently taking place, and cultural boundaries have always been challenged and renegotiated (Becker 2017). As a striking example, consider the historic development from homosexuality as a deadly sin punished under the pain of death to the legal acceptance of same-sex marriage in the modern societies today. Each of these shifts in boundaries has the potential to trigger the delegitimization of what exists. What has previously been considered as normal and just may appear strange or offensive. A new social consensus may deprive leaders of their legitimating basis. Consequently, it seems advisable for leadership to acknowledge counter-narratives and to renegotiate its own legitimacy on the basis of a changing zeitgeist. Symbolic acts, such as Daimler CEO Zetsche in sneakers (Weinzierl 2018) or the radical turn of a Volkswagen CEO (Herbert Diess) toward electromobility ("Die Welt" 2018), may serve as examples. On the other hand, there is danger ahead when the social mesh is cut by leaders and executives, and the grid of Excel becomes the prison of the organization (Case and Maner 2014). Companies barricade themselves, before they die (Dueck 2019).

7 Taking Value-Based Leadership to the Streets

We have seen that value-based leadership is leadership that enables the sustainable survival of groups and organizations (companies) under ever-changing resource conditions. Leadership thus means ensuring coordinated goal-oriented action to reliably solve group problems over a longer period of time and under varying conditions.

In doing so, one should abandon the idea that there is "one best way." Nevertheless, it can make sense to provide a wider framework for leadership and to approach leadership problems in a structured way, both in terms of one's own leadership practices and as an orientation for those indirectly and directly involved. Therefore the "Triple-Two Model of Sustainable Leadership" is proposed as a guideline (Becker 2013, p. 138 ff.) (Fig. 5).

7.1 Guiding and Alignment

The more complex the problem and the more dynamic the conditions, the less simple leadership concepts such as instruction and execution, carrot and stick, work. The more complex the task, the more undefined the situation, and the more qualified the employees, the more a participative, delegative, and democratic style of leadership is required. It is then no longer a matter of giving instructions or controlling execution, but of ensuring coordinated problem-solving (alignment) by means of shared visions. Consequently, the focus is no longer on specific leadership intervention, but on reliable institutional arrangements by which provide orientation for the group members and their activities.

The Triple Two of Sustainable Leadership		
Guiding	**Conception** Providing a meaningful strategic route from history to future	**Communications** Enabling multiple levels of communication
Motivational	**Mastery** Fostering personal development	**Belonging** Making followers a valued part of the group
Social	**Empathy** Ensuring attention to the feelings and accomplishments of others	**Reciprocity** Balancing both social and economic interests

Becker, Lutz (2013) Projektmanagement als Führungskonzeption; in: Wagner, R./Grau, N.: Basiswissen Projektmanagement - Grundlagen der Projektarbeit, Symposion: Düsseldorf

Fig. 5 The triple two of sustainable leadership

7.1.1 Conception

Conceptual leadership is understood as an integral design framework for leadership and strategy and all activities derived, internally and externally. The conception is a typically written system of mission statement, goals, strategies, and rules as a guide for all involved. Somehow similar to what our aforementioned mobster carried with him.

This means that everything that happens in the company is subordinated to the concept and measured against it. The conceptual approach provides a framework within which employees can and should act as freely and autonomously as possible. De facto, it is a matter of fiducially holding the interests of the various stakeholders, which consequently also include future generations or nature, and of agreeing on a binding framework of values and virtues. That all against the background of current and anticipated internal and external conditions to which the attention of the group or organization is to be directed. The conceptual approach should ensure consistency in communication and the social coordination of the team under changing conditions and ensure that the organization is not thrown off course by the self-interests, whims, and weaknesses of individuals. The concept creates rules and decision-making premises which, ideally, can be relied upon by all stakeholders involved.

7.1.2 Communications

Social systems are constituted by communications (Luhmann 1984). "Resonance" (Rosa 2016) arises here between actors through the alignment of goals and interests, shared values, a common history, or coordinated actions that shape a common picture of reality. The point is that it enables certain coordinated responses to environmental stimuli and the development of viable solutions to group problems. Therefore, it is the leaders' task to challenge the organization by questioning values in order to create new occasions for communication and alignment.

7.2 Motivation

The constant improvement of one's repertoire for mastering problems and the need for social belonging are strong motivators.

7.2.1 Mastery

By mastery, we understand the development of capabilities and competencies to mastering the challenges of the organization. It is regarded as a basic human need to further develop individual repertoires and abilities.

7.2.2 Belonging

Participation in and acceptance by the community is, as we have seen, an important driver of human action. It is basic human motives such as being recognized, being liked, and active participation that motivate us in our depths. This is where leadership is required to ensure cohesion and inclusion. However, there is a danger that leaders who do not adhere to the explicit and implicit rules of the game lose their ties to the group and thus give away potential to promote the group.

7.3 Social

If we understand leadership as something emergent, it becomes clear that the social quality is a decisive factor for the success of leadership.

7.3.1 Empathy

Empathy is an automatism that enables us to interpret the actions, emotions, and intentions of others and to be able to take the perspective of the other person. Our narrative consciousness helps us to do this, because it invents, produces, and simulates links, alternatives, surprises, excuses, solutions, and dei ex machina all at once (Breithaupt 2009, p. 138). Without empathy, you cannot move people in the long run.

7.3.2 Reciprocity

Leadership, as we have seen, goes hand in hand with the ability to accumulate resources: power, time, job performance, collective intelligence, esteem, attention, and, last but not least, material resources. But leaders must also be able to, in turn, distribute these resources fairly back within the organization. As we could see from the ancestors challenge of distribution their common prey fairly, followers focus a great deal of their attention on getting a fair share of their contribution resp. the resources they have generated back.

8 Final Remark

The concept of value is, as we have seen, amorphous. Nevertheless, codified values enable orientation and are thus the basis for negotiating structures and strategies in organizations. At the same time, such values legitimize leadership as such as well as certain leadership practices and interventions.

Leadership competencies also seem to go hand in hand with the ability to make value judgments and to justify them conclusively to those being led as well as to external stakeholders. In this way, leadership evades the absurd primacy, so often staged, of having to restrict people's scope for action or even make them "compliant."

However, values and value standards are not endogenous, but develop in processes of engagement with relevant environments and stabilizing cultural artifacts (Becker and Montiel Alafont 2015). This reveals that values, value concepts, and appreciation toward people, actions, and objects are subject to an ever-changing "zeitgeist." If the standards change in this debate, i.e., if the other and the new are considered valuable, then the economic mechanisms of value creation also change. We are only prepared to invest in something that fulfills a value for us.

However, changing values and diverging value concepts of leaders and internal and external stakeholders can also lead to the slippery slope of delegitimation. Utilitaristic-hedonistic value concepts seem to be just as obvious candidates for delegitimation processes of this kind as the extractive handling of economic values generated from within the organization. Focusing only on output may be fatal in the long run.

References

Acemoglu D, Robinson JA (2019) The narrow corridor. States, societies and the fate of liberty. Penguin Books, London

BBC (2007) Mafia's 'Ten Commandments' found; http://news.bbc.co.uk/2/hi/europe/7086716.stm. Accessed 27 June 2022

Becker L (2013) Projektmanagement als Führungskonzeption. In: Wagner R, Grau N (eds) Basiswissen Praktisches Projektmanagement. Symposion, Düsseldorf

Becker L (2017) Transformation, Kultur und das Digitale: Transformative Wissenschaft als Grenzgang. In: Pfriem R, Schneidewind U, Barth J, Graupe S, Korbun T (eds) Transformative Wirtschaftswissenschaft im Kontext nachhaltiger Entwicklung. Metropolis, Marburg

Becker L (2019) Schumpeters blinder Fleck. Das Spannungsfeld zwischen Markt und Unternehmer im Zeichen der Plattform-Ökonomie. In: Frambach H, Koubek N, Kurz HD, Pfriem R (eds) Schöpferische Zerstörung und der Wandel des Unternehmertums. Zur Aktualität von Joseph A. Schumpeter. Metropolis, Marburg

Becker L, Montiel Alafont FJ (2015) Warum in interkulturellen Projekten das wahre Leben tobt. In: Becker L, Gora W, Wagner R (eds) Erfolgreiches Interkulturelles Projektmanagement. Symposion, Düsseldorf
Becker L, Ray A (2017) Ehrbarer Kaufmann oder verantwortungsvoller Unternehmer? Mythen, Spannungen und Interessenskonflikte im Umgang mit Verantwortung im Marketing. In: Stehr C, Struve F (eds) CSR und Marketing. Nachhaltigkeit und Verantwortung richtig kommunizieren. Springer Gabler, Wiesbaden, pp 41–57
Beckert J (2018) Imaginierte Zukunft. Fiktionale Erwartungen und die Dybanik des Kapitalismus. Suhrkamp, Berlin
Breithaupt F (2009) Kulturen der Empathie. Suhrkamp, Frankfurt am Main
Carlyle T (1841) On heroes and hero worship and the heroic in history. James Fraser, London
Case CR, Maner JK (2014) Divide and conquer: when and why leaders undermine the cohesive fabric of their group. J Pers Soc Psychol 107(6):1033–1050
Childe VG (1951) Social evolution. Watts, London
Crutzen P, Stoermer EF (2000) The anthropocene. Glob Chang Newsl 41:17–18
Die Welt (2018) VW-Chef Diess will E-Dienstwagen für Manager einführen. https://www.welt.de/regionales/niedersachsen/article181392128/VW-Chef-Diess-will-E-Dienstwagen-fuer-Manager-einfuehren.html?wtrid=onsite.onsitesearch. Accessed 02 Sept 2018
Dueck G (2019) DD352: Vor ihrem Tod igeln sich Unternehmen ein. https://www.omnisophie.com/dd352-vor-ihrem-tod-igeln-sich-unternehmen-ein/. Accessed 29 Dec 2019
Fayol H (2018) Administration industrielle et générale – prévoyance organisation – commandement, coordination – contrôle. H. Dunod et E. Pinat, Paris (Original 1916)
Flannery KV (1972) The cultural evolution of civilizations. Annu Rev Ecol Syst:399–426. https://doi.org/10.1146/annurev.es.03.110172.002151
Gutenberg E (1929) Die Unternehmung als Gegenstand betriebswirtschaftlicher Theorie. Spaeth & Linde, Berlin/Wien
Harari NY (2017) Homo Deus: Eine Geschichte von Morgen. C. H. Beck, München
Kristiansen K (2013) Religion and society in the bronze age. In: Bredholt Christensen L, Hammer O, Warburton DA (eds) The handbook of religions in ancient Europe. Acumen, Stocksfield, pp 77–92. https://www.academia.edu/5698976/Religion_and_society_in_the_Bronze_Age?source=swp_share. Accessed 10 Jan 2020
Langer A (2007) Fund bei Verhaftung Polizei entdeckt die zehn Gebote der Mafia Der Spiegel 09.11.2008. https://www.spiegel.de/panorama/justiz/fund-bei-verhaftung-polizei-entdeckt-die-zehn-gebote-der-mafia-a-516480.html
Luhmann N (1984) Soziale Systeme. Suhrkamp, Frankfurt am Main
Lumsden CJ, Wilson EO (2005) Genes, mind, and culture – the coevolutionary process: 25th anniversary edition. World Scientific, Hackensack
MacGregor Burns J (1978) Leadership. Harpers & Row, New York
Marx K (2018) Das Kapital. Alle drei Bände – Kritik der politischen Ökonomie: Der Produktionsprozess des Kapitals + Der Zirkulationsprozeß des Kapitals + Der Gesamtprozess der kapitalistischen Produktion. e-artnow, Prag (Original, 1867–1894) E-Book. Apple Books. https://books.apple.com/de/book/das-kapital/id932306075. Accessed 01 July 2019
McLaughlin P (2012) The second Darwinian revolution: steps toward a new evolutionary environmental sociology. Nat Cult 7(3):231–258
Olivelle P (2013) King, governance, and law in ancient India: Kauṭilya's Arthaśāstra. Oxford University Press, Oxford
Price ME, van Vugt M (2014) The evolution of leader – follower reciprocity: the theory of service-for-prestige. Front Hum Neurosci. https://doi.org/10.3389/fnhum.2014.00363
Richter S (2012) Mensch und Markt. Murmann, Hamburg

Ridley M (2011) The rational optimist. Fourth Estate, London
Rosa H (2016) Resonanz: Eine Soziologie der Weltbeziehung. Suhrkamp, Frankfurt
Scheler M (1971) Frühe Schriften. Francke, Bern/München
Stogdill RM (1974) Handbook of leadership: a survey of the literature. Free Press, New York
Taylor FW (1911) The principles of scientific management. iBooks. https://itunes.apple.com/de/book/the-principles-of-scientific-management/id501276645?mt=11. Accessed 10 Jan 2020
van Vugt M, Ahuja A (2010) Selected. Why some people leas, why others follow, and why it matters. Profil Books, London
van Vugt M, Hogan R, Kaiser RB (2008) Leadership, followership, and evolution – some lessons from the past. Am Psychol 63(3):182–196
Voigt C, Voigt J, Voigt JF, Voigt R (2005) Unternehmensbewertung. Springer Gabler, Wiesbaden
von Rosen C (2008) När-democracy: equality and leadership in a marginalised Gotlandic community. In: Emanuelsson M, Johansson E, Ekman A-K (eds) Peripheral communities crisis, continuity and long-term survival. Department of Urban and Rural Development, Swedish Agricultural University, Uppsala, pp 115–130
Weber M (1922) Wirtschaft und Gesellschaft – Grundriß der verstehenden Soziologie. https://www.textlog.de/weber_wirtschaft.html
Weinzierl S (2018) Dieter Zetsche wird 65 – Der Erfolgsschnauzer der Autowelt. https://www.produktion.de/wirtschaft/dieter-zetsche-wird-65-der-erfolgsschnauzer-der-autowelt-287.html. Accessed 02 May 2018
Witt FH (1994) Theorietraditionen der betriebswirtschaftlichen Forschung – Deutschsprachige Betriebswirtschaftslehre und angloamerikanische Management- und Organisationsforschung. Gabler, Wiesbaden
Witt U (2003) The evolving economy: essays on the evolutionary approach to economics. Edward Elgar, Cheltenham
Witt U (2006) Evolutionary concepts in economics and biology. J Evol Econ 16(5):473–476
Zeuch A (2015) Alle Macht für niemand. Aufbruch der Unternehmensdemokraten, Murmann, Hamburg

Prof. Dr. rer. oec. Lutz Becker heads the Business School and, as Dean of Studies, the Master's program "Sustainable Marketing and Leadership" at the Fresenius University of Applied Sciences in the Department of Business and Media in Cologne. Research interests: Digital and Social Transformation, Strategy and Leadership, Sustainable Business Development, and Narrative and Innovation.

Employee Commitment in Small- and Medium-Sized Enterprises (SMEs): Investigation of Influencing Factors Using the Example of Generation Y

Larissa Loose and Marion Preuß

Abstract

As a result of demographic developments and the resulting shortage of skilled workers in Europe, companies should focus on retaining their employees. This is particularly important for small- and medium-sized enterprises (SMEs) due to their often limited financial resources. Therefore, the aim of this study is to determine which factors are important for Generation Y employees (born between 1980 and 2000) to retain their loyalty to a small- and medium-sized enterprise.

To test the validity of the key factors influencing employee retention from various studies presented in a literature- and theory-based structural equation model, Millennials working in small- and medium-sized companies responded to a survey using a five-point Likert scale. The empirical data were analyzed using the partial least square (PLS) method.

The study shows that perceived organizational support (POS), corporate social responsibility (CSR), and job satisfaction contribute a crucial role to Generation Y retention. Overall, the findings provide important insights for SMEs and have implications for human resource management (HRM) practices.

L. Loose (✉) · M. Preuß
FOM Hochschule für Oekonomie & Management, Hamburg, Germany
e-mail: marion.preuss@fom.de

J. Lange (ed.), *Value-Oriented Leadership in Theory and Practice*,
https://doi.org/10.1007/978-3-662-65883-3_4

1 Relevance of Employee Retention of Generation Y in SMEs

"The most valuable assets of a 20th-century company were its production equipment. The most valuable asset of a 21st-century institution, whether business or non-business, will be its knowledge workers and their productivity" (Drucker 2007). As early as the end of the twentieth century, Peter Drucker predicted that the know-how and productivity of a company's employees would be its competitive advantage today.

Therefore, the wishes and needs of employees should become the focus of companies, especially due to demographic developments. As a result of low birth rates and higher life expectancy, the European Union is affected by demographic aging (Eurostat 2019). This in turn leads to a lower proportion of people of working age. In 2018, the proportion of people aged 15–64 in society was 64.7% (total population 512.4 million). While the share of 65-year-olds was almost 20%, the share of young people was only 15.6%.

These developments are leading to a shortage of skilled workers, also referred to as the "war for talent." Therefore, employee retention is gaining importance, especially for small- and medium-sized enterprises (SMEs) with limited financial resources, which in 2017 included around 24.5 million in the European Union (Statista 2019) (Table 1).

With regard to the "war for talent," the employees of Generation Y, born between 1980 and 2000 (Lenka and Naim 2018), receive the most attention. This generation grows up in homes with stable financial circumstances and is shaped by new technological media such as the Internet and social media, among other things (Lenka and Naim 2018). Furthermore, the literature describes Millennials as ego-centered, self-confident, materialistic, and disloyal to employers (Lyons and Papavasileiou 2015). Compared to Baby Boomers (born between 1946 and 1964) and Generation X (born between 1965 and 1979), there are differences in their work values and work style (Lenka and Naim 2018). Future research will reveal the extent to which Generation Y differs from Generation Z (born in 2001), who will soon enter the workforce (Montana and Petit 2008). Due to the changing work values and requirements of Generation Y, companies' human resource management faces challenges (Brant and Castro 2019). Therefore, companies should introduce various measures to satisfy this generation and strengthen retention.

The aim of this study is to investigate which factors are important for the employee retention of Generation Y in an SME. Recommendations for SMEs can be derived from the results.

Table 1 Differentiation criteria for SMEs (European Commission 2003)

	Number of employees	Annual turnover in EUR	Balance sheet total in EUR
Microenterprises	Until 9	Up to two million	Up to two million
Small enterprises	Until 49	Up to ten million	Up to ten million
Medium-sized companies	Until 249	Up to 50 million	Up to 43 million

2 Literature Review

In the context of employees' attitudes and identification with their work, job satisfaction is the most studied construct (Hulin et al. 2017). During the period from 1975 to 1990, the construct "organizational commitment" was also researched. According to Boulian et al. (1974), this refers to the strength of the employee's identification with one's employer and the degree of the involvement. Until the end of this period, commitment, along with job satisfaction, was among the main attitudinal determinants of staff turnover (Hulin et al. 2017).

In 1974, Boulian et al. examined organizational commitment and job satisfaction in the context of personnel turnover using American mental health trainees. Commitment proved to be the most important variable in distinguishing between employees who stayed with the organization and those who quit. Steers (1977) determined the influencing factors and effects of commitment in his study. Thus, personal and job characteristics as well as work experiences influence commitment, which in turn influences the employee's intention and desire to stay with the company. Eisenberger et al. (1986), on the other hand, focused on the relationship of employee's perceived organizational support and affective commitment to the company.

Mottaz (1988) also reviewed the factors influencing organizational commitment. According to this, intrinsic rewards such as the content of the job itself are decisive.

Allen and Meyer (1990) marked the beginning of a new era. While in the previous decade organizational commitment as a whole was relevant, Allen and Meyer developed the three-component model. According to this, organizational commitment is composed of affective (emotional attachment), normative (perceived obligation), and calculative (associated switching costs) commitment. This model forms the basis for further studies (Budhwar et al. 2007).

Eby et al. (1999) related their study to affective commitment and identified intrinsic motivation as a mediator of both affective commitment and job satisfaction. Both constructs have a negative impact on employee turnover. Additionally, job satisfaction is positively related to affective commitment.

Coetzer et al. (2010) focused their study on the effects of formal training and development opportunities on the behavior of employees from SMEs. Affective commitment was not found to be an influencing factor on switching intentions, but the sample was highly educated senior employees, so generalization is not possible. The study by Johnstone et al. (2013) shows that employees in small firms are more strongly committed to it than those in large firms. Moreover, organizational commitment is higher in companies with high employee satisfaction than in companies with low satisfaction.

Around 2010, the topic around Generation Y and the differences in work values compared to other generations came up. Campbell et al. (2010) examined and compared the work values of Baby Boomers, Generation X, and Generation Y, using American high school graduates from 1976, 1991, and 2006 to isolate generational differences from age differences. The strongest change here is seen in the value placed on leisure time. This is reflected in Generation X's and Y's frequently described desire for work-life balance. According to Bal et al. (2016), work content such as task variety and autonomy is important to Generation Y. This in turn influences both affective commitment and intention to leave.

Göttel et al. (2016) investigated the influence of a relatively unexplored factor "internal corporate social responsibility" (CSR) on affective and normative commitment. The study confirmed the relationship between CSR and affective commitment.

In summary, from the state of research, there is currently no acquainted study on the factors influencing employee retention based on Generation Y in SMEs.

3 Empirical Analysis of the Relevant Factors Influencing Employee Retention

3.1 Conceptual Background and Hypothesis Development

Based on the current state of research, the following section develops a hypothesis-based structural equation model to identify the factors influencing employee retention of Generation Y in SMEs.

Intrinsic motivation is defined by Hackman and Oldham (1975) as the degree to which an employee is motivated to do their job effectively on their own. This is influenced, for example, by the job challenge, the clarity of tasks, or how feedback is received. In their study, Eby et al. (1999) confirmed a positive relationship between intrinsic motivation and an employee's job satisfaction using meta-analytic correlations and a structural equation model. Therefore, the following hypothesis can be formulated:

H1: The more intrinsically motivated a Generation Y employee is, the more satisfied they are with their job in the SME.

The European Commission (2001) describes corporate social responsibility (CSR) as a concept whereby companies voluntarily integrate social and environmental issues into their business operations and toward their stakeholders. According to Gómez-Navarro et al. (2017), economic performance is also an important criterion of CSR because it allows conclusions to be drawn about the extent to which a company has "created wealth for stakeholders" (Global Reporting Initiative 2016).

In the social context, for example, transparent communication is important for Generation Y as they want to be involved in important issues (Stewart et al. 2017). Furthermore, corporate engagement ($p = 0.67$) and job security ($p = 0.71$) have a positive impact on social responsibility (Göttel et al. 2016, 2017). Since social responsibility is gaining importance within Generation Y, based on the social exchange theory, a positive relationship between CSR and an employee's satisfaction can be assumed. The next hypothesis is derived from this:

H2: The more an SME implements the concept of social responsibility, the more satisfied a Generation Y employee is with their job.

According to Eisenberger et al. (1986), perceived organizational support (POS) refers to the extent to which an employee feels that one's employer cares about their well-being and values their efforts. For an organization to be perceived as supportive, it may be important to provide equity, supervisor support, good rapport between colleagues, and rewards. Allen et al. (2003) in their study examined the influences on perceived organizational support (POS) and role in the termination process. The result is that there is a positive correlation between POS and job satisfaction ($p = 0.42$) (Allen et al. 2003). Applied to Generation Y in SMEs, the following hypothesis emerges:

H3: Perceived organizational support has a positive impact on job satisfaction among Generation Y employees.

According to Price and Mueller's (1981) definition, job satisfaction means the extent to which employees like their job. Kinnie et al. (2005) examined the impact of employee satisfaction with different HR measures using three different work groups on affective commitment, and multivariate analysis confirmed a positive relationship. The meta-analysis by Herscovitch et al. (2002) also confirmed a strong positive correlation between job satisfaction and affective commitment ($p = 0.65$). The corresponding hypothesis is:

H4: The more satisfied a Generation Y employee is with one's job in an SME, the stronger the affective commitment is.

Allen and Meyer (1991) define affective commitment as the emotional attachment and identification of an employee with the company. This means that employees stay in a company because they want to. While Steers (1977) identified a positive relationship between affective commitment and an employee's intention to stay with the company ($p = 0.31$ and 0.38), Herscovitch et al. (2002) confirmed with the help of a meta-analysis that low affective commitment leads to increased intensions to leave. Therefore, the following hypotheses can be formulated:

H5: The more pronounced the affective commitment of a Generation Y employee in an SME, the greater the intention to stay in the company.

H7: The lower the affective commitment of a Generation Y employee in an SME, the greater the intention to leave.

Intention to stay indicates the extent to which an employee intends to maintain employment with the current employer, while intention to leave refers to the employee's plan to quit (Price 2001). As a result of the definitions, the following hypotheses are made:

H6: The more pronounced the intention of a Generation Y employee to remain in the SME, the longer an employment relationship lasts.

H8: The more pronounced an employee of Generation Y's intention to change jobs, the more likely one is to voluntarily terminate the employment relationship.

The relationships formulated in H1–H8 form the structure of the model shown in Fig. 1, which examines the factors influencing employee retention of Generation Y in SMEs.

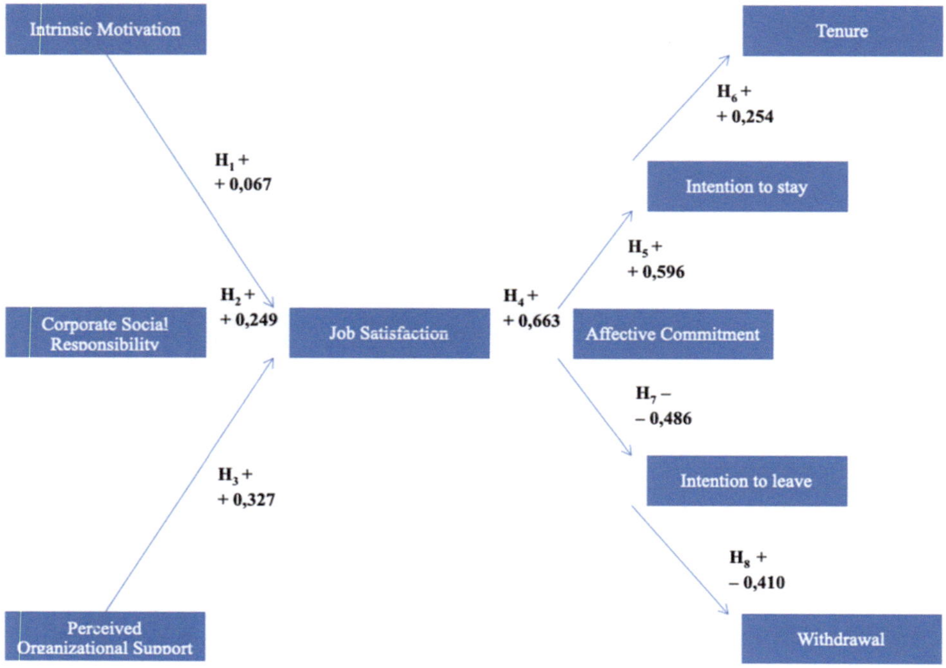

Fig. 1 Model for investigating the determinants of employee retention

3.2 Applied Methodology

The model setup was validated with the results of an online survey. The prerequisite for participation in the study was that the respondents were born between 1980 and 2000 and were employed in a German SME at the time of the survey.

3.2.1 Sample

A total of 102 people answered the survey completely (response rate 5.3%). After checking the data for missing values and plausibility, the present sample is $n = 99$ (63% women, 37% men).

The average age is 29 (born in 1989) and reflects different levels of education, although the proportion of academics (bachelor, master, or diploma) is higher. While almost half of the sample is employed in a company with 50–249 employees, another 42% work in a company with 10–49 employees and only 9% in a company with less than 10 employees. Overall, this $n = 99$ sample is 95% accurate in reflecting the average opinion of Generation Y in SMEs on key retention factors within a 10% margin of error.

3.2.2 Procedure

A Likert scale was used to measure the respondents' position. The survey participants answered the questions and statements on a five-point rating scale (1, does not agree at all; 2, agrees a little; 3, agrees some; 4, agrees quite a bit; 5, agrees completely) (Likert 1932).

In order to achieve high data quality, the questionnaire was tested in advance. This allowed changes to the wording and ensured that the questionnaire was understandable for the target group (Presser et al. 2004).

Two multivariate analysis methods with confirmatory application are available for estimating a structural equation model: variance structure analysis and covariance structure analysis (Dijkstra and Henseler 2015). The present study uses the variance-based partial least square (PLS) method and the latest software SmartPLS 3.0 (Henseler et al. 2015). It is an exploratory method, which is used to explain complex models with a large number of indicators that have also not been sufficiently explored. Moreover, in the present work, a small sample and no normally distributed data are available. Nevertheless, PLS allows the estimation of the model as it is an iterative estimation procedure (Dijkstra and Henseler 2015). Moreover, PLS also allows for latent variables operationalized with a formative measurement model (Fornell and Bookstein 1982) and moderator effects (Hair et al. 2014).

3.3 Statistical Verification and Results

3.3.1 Descriptive Statistical Analysis

The mean value, standard deviation, minimum (=1), and maximum (=5) of each item will be examined considering the whole data set. The mean values should be between 2 and 4 in relation to the existing Likert scale to ensure a differentiated representation of the different opinions (Albaum 1997). The analysis shows that eight items need to be removed. The reason for this is that these have only a small standard deviation (less than 1), so they do not differentiate enough. For example, for item IM01_01 (= a job that is interesting.), the reason may be that an interesting job is part of the basic requirement of a Generation Y worker. Therefore, it does not contribute to intrinsic motivation, and the survey does not result in different expressions.

After removal, all scores are within the valid minimum/maximum range. This means that the respondents used the rating scale evenly and it is unlikely to bias the data analysis.

3.3.2 Analysis of the Measurement Models

The reflective measurement model is tested with regard to its validity and reliability. To check the indicator reliability, the external loadings of the items are considered. These should exceed the threshold value of 0.707 (Hair et al. 2014). Then the loadings are usually also significant. To check this, a one-sided significance test with an appropriate significance level of 10% is conducted using bootstrapping with 300 iterations and 600 subsamples (Sarstedt and Ringle 2010).

The result of the test is that nine items are not significant and must be removed. For example, the loadings of the items AC01_05_rev (= I do not feel like "part of the family" at my employer), CS09_05 (= My employer stands for rewarding employees partly through performance-based bonuses), and OS04_06 (= My colleagues and I spend time together outside of work) are less than 0.5 and thus do not exceed the threshold. In addition, the internal consistency of the combined indicators and their convergent and discriminant validity were checked.

Both composite reliability and Cronbach's alpha can be used as quality measures of internal consistency and should take a value of at least 0.7 (Hair et al. 2014).

Convergent validity is verified using the AVE (average variance extracted) (Hair et al. 2016). An AVE value of at least 0.50 ensures that the construct explains at least half of the variance of the indicators.

The constructs meet the minimum values for AVE and composite reliability (Table 2). Only Cronbach's alpha for organizational support and affective commitment are below the required value of 0.70. However, since the other two quality measures are fulfilled, this Cronbach's alpha value is accepted.

The Fornell-Larcker criterion is used to test discriminant validity (Henseler et al. 2015). This criterion is considered to be met if the root of the average variance extracted (AVE) of a latent variable is greater than any correlation of this variable with all other variables in the model (Henseler et al. 2015). The results show that all variables are independent constructs.

After assessing the reflective measurement model, the formative measurement model is examined, for which other quality criteria are used.

To ensure that the formative indicators do not correlate with each other, the variance inflation factor (VIF) is used to check for collinearity (Hair et al. 2014). If the VIF is less than 5, it can be assumed that there is no correlation problem. This measure of goodness is met in this study as the VIF of the formative indicators is between 1 and 3. To assess the relevance of the indicators, the weights and, as in the reflective measurement model, the significance are considered. According to Hair et al. (2016), the path coefficient should have a value of at least 0.1, but it is important that indicators with low weights are not

Table 2 Values of the convergence criteria and Cronbach's alpha of the reflectively specified constructs

Construct	Average variance extracted (AVE)	Cronbach's alpha	Composite reliability
Intention to stay	0.808	0.764	0.893
Affective commitment	0.558	0.418	0.705
CSR	0.579	0.853	0.891
Job satisfaction	0.713	0.795	0.880
Organizational support	0.514	0.590	0.777
Intention to leave	0.863	0.842	0.926

directly eliminated because all indicators together define the latent variable. In reviewing the weights and significance of the formative indicators, it is noticeable that several indicators have low, non-significant weights. Before these are finally eliminated, it is checked whether these indicators have a relatively high and significant load (>0.50). This is the case for six items, so they are not removed. These are CS02_01 (= My employer is very transparent about the organization's goals and activities), IM05_01 (= My job requires the use of a variety of complex or demanding skills), IM05_03 (= My job requires doing many different tasks and using a variety of different skills to do so), IM07_01 (= My job is one in which many people are affected by how well I do it), IM07_03 (= The results of my work affect other people's lives or well-being), and IM10_03 (= Managers or other coworkers let me know how well I do my job). Since eight items such as IM01_03 (= A job where the skills you learn do not become obsolete) and IM01_07 (= A job where you have the opportunity to be creative) have low, non-significant loadings, they are eliminated. Against the background of the tested quality criteria, it can be assumed that the existing reflective and formative measurement models are of sufficient quality.

3.3.3 Analysis of the Structural Model

After the quality assessment of the measurement models has been completed, their relationships to each other are considered in the structural model. Since PLS is not based on distributional assumptions, non-parametric tests are applied (Sarstedt and Ringle 2010). For the endogenous constructs, the coefficient of determination R^2 is considered as a goodness-of-fit measure. This indicates what proportion of the variance of the endogenous construct is explained by the exogenous ones (Hair et al. 2016). The larger the R^2 is, the better the construct is explained by the exogenous latent variables. While values as high as 0.67 are described as substantial, values as low as 0.33 are considered medium, and values as low as 0.19 are considered weak (Chin 1998). Table 3 shows the values of R^2 for the endogenous constructs. It can be seen that the coefficient of determination of CSR can be described as substantial, while it assumes substantial to medium values for the construct's intention to stay and organizational support. The values of affective commitment and

Table 3 Quality criterion R^2

Construct	R^2
Intention to stay (ITS)	0.533
Affective commitment (AC)	0.440
Duration of employment (DOE)	0.065
Corporate social responsibility (CSR)	0.708
Intrinsic motivation (IM)	0.242
Job satisfaction (JS)	0.251
Withdrawal (WD)	0.168
Perceived organizational support (POS)	0.537
Intention to leave (ITL)	0.430

Table 4 Results overview of the hypotheses

Hypothesis	Path coefficient	t-value	f^2	Result
H1: IM → JS	0.067	0.672	0.006	Rejected
H2: CSR → JS	0.249	2.001	0.064	Acknowledged
H3: POS → JS	0.327	2.923	0.110	Acknowledged
H4: JS → AC	0.663	13.833	0.786	Acknowledged
H5: AC → ITS	0.596	10.349	0.700	Acknowledged
H6: ITS → DOE	0.254	2.801	0.069	Acknowledged
H7: AC → ITL	−0.486	6.719	0.380	Acknowledged
H8: ITL → WD	−0.410	4.597	0.203	Rejected

intention to leave are in the moderate range. For the constructs intrinsic motivation and job satisfaction, the coefficient of determination takes weak values, and the values of tenure and quitting are even below the weak level. Path coefficient analysis can be used to assess the strength of the relationships between the latent variables and the significance of the path relationships (Henseler et al. 2009). To test the strength of the influence of an exogenous construct on an endogenous one, the effect size f^2 is determined. Thresholds of 0.02, 0.15, and 0.35 define whether the exogenous latent variable has a weak, moderate, or strong influence on the endogenous construct (Chin 1998).

The calculation of the path coefficients and the corresponding t-values shows that six out of eight hypotheses (H2, H3, H4, H5, H6, H7) can be confirmed, while H1 and H8 are rejected. The results are presented in Table 4.

With regard to the effect size f^2, it should be noted that only in the path relationships "Affective commitment → Intention to stay," "Affective commitment → Intention to leave," and "Job satisfaction → Affective commitment" does the respective exogenous latent variable have a strong influence on the endogenous one. Perceived organizational support has a weak to medium influence on job satisfaction, while the relationship "Intention to leave → Withdrawal" has a medium effect size.

Another model assessment method is forecast relevance Q^2. This determines the predictive ability of a model and is performed via blind folding for the endogenous latent variables specified reflectively or as a single item (Hair et al. 2014). In this research, all Q^2 values for the endogenous constructs are greater than 0 (values between 0.15 and 0.40). This indicates the predictive relevance of the measurement models (Hair et al. 2014).

4 Conclusion on Employee Retention of Generation Y in SMEs

The results largely corroborate findings from previous literature on Generation Y. The study confirms the importance of perceived organizational support, corporate social responsibility, and job satisfaction for employee retention.

The results regarding the influence of CSR and intrinsic motivation can be classified as new or different. Internal and external corporate social responsibility is an influencing factor that has been little studied to date and is becoming increasingly important as a topic (Göttel et al. 2016).

4.1 Restrictions

The sample is mainly generated from the trade and services sector. It is therefore unclear to what extent the results can be transferred to the employees of an SME from another sector. For further critical appraisal, the scientific quality criteria of validity and reliability are used. For this purpose, both convergent and discriminant validity are assessed. As described, these quality criteria are fulfilled for the reflective measurement model. For the formative measurement model, discriminant validity is present if two constructs do not correlate completely (Henseler et al. 2015). For this, the correlation coefficient should not be greater than 0.9 (Gold et al. 2001). The analysis shows that this criterion is also given. Consequently, convergence validity can be regarded as proven.

Internal consistency is used to test reliability (Taber 2017). Cronbach's alpha is calculated for this purpose. Except for the constructs organizational support and affective commitment, Cronbach's alpha assumes desirable values of greater than 0.7 for all constructs (Taber 2017). Since Cronbach's alpha tends to underestimate the true value, the composite reliability is still considered for organizational support and affective commitment (Dijkstra and Henseler 2015). This exceeds the minimum value of 0.6 for both constructs, meaning that all results indicate a high internal consistency and thus the reliability of the measurement is given. Overall, an acceptable model fit can be assumed.

4.2 Future Research

This study provides the first important insights for SMEs to meet the requirements of Generation Y and to retain them in the company. In order for SMEs to gain an even better understanding of Millennials, the influence of current economic developments should also be examined. In this regard, the influence of digitalization or developments in Industry 4.0 on employee retention should be further investigated. This is because "Industrie 4.0 solutions dovetail production with state-of-the-art information and communication technology and create intelligent value chains," which ensure that the way of working changes (Press and Information Office of the Federal Government 2018).

Since this study was able to confirm the positive influence of corporate social responsibility on job satisfaction, further studies should look more deeply into the influence of CSR, especially considering that issues such as sustainability are becoming increasingly important for society.

Since in the present sample the proportion of academics predominated at around 50% and only around a quarter had completed vocational training, it is interesting to focus in a further study on those employees who have completed vocational training in an SME. This will make it possible to investigate whether those who have completed vocational training may not be seeking a professional career and thus have different requirements for an SME.

References

Albaum G (1997) The Likert scale revisited: an alternate version. J Mark Res Soc 39(2):331–348
Allen NJ, Meyer JP (1990) The measurement and antecedents of affective, continuance and normative commitment to the organization. J Occup Psychol 63:1–18
Allen NJ, Meyer JP (1991) A three-component conceptualization of organizational commitment. Hum Resour Manag Rev 1(1):61–89
Allen DG, Griffeth RW, Shore LW (2003) The role of perceived organizational support and supportive human resource practices in the turnover process. J Manag 29(1):99–118
Bal PM, Blomme RJ, Lub XD, Schalk R (2016) One job, one deal … or not: do generations respond differently to psychological contract fulfilment? Int J Hum Resour Manag 27(6):653–680
Boulian PV, Mowday RT, Porter LW, Steers RM (1974) Organizational commitment, job satisfaction, and turnover among psychiatric technicians. J Appl Psychol 59(5):603–609
Brant KK, Castro SL (2019) You can't ignore millennials: needed changes and a new way forward in entitlement research. Hum Resour Manag J 29(4):527–538
Budhwar P, Malhotra N, Prowse P (2007) Linking rewards to commitment: an empirical investigation of four UK call centres. Int J Hum Resour Manag 18(12):2095–2128
Campbell SM, Hoffman BJ, Lance CE, Twenge JM (2010) Generational differences in work values: leisure and extrinsic values increasing, social and intrinsic values decreasing. J Manag 36(5):1117–1142
Chin WW (1998) The partial least squares approach for structural equation modeling. In: Marcoulides GA (ed) Methodology for business and management. Modern methods for business research. Psychology Press, New York, pp 295–336
Coetzer A, Guenole N, Pajo K (2010) Formal development opportunities and withdrawal behaviors by employees in small and medium-sized enterprises. J Small Bus Manag 48(3):281–301
Commission of the European Communities (2001) Promoting an European framework for corporate social responsibility. Green Pap:1–37
Dijkstra TK, Henseler J (2015) Consistent partial least squares path modeling. MIS Q 39(2):297–316
Drucker P (2007) Management challenges for the 21st century. Routledge, London
Eby LT, Freeman DM, Lance CE, Rush MC (1999) Motivational bases of affective organizational commitment: a partial test of an integrative theoretical model. J Occup Organ Psychol 72:463–483
Eisenberger R, Huntington R, Hutchison S, Sowa D (1986) Perceived organizational support. J Appl Psychol 71(3):500–507
European Commission (2003) Commission recommendation of 6 May 2003 concerning the definition of micro, small and medium-sized enterprises. Off J Eur Union 124:36–41
Eurostat (2019) Population structure and ageing. https://ec.europa.eu/eurostat/statistics-explained/index.php?title=Population_structure_and_ageing&oldid=72315. Accessed 15 Mar 2020
Fornell C, Bookstein FL (1982) Two structural equation models: LISREL and PLS applied to consumer exit-voice theory. J Mark Res 19:440–452
Global Reporting Initiative (2016) GRI 201: economic performance 2016. https://www.globalreporting.org/standards/media/1039/gri-201-economic-performance-2016.pdf. Accessed 15 Mar 2020

Gold AH, Malhotra A, Segars AH (2001) Knowledge management: an organizational capabilities perspective. J Manag Inf Syst 18(1):185–214

Gómez-Navarro T, García-Melón M, Guijarro F, Preuss M (2017) Methodology to assess the market value of companies according to their financial and social responsibility aspects: an AHP approach. J Oper Res Soc 68:1–12

Göttel V, Mory L, Wirtz BW (2016) Factors of internal corporate social responsibility and the effect on organizational commitment. Int J Hum Resour Manag 27(13):1393–1425

Göttel V, Mory L, Wirtz BW (2017) Corporate social responsibility: the organizational view. J Manag Gov 21(1):145–179

Hackman RJ, Oldham GR (1975) Development of the job diagnostic survey. J Appl Psychol 60(2):159–170

Hair JF, Ringle CM, Sarstedt M (2014) Partial least squares structural equation modeling: rigorous applications. Better Results High Accept Long Range Plan 47(6):1–12

Hair JF, Hult GTM, Ringle CM, Sarstedt M (2016) A primer on partial least squares structural equation modeling (PLS-SEM). SAGE Publications, Thousand Oaks

Henseler J, Ringle C, Sinkovics R (2009) The use of partial least squares path modeling in international marketing. In: Sinkovics R, Ghauri P (eds) New challenges to international marketing. Emerald Group Publishing Limited, Bingley, pp 277–319

Henseler J, Ringle CM, Sarstedt M (2015) A new criterion for assessing discriminant validity in variance-based structural equation modeling. J Acad Mark Sci 43(1):115–135

Herscovitch L, Meyer JP, Stanley DJ, Topolnytsky L (2002) Affective, continuance, and normative commitment to the organization: a meta-analysis of antecedents, correlates, and consequences. J Vocat Behav 61(1):20–52

Hulin CL, Judge TA, Weiss HM, Kammeyer-Mueller JD (2017) Job attitudes, job satisfaction, and job affect: a century of continuity and of change. J Appl Psychol 102(3):356–374

Johnstone S, Muñoz Torres R, Saridakis G (2013) Do human resource practices enhance organizational commitment in SMEs with low employee satisfaction? Br J Manag 24(3):445–458

Kinnie N, Hutchinson S, Purcell J, Rayton B, Swart J (2005) Satisfaction with HR practices and commitment to the organisation: why one size does not fit all. Hum Resour Manag J 15(4):9–29

Lenka U, Naim MF (2018) Development and retention of generation Y employees: a conceptual framework. Empl Relat 40(2):433–455

Likert R (1932) A technique for the measurement of attitudes. Arch Psychol 140:5–55

Lyons ST, Papavasileiou EF (2015) A comparative analysis of the work values of Greece's 'millennial' generation. Int J Hum Resour Manag 26(17):2166–2186

Montana PJ, Petit F (2008) Motivating and managing Generation X and Y on the job while preparing for Z: a market oriented approach. J Bus Econ Res 6(8):35–40

Mottaz CJ (1988) Determinants of organizational commitment. Hum Relat 41(6):467–482

Presse- und Informationsamt der Bundesregierung (2018) Plattform Industrie 4.0. https://www.bundesregierung.de/breg-de/service/publikationen/plattform-industrie-4-0-727316. Accessed 15 Mar 2020

Presser S, Couper MP, Lessler JT, Martin E, Martin J, Rothgeb JM, Singer E (2004) Methods for testing and evaluating survey questions. Public Opin Q 68(1):109–130

Price JL (2001) Reflections on the determinants of voluntary turnover. Int J Manpow 22(7):600–624

Price JL, Mueller CW (1981) A causal model of turnover for nurses. Acad Manag J 24(3):543–565

Sarstedt M, Ringle CM (2010) Treating unobserved heterogeneity in PLS path modeling: a comparison of FIMIX-PLS with different data analysis strategies. J Appl Stat 37(8):1299–1318

Statista Inc (2019) Number of small and medium-sized enterprises (SMEs) in the European Union in 2018, by size (in 1000s). https://www.statista.com/statistics/878412/number-of-smes-in-europe-by-size/. Accessed 15 Mar 2020

Steers RM (1977) Antecedents and outcomes of organizational commitment. Adm Sci Q 22:46–56
Stewart JS, Oliver EG, Cravens KS, Oishi S (2017) Managing millennials: embracing generational differences. Bus Horiz 60(1):45–54
Taber KS (2017) The use of Cronbach's Alpha when developing and reporting research instruments in science education. Res Sci Educ 48(6):1273–1296

Larissa Loose has been an e-commerce brand manager for an international company since 2018. In 2016, Loose completed her Bachelor of Arts in Business Administration and in 2018 her Master of Science in Marketing and Communication. She wrote her master's thesis on the topic published here.

Prof. Dr. Marion Preuß is a professor of general business administration, in particular human resources and project management, at the FOM University of Economics and Management in Hamburg. Prof. Preuß can look back on many years of practical experience in the real estate industry, where she has held management positions in national and international departments. Her teaching and research focus on a wide range of topics, including HR management, project management and IT basics, information and communication management, scientific methodology and data analysis, and sales and marketing management. Prof. Preuß is also a reviewer of the *International Journal of Strategic Property Management*. Furthermore, she is a member of the German Statistical Society.

Assessing the Value Perception of Employees of the 50 Plus Generation: An AHP Approach

Marion Preuß

Abstract

Within the present research, the relevance of the perceived values of older cohorts of employees aged 50 and over for companies is to be demonstrated. The older cohorts will represent a growing proportion of the age structure in companies in the coming years, so that a closer look at the values perceived as important by this generation and their responsibilities for implementation plays a decisive role. The research paper addresses these issues in detail and develops a hierarchy using the analytic hierarchy process method. In this process, approximately 1000 pairwise comparisons are performed by the experts consulted in order to evaluate a weighting of criteria, sub-criteria, and alternatives in relation to the overall objective of employee motivation of the 50 plus workforce. The results are consistent and homogeneous and thus derive reliable information for companies.

1 Relevance of the Value Perception of Older Employees in Companies

Due to the demographic development in Europe and thus in Germany, the total number of the population is decreasing, while the number of older cohorts is increasing (Cervelló et al. 2016). This also results in an overall shrinkage of the workforce with a simultaneous increase in the number of older employees in companies. While currently 62.2 million

M. Preuß (✉)
FOM Hochschule für Oekonomie & Management, Hamburg, Germany
e-mail: marion.preuss@fom.de

J. Lange (ed.), *Value-Oriented Leadership in Theory and Practice*,
https://doi.org/10.1007/978-3-662-65883-3_5

employed persons in companies are calculated with a share of about 22% of the oldest cohorts 60–74 years, the projected number in 2050 decreases to 56.1 million total working population with an increasing share of the aforementioned oldest working population with a percentage of 27% (BIB Bundesinstitut für Bevölkerungsforschung 2020).

Accordingly, the relevance of older employees in companies will continue to increase in the future. There is no consistent definition of the "older" employee. In employment and labor policy, an age limit of employees is often set from 50 years upward, whereas in companies, age limits from 55 years upward are also found (Brandenburg and Domschke 2007; ComNet – Landesinstitut für Arbeitsgestaltung 2020). Within the present research, the focus is insofar placed on the generation 50 plus, in order to achieve a large intersection of the existing different definitions.

For Klinger et al. (2015), the innovative capacity of companies ensures their success and must be achieved with the involvement of older employee cohorts. The external conditions, such as economic and political framework conditions, as well as the internal conditions, divided into tangible prerequisites, such as the company's capital, and intangible resources, including products, services, and product stewardship, form the basis. This innovative capacity of companies and aging workforces is focused here as one of the important prerequisites for overcoming demographic challenges. Zacher et al. (2009) also examine work design and conclude that age-related differences should be considered in the career goals of employees. For the older cohorts here, job commitment is significantly more important than for the younger subjects. Roth et al. (2007) focus on training, leadership, and age heterogeneous design opportunities in their research on maintaining innovation and performance and exploiting the existing potential of older employees. Grauer (1998) focuses his research on opportunity orientation in the context of corporate governance.

In this respect, implementing this innovation capability, the motivation of older employees must serve as the starting point for the success of the company. Workforces are motivated and willing to perform when they have the opportunity to pursue their personal significant values within their professional activities (Bossmann and Eck 2013).

Due to the heterogeneity of the 50 plus age cohort, the values of older employees also differ within companies. Values such as quality awareness, security, long-term orientation, stability, relief, reliability, appreciation and recognition, self-assertion, and self-care are the focus of these generation cohorts and are significantly pronounced (Federal Ministry for Family Affairs, Senior Citizens, Women and Youth, Federal Ministry of Economics and Technology 2010; Bossmann and Eck 2013). Furthermore, clarity, purity, authenticity, emotional well-being, as well as economic awareness play a concise role (Bossmann and Eck 2013; Pompe 2013). In addition, commitment within social areas as civic activity in the community, in professional interest groups, as well as in ecological protection and as economic self-help in line with values such as experiential knowledge, work ethic, and loyalty also has a high value for the 50 plus generation (Boockmann and Zwick 2004; Landeshauptstadt Düsseldorf 2011).

In this respect, it can be seen from the aforementioned value domains of older workers that enduring values represent a decisive relevance (Oppermann 2008; Wendt et al. 2019).

Overall, in this respect, the motivation of employees in the 50 plus age cohort that ensures the success of the company as a management task should be the focus of further investigations in this research. In this context, the influence of the enforcement of the values of the older cohorts on motivation will be analyzed. The basis for this is the responsibility of work design on the part of the economy or politics, the companies, and the individual employee in the economic, ecological, and social areas of companies (Dyllick 2003; Global Reporting Initiative GRI 2016; Gómez-Navarro et al. 2017).

2 Valuation of Employee Values

The economic valuation is carried out, among other things, on the basis of economic and financial information of the companies. One-period models can be used for this purpose. This technique considers the company's success on the basis of a current account from the balance sheet or the profit and loss account. Furthermore, multi-period models can be used, which are dynamically derived from the company's earnings (Demirakos et al. 2004; Gómez-Navarro et al. 2017). Economic values are focused by the 50 plus workforce and in this respect provide the framework for high motivation and motivation of the older cohorts within companies (Bossmann and Eck 2013).

Sustainable values are anchored, among other things, in the corporate social responsibility (CSR) concept (Gómez-Navarro et al. 2017): this describes a concept that establishes ecological as well as social content within companies' business activities and interactions with their stakeholders as a voluntary basis (European Commission 2019). These values and their implementation play a significantly greater role for older cohorts of workers than for younger cohorts (Sect. 1). Nevertheless, CSR is viewed critically by some authors and interpreted less as ecological and social responsibility and more as a means to an end (Walker and Wan 2012; Rimser 2014). However, evidence is emerging that the implementation of CSR and thus the fulfilment of ecological and social values contribute to corporate success (Loew et al. 2004; Arendt and Brettel 2010; Du et al. 2010). The evaluation or achievement of corporate success is evidenced, for example, by Chatterji et al. (2009) or Gómez-Navarro et al. (2017). According to Sheikh and Beise-Zee (2011) or Lintemeier and Rademacher (2016), the continuous dialog of these values with the company's stakeholders, i.e., also with the older employees, is one of the most important pillars of CSR. The dialog is carried out, among other things, through sustainability reports that highlight the actions taken on the part of the company (Quick and Knocinski 2006; Duran-Encalada and Paucar-Caceres 2012; Baviera-Puig et al. 2015). Reflection is shown, for example, through the Global Reporting Initiative, a global non-profit organization (2016).

3 Empirical Analysis of Relevant Value Variables in Relation to Employee Motivation of the Generation 50 Plus

3.1 Applied Methodology: Analytic Hierarchy Process (AHP)

The AHP methodology was developed by Thomas L. Saaty in 1980. It is a decision-making analysis and implementation technique that can be used in a variety of research areas (Aznar et al. 2011b; Afshari and Mafi 2014). For Saaty and Vargas, this technique is a universal theory for measuring constructs developed via pairwise comparisons in multi-level hierarchy constructs (Saaty and Vargas 2001; Saaty 2005). The basis is the creation of a hierarchy with the goal at the highest level of the hierarchy, followed by the criteria and sub-criteria in the levels that follow, and finally the alternatives in the last lower level of the hierarchy to satisfy the overall goal. Within the different levels of the hierarchy, the variables are evaluated and weighted by pairwise comparisons performed by the selected experts. These pairwise comparisons are performed in the framework of matrices whose ratio scales give rise to eigenvectors (Saaty and Vargas 2001), which are performed both positively and reciprocally, as shown below:

$$a_{ij} = {}^{1}\!/_{a_{ji}} \tag{1}$$

$$\text{if } a_{ij} = x \text{ then } a_{ji} = {}^{1}\!/_{x}, {}^{1}\!/_{9} \leq x \leq 9 \tag{2}$$

Provided that the assessment of the consistency relationship is plausible, the results of the pairwise comparisons can be used and serve as the basis of the research findings. If consistency is not warranted, the aforementioned research is discarded or repeated accordingly (Saaty 1990). The pairwise comparisons are created from tangible dimensions or a fundamental scale that replicates the comparative advantage of subjects' preferences, appraisals, feelings, evaluations, etc. The AHP methodology is considered a nonlinear pattern to map deductive as well as inductive views. This procedure is intended to use different influences on reflection simultaneously to allow subjection and feedback from the experts and make numerical deductions from them. The methodology includes four different principles: comparison of homogeneous components, reciprocal relationship of the elements, hierarchy dependence, and validity of the rank, value of the result, and their dependence on the structure (Saaty and Vargas 2001; Cervelló et al. 2016).

3.1.1 AHP Hierarchy

The first stage of the AHP process is to create the hierarchy. To form this hierarchy, the overall decision-making objective must be defined, followed by the criteria that compare relative importance in relation to the objective. These criteria are then further decomposed into sub-criteria in the subsequent level, which in turn relate to the criteria. In the last level, the alternatives for the realization of the goal are mapped; these are compared with the sub-criteria (Saaty 1990; Cervelló et al. 2016).

3.1.2 AHP Priorities

The prioritization of the different elements of the hierarchy is a fundamental part of the second stage of the AHP methodology. In this respect, the pairwise comparisons must be carried out on the basis of the given elements. By presenting the matrix, the structure for the analysis of consistency is established. This enables the extraction of further information as a result of the fulfilment of all the likely comparisons and provides the assessment of the stability of all outcomes. The matrix reflects both the dominant and dominated features of the priorities (Saaty 1990; Cervelló et al. 2016).

3.1.3 The Fundamental Scale

Since experts make pairwise comparisons based on their own preferences, etc., an evaluation based on values of Saaty's (2009) fundamental scale is required here. The fundamental scale includes the numerical scale from 1 – for an equality of variables – to 9, for an extremely high importance of one variable over another variable, and reciprocal. A rating represents a pair of items in relation to a common characteristic. The smaller component is considered as a unit, and subjects rate how many times more important or dominant one item is over the other using one of the indicated values from the fundamental scale (Saaty 2009; Cervelló et al. 2016):

Given the pairwise comparisons between the elements of the hierarchy, the matrix structure A is as follows:

$$\mathbf{A} = \left[a_{ij} \right], 1 \leq i, j \leq n \tag{3}$$

3.1.4 The Synthesis

Finally, to achieve the overall goal of the hierarchy, it is critical to harmonize or synthesize the pairwise comparisons. Here, the overall assessment of the relative priorities from one level of the hierarchy to the next higher level is presented. Accordingly, the experts' assessments are synthesized with the aim of obtaining a normalized matrix (Saaty 1990; Cervelló et al. 2016).

3.1.5 The Consistency

For decision-making, it is essential to assess the quality of consistency in order to ensure that the decision proves stable in the context of pairwise comparisons and is not based on the consequence of a random outcome (Aznar et al. 2011a). Nevertheless, perfect consistency is not realistic, as the judgments by the experts are made based on personal preferences. In this respect, the weightings of the elements by the experts must lie within a tolerable range between acceptance of inconsistency and complete consistency. The consistency is measured by means of the consistency ratio. The value of the consistency ratio should not exceed a ratio of more than 10%. If the ratio exceeds this tolerance value, the subjects' decisions are interpreted as random with the consequence of revising the results (Saaty 1990): Therefore, the consistency matrix must satisfy the posterior characteristic:

$$a_{ik} \times a_{kj} = a_{ij} \tag{4}$$

$$\text{is fulfilled for all } 1 \leq i, j, k \leq n$$

As a result of combining the positive reciprocal matrices, the equality is as follows (Saaty 2009; Cervelló et al. 2016):

$$\partial\lambda_{\max} / \partial \mathrm{a}_{\mathrm{ij}} = \partial\lambda_{\max} / \partial \mathrm{a}_{\mathrm{ji}} \tag{5}$$

$$\text{for all } i \text{ and } j$$

3.2 Selection of Variables for the Case Study Evaluation Sample

The assessment of the values of the older generation cohorts 50 plus within the companies is based on three dimensions – economic dimension for the material values and ecological and social dimensions for the sustainable CSR values (Gómez-Navarro et al. 2017).

3.2.1 Criteria for the Economic Dimension

The economic values are presented in accordance with the GRI Standard (2016). The directly generated and distributed monetary values are considered and broken down into the sub-criteria of revenues, operating costs, employee compensation, donations, and retained earnings (Table 1).

3.2.2 Criteria for the Ecological and Social Dimension

The ecological and social values as CSR sustainability dimensions are also taken from the GRI Standard (2016), analogous to the economic value dimensions. The overarching criteria here are the ecological and social values with the sub-criteria energy, emissions,

Table 1 Criteria and sub-criteria of economic values

Criteria	Sub-criteria	Explanation
Economic values	Revenues	Revenue from the sale of goods and services
	Operating costs	Expenses for maintenance and administration of the company
	Employee compensation	Salary structure of the workforce
	Donations	Voluntary benefits of the company
	Retained earnings, payments to investors and government	Retained earnings of the company

effluents, waste and products, services for the ecological dimension, and, furthermore, occupational safety, health protection, diversity, equal opportunities, equal pay, local community, corruption, and product stewardship for the social dimension (Tables 2 and 3).

The criteria of economic, ecological, and social values are examined in relation to the overriding objective of motivating the older 50 plus workforce in companies, which is largely responsible for the company's success (Sect. 1). Furthermore, the relative importance of the sub-criteria to the respective criterion is compared. The value levels of the alternatives economic, corporate, and individual level are in turn compared with the aforementioned sub-criteria (Table 4).

Table 2 Criteria and sub-criteria of ecological values

Criteria	Sub-criteria	Explanation
Ecological values	Energy	Direct energy demand of the company
	Emissions, effluents, waste	Direct and indirect greenhouse gas emissions
	Products, services	Initiatives to improve the efficiency of goods and services

Table 3 Criteria and sub-criteria of social values

Criteria	Sub-criteria	Explanation
Social values	Occupational safety, health protection	Prevention of serious accidents and illnesses of employees
	Diversity	Ensuring the ability to work of all employee groups in the company
	Equal opportunities	Ensuring equal opportunities for employees within the company
	Equal pay	Ratio of remuneration by employee category
	Local community	Promotion and development of the company's local commitment
	Corruption	Corporate structures to prevent incidents of corruption
	Product stewardship	Investigation of the impact of goods and services on the safety of customers

Table 4 Value levels of the alternatives

Levels	Alternatives	Explanation
Value levels	Economic level	System level of the economy, politics
	Corporate level	Institutional level of corporate relations and voluntary commitments
	Individual level	Ethical level of one's own understanding of values and responsibilities

Rankings are then generated for the value levels, from which it can be seen which responsibilities contribute to the fulfilment of the (sub-)criteria for the motivation of employees 50 plus. The corresponding hierarchy of the AHP process is as follows (Fig. 1):

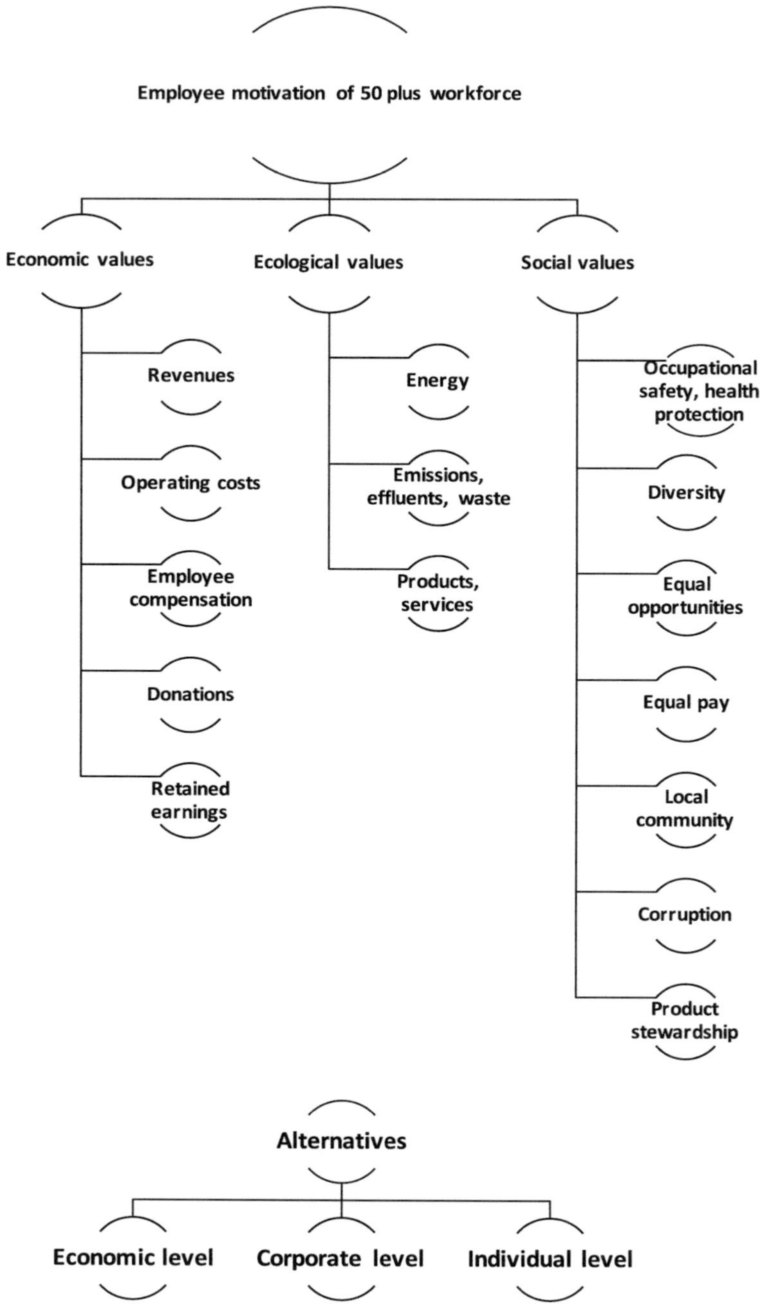

Fig. 1 AHP hierarchy for employee motivation of the 50 plus workforce

3.3 Statistical Verification and Results of the Case Study

3.3.1 Selection of Experts for the Case Study

The selection of experts is required to carry out the study. The prerequisite is that they must have reached the age of at least 50 years. In addition, professional experience is required to enable the experts to assess and conduct the pairwise comparisons of the criteria, sub-criteria, and alternatives in order to achieve the overall objective of motivating the 50 plus workforce in relation to the values and responsibilities of older employees. A total of 12 participants who meet these requirements will be selected for this study. They come from different professional contexts (Table 5).

Before as well as during the execution of the study, the subjects are provided with an agenda that presents the definitions of the (sub-)criteria and alternatives (Sect. 3.2, Tables 1, 2, 3 and 4). The pairwise comparisons are carried out in the hierarchical order and take on average about 1 hr. per participant. Afterward, the results are presented to the experts, checked again for correctness, and approved.

3.3.2 Conducting the Case Study

The contents of the construct are derived on the basis of the current literature (Sect. 3.2) and transferred to the AHP hierarchy. Within the hierarchy, the experts' prioritizations are then mapped by pairwise comparisons. These are carried out in the order shown in Table 6.

In this respect, 82 pairwise comparisons take place per expert, thus a total of 984 weightings for the 12 selected participants. The weights of the pairwise comparisons are presented using Saaty's (2009) fundamental scale from 1 to 9 as well as reciprocally 1/2–1/9. The pooling of the expert results is done using the geometric mean for all pairwise comparisons as the mean and stable proportional, so that a synthesis or harmonization of all weights can then be done as the normalized matrix of the study. All the results

Table 5 Overview of the experts

Expert	Professional background
1	Mechanical engineer
2	Nursing
3	Pharmacist
4	Personnel consultant
5	Management consultant
6	Commercial clerk
7	Marketing manager
8	Aircraft electronics technician
9	Nursing
10	Nursing
11	IT specialist
12	Professor

Table 6 Structure of the pairwise comparisons of the hierarchy levels

Hierarchy level	Art	Reference to
Criteria	Economic, ecological, social values	Aim of employee motivation
Sub-criteria	Revenues, operating costs, employee compensation, donations, retained earnings	Criterion of economic values
Sub-criteria	Energy, emissions, effluents, waste, products, services	Criterion of ecological values
Sub-criteria	Occupational safety, health protection, diversity, equal opportunities, equal pay, local community, corruption, product stewardship	Criterion of social values
Alternatives	Economic, corporate, individual level	Economic sub-criteria revenues, operating costs, employee compensation, donations, retained earnings
Alternatives	Economic, corporate, individual level	Ecological sub-criteria energy, emissions, effluents, waste, products, services
Alternatives	Economic, corporate, individual level	Social sub-criteria occupational safety, health protection, diversity, equal opportunities, equal pay, local community, corruption, product stewardship

of the investigation are consistent and within the 10% ratio specified by Saaty (1990), so that it is possible to use all the weights. In order to be able to map a more extensive consistency, a maximum consistency of 5% for a 3 × 3 matrix is assumed in the present investigation; for the larger matrices, the 10% quota is specified. Even under these tightened conditions, a high consistency of the pairwise comparisons is given, so that the research results can be recognized as stable.

3.3.3 Results of the Case Study

On the first criteria level in relation to the objective of achieving a high level of motivation of the 50 plus workforce, it can be shown that the criterion of social values has the highest value (40%), followed by economic values (33%) and ecological values (27%) (Table 7).

In the second sub-criteria level in terms of economic values as a criterion, employee compensation (31%) and retained earnings for payments to lenders and the state (20%) are rated as highly significant. Donations (15%) play a rather subordinate role (Table 8).

At the sub-criteria level in relation to ecological values, products and services are rated highly (39%), with the lowest rating for the sub-criterion energy (24%) (Table 9).

Table 7 Pairwise comparisons of criteria

Reference: target	Economic values	Ecological values	Social values	Eigenvector
Economic values	1.00	1.24	0.79	0.33
Ecological values	0.81	1.00	0.67	0.27
Social values	1.26	1.50	1.00	0.40
Consistency ratio	0.00%	<5%		1.00

Table 8 Pairwise comparisons of the economic sub-criteria

Reference: criteria	Revenues	Operating costs	Employee compensation	Donations	Retained earnings	Eigenvector
Revenues	1.00	1.81	0.51	1.27	0.78	0.19
Operating costs	0.55	1.00	0.61	1.17	0.78	0.15
Employee compensation	1.95	1.64	1.00	1.99	1.57	0.31
Donations	0.79	0.85	0.50	1.00	0.80	0.15
Retained earnings	1.28	1.28	0.64	1.25	1.00	0.20
Consistency ratio	1.27%	<10%				1.00

Table 9 Pairwise comparisons of the ecological sub-criteria

Reference: criteria	Energy	Emissions, effluents, waste	Products, services	Eigenvector
Energy	1.00	0.61	0.62	0.24
Emissions, effluents, waste	1.65	1.00	0.94	0.37
Products, services	1.60	1.07	1.00	0.39
Consistency ratio	0.09%	<5%		1.00

The sub-criteria level in relation to social values also shows significant relevance for product stewardship (19%), whereas diversity is weighted as weakly relevant (8%) (Table 10).

In the next hierarchical level of alternatives in relation to the economic, ecological, and social sub-criteria, it can be seen that the predominant pairwise comparisons show the responsibilities in the first instance with the companies, followed by the employees as the second priority and the economic level as the third priority.

The subsequent harmonization or synthetization of all weightings in the different hierarchical levels finally leads to the following research results (Table 11).

From this matrix of the overall rankings, it can be seen that the experts see a high level of responsibility for implementing the values of the 50 plus generation first and foremost with the companies. The next rank is then represented by the cohort of older workers themselves, and finally an additional responsibility is weighted at the economic level, i.e., the economy and politics. Social values are of particular relevance, followed by economic

Table 10 Pairwise comparisons of the social sub-criteria

Reference: criteria	Occupational safety, health protection	Diversity	Equal opportunities	Equal pay	Local community	Corruption	Product stewardship	Eigenvector
Occupational safety, health protection	1.00	2.46	1.08	0.90	2.15	0.64	0.65	0.15
Diversity	0.41	1.00	0.48	0.66	0.93	0.60	0.48	0.08
Equal opportunities	0.93	2.08	1.00	1.10	1.85	0.87	0.85	0.16
Equal pay	1.11	1.53	0.91	1.00	1.77	0.82	0.82	0.15
Local community	0.47	1.07	0.54	0.56	1.00	0.45	0.55	0.09
Corruption	1.57	1.67	1.15	1.22	2.22	1.00	0.98	0.18
Product stewardship	1.55	2.08	1.17	1.21	1.82	1.02	1.00	0.19
Consistency ratio	0.76%	<10%						1.00

Table 11 Ranking of the alternatives for achieving the objectives

Overall rankings	Economic values	Ecological values	Social values	Criteria	Rank criteria	Rank alternatives
Economic level	0.23	0.29	0.29	Economic values	0.33	0.27
Corporate level	0.46	0.36	0.38	Ecological values	0.27	0.40
Individual level	0.31	0.35	0.33	Social values	0.40	0.33

and finally ecological values. Overall, however, it can be seen that the rankings are homogeneous, so that the differences within the ranks are weighted marginally differently.

In this respect, the overall result shows the extent of the demands of the older employee cohorts and suggests that a complex implementation of the different values on the macro and micro levels of action must take place in order to be able to increase the employee motivation of the 50 plus workforce.

4 Conclusion on the Assessment of the Perception of Values of the Generation 50 Plus

The study conducted indicates that the motivation of older cohorts of employees aged 50 and above is complex in nature. For the evaluation of the relevance of values as well as the responsibility for the implementation of values to increase motivation as an overriding goal, a hierarchical construct has been developed in an elaborate procedure within the framework of the analytic hierarchy process. The various criteria, sub-criteria, and alternatives as variables are derived from different national and international literature and have also been executed following the Global Reporting Initiative guidelines. Different experts of the concerned age cluster 50 plus have carried out a total of almost 1000 weightings by means of pairwise comparisons within the AHP construct. The consistency ratios are consistently very low, so that there is a high stability of the weightings. Overall, the results are homogeneous: the older generation cohorts assume the implementation of economic, ecological, and social values to be highly significant. Here, responsibility is assumed to lie primarily with the companies, then with the employees themselves, and finally at the economic level.

In the future, older employee cohorts will represent an increasingly large proportion of the age structure of companies, so that a great deal of focus should be placed on this employee cluster. Increasing the motivation of this age cohort will have a significant impact on the success of the company (Sect. 1).

In this respect, this research makes a significant contribution to revealing employees' value perceptions and to highlighting the significant complexity of the different value areas. The AHP hierarchy as well as the final results of the experts' weightings can lead to a targeted implementation in the companies.

References

Afshari M, Mafi E (2014) Land capability assessment for regional planning using AHP und GIS at Shandiz urban region, Northeast Iran. Environ Urban ASIA 5(I):105–118

Arendt S, Brettel M (2010) Understanding the influence of corporate social responsibility on corporate identity, image, and firm performance. Manag Decis 48(10):1469–1492

Aznar J, Cervelló R, Romero A (2011a) New Spanish banking conglomerates. Application of the analytic hierarchy process (AHP) to their market value. Int Res J Financ Econ 78:70–82

Aznar J, Guijarro F, Moreno-Jiménez JM (2011b) Mixed valuation methods: a combined AHP-GP procedure for individual and group multicriteria agricultural valuation. Ann Oper Res 190:221–238

Baviera-Puig A, Gómez-Navarro T, García-Melón M, García-Martínez G (2015) Assessing the communication quality of CSR reports. A case study on four Spanish food companies. Sustainability 7(8):11010–11031

BIB Bundesinstitut für Bevölkerungsforschung (2020) (Hrsg) Erwerbsbevölkerung nach Altersgruppen, 1960–2050. https://www.demografie-portal.de/DE/Fakten/erwerbsbevoelkerung.html. Accessed on 07.09.2020

Boockmann B, Zwick T (2004) Betriebliche Determinanten der Beschäftigung älterer Arbeitnehmer. Z Arbeitsmarktforsch – J Labour Mark Res, (IAB). Nürnberg 37(1):53–63

Bossmann U, Eck A (2013) Wollen und Sollen: Interessen, Motive, Werte und Bedürfnisse jüngerer und älterer Mitarbeiter. In: Schweitzer J, Bossmann U (Hrsg) Systemisches Demografiemanagement. Springer, Wiesbaden, S 63–76

Brandenburg U, Domschke JP (2007) Wann ist man „älterer Arbeitnehmer"? In: Die Zukunft sieht alt aus. Gabler, Berlin/Heidelberg. Online ISBN 978-3-8349-9532-2: S 63–67

Bundesministerium für Familie, Senioren, Frauen und Jugend, Bundesministerium für Wirtschaft und Technologie (2010) Potenziale nutzen – die Kundengruppe 50plus – Ein Gewinn für Unternehmen und ältere Kundinnen und Kunden. Publikationsversand der Bundesregierung, Rostock

Cervelló R, Guijarro F, Pfahler T, Preuss M (2016) An analytic hierarchy process (AHP) framework for property valuation to identify the ideal 2050 portfolio mixes in EU-27 countries with shrinking populations. Qual Quant Int J Methodol 50(1):2313–2329

Chatterji AK, Levine DI, Toffel MW (2009) How well do social ratings actually measure corporate social responsibility? J Econ Manag Strateg 18(1):125–169

ComNet – Landesinstitut für Arbeitsgestaltung (Hrsg) (2020) Wie definiere ich „ältere Mitarbeiter" und wann spricht man von einer hohen Anzahl älterer Mitarbeiter (prozentual)? https://www.komnet.nrw.de/_sitetools/dialog/25256. Accessed on 14.04.2020

Demirakos E, Strong N, Walker M (2004) What valuation models do analysts use? Account Horiz 18(4):221–240

Du S, Bhattacharya CB, Sen S (2010) Maximizing business returns to corporate social responsibility (CSR)–the role of CSR communication. Int J Manag Rev 12(1):8–19

Duran-Encalada AJ, Paucar-Caceres A (2012) A system dynamics sustainable business model for Petroleos Mexicanos (Pemex): case based on the global reporting initiative. J Oper Res Soc 63(8):1065–1078

Dyllick T (2003) Konzeptionelle Grundlagen unternehmerischer Nachhaltigkeit. In: Linne G, Scharz M (Hrsg) Handbuch Nachhaltige Entwicklung. VS Verlag für Sozialwissenschaften, Wiesbaden, S 235–243

Europäische Kommission (2019) Kommission stößt Debatte über nachhaltige Entwicklung in Europa an. https://ec.europa.eu/germany/news/20190130-nachhaltige-entwicklung_de. Accessed on 15.04.2020

Global Reporting Initiative GRI (2016) GRI 101: Grundlagen 2016. Global Sustainability Standards Board (GSSB), Amsterdam

Gómez-Navarro T, García-Melón M, Guijarro F, Preuss M (2017) Methodology to assess the market value of companies according to their financial and social responsibility aspects: an AHP approach. J Oper Res Soc 69(10):1599–1608

Grauer F (1998) Gestaltungsaspekte eines integrativen Personalmanagements. In: Personalmanagement für ältere Mitarbeiter. Deutscher Universitätsverlag, Wiesbaden, S 162–211

Klinger C, Stracke S, Müller C, Nerdinger FW (2015) Innovativ und leistungsfähig mit alternden Belegschaften. In: Nerdinger F, Wilke P, Stracke S, Drews U (Hrsg) Innovation und Personalarbeit im demografischen Wandel. Springer Gabler, Wiesbaden, S 27–37

Landeshauptstadt Düsseldorf, Amt für Statistik und Wahlen, Statistik und Stadtforschung (2011) Befragung „Generation 50plus: Lebensqualität und Zukunftsplanung in Düsseldorf" – Beiträge zur Statistik und Stadtforschung. Landeshauptstadt Düsseldorf, Düsseldorf

Lintemeier K, Rademacher L (2016) Stakeholder relations. Nachhaltigkeit und Dialog als strategische Erfolgsfaktoren. In: Altenburger R, Mesicek R (Hrsg) CSR und stakeholder management. Managementreihe corporate social responsibility. Springer Gabler, Berlin/Heidelberg, S 29–58

Loew T, Ankele K, Braun S, Clausen J (2004) Bedeutung der CSR-Diskussion für Nachhaltigkeit und die Anforderungen an Unternehmen. iöw – Institut für Ökologische Wirtschaftsforschung, Münster

Oppermann R (2008) LOHAS und Best Ager – Hauptzielgruppe für Bio-Produkte aus der Region? In: Rahmann G (Hrsg) Ressortforschung für den Ökologischen Landbau. Johann Heinrich von Thünen-Institut – Bundesforschungsinstitut für Ländliche Räume, Wald und Fischerei (vTI), Braunschweig, S 91–102

Pompe HG (2013) Die Zielgruppen 50plus. In: Marktmacht 50plus. Springer, Wiesbaden, S 73–93

Quick R, Knocinski M (2006) Sustainability reporting – empirical findings on the reporting practices of HDAX companies. J Bus Econ 76:615–650

Rimser M (2014) Generation Resource Management: Nachhaltige HR-Konzepte im demografischen Wandel. Springer, Wiesbaden

Roth C, Wegge J, Schmidt KH (2007) Konsequenzen des demographischen Wandels für das Management von Humanressourcen. Z Pers 6:99–116

Saaty TL (1990) Decision making for leaders. RWS Publications, Pittsburgh

Saaty TL (2005) Making and validating complex decisions with the AHP/ANP. J Syst Sci Syst Eng 14(1):1–36

Saaty TL (2009) Theory and applications of the analytic network process – decision making with benefits, opportunities, costs and risks. RWS Publications, Pittsburgh

Saaty TL, Vargas L (2001) Models, methods, concepts & applications of the analytic hierarchy process. Kluwer Academic Publishers, Stanford

Sheikh SR, Beise-Zee R (2011) Corporate social responsibility or cause-related marketing? The role of cause specificity of CSR. J Consum Mark 28(1):27–39

Walker K, Wan F (2012) The harm of symbolic actions and green-washing: corporate actions and communications on environmental performance and their financial implications. J Bus Ethics 109:227–242

Wendt B, Höppner G, Görgen B, Grundmann M (2019) Nachhaltigkeit und Alter – Konturen und Spannungsfelder eines vernachlässigten Forschungsfeldes. Soziol Nachhalt – Beitr sozial-ökon Transformationsforsch 4:68–90

Zacher H, Degner M, Seevaldt R, Frese M, Lüdde J (2009) Was wollen jüngere und ältere Erwerbstätige erreichen? Z Personalpsychol 8:191–200

Prof. Dr. Marion Preuß is a professor of general business administration, in particular human resources and project management, at the FOM Hochschule für Oekonomie & Management in Hamburg. Prof. Preuß can look back on many years of practical experience in the real estate industry, where she has held management positions in national and international departments. Her teaching and research focus on a wide range of topics, including HR management, project management and IT basics, information and communication management, scientific methodology and data analysis, and sales and marketing management. Prof. Preuß is also a reviewer of the International Journal of Strategic Property Management. Furthermore, she is a member of the German Statistical Society.

Part II

Conceptual Implementation

If you want to know how to embed value-based leadership conceptually and structurally in your business and organization, you may find the articles in this section helpful.

After the constructively critical considerations of the concept of values or also of value-oriented leadership, which, however, ultimately underlined its relevance, we also remain constructively critical in the contribution by Prof. Dr. Anja Lüthy. The clear message of this contribution is that a mission statement, especially in the form in which it is currently often implemented in practice, is not sufficient for value-based leadership. The real leadership behind the good sounding text is more important. Ms. Lüthy applies an absolutely on-target critique of mission statements that opens eyes and "straightens" perspective. Egocentric utopias that do not reflect the true reality and identity of a company do not help anyone.

As already made clear in the first article, the objective- and structure-oriented corporate management and the employee-oriented personal management must always be combined in order to really lead in a value-oriented way or to be a value-oriented company. Without appreciative, empathetic superiors, it is not possible, but the structural corporate management should also be further developed with regard to a "caring company." This article helps us to understand, and possibly even internalize, the absolutely necessary connection between value-oriented corporate and personal leadership. The characteristics and properties of value-oriented leadership on different levels are clarified in a vivid and practice-oriented way. In addition to current references to the current Corona crisis, real application of the contents is simplified by a detailed case study as well as constant hints and tips.

With the contribution by Ehrenberger, Mäder, and Berna, we delve deeper into a special area of structure- and objective-oriented value-based corporate management. Values and related aspects and parameters are non-financial factors, the management and control of which pose a problem for many companies – particularly in view of the more financial management and control systems that have prevailed to date. Nevertheless, a complete value-oriented management also needs possibilities for measurement, management, and control. So-called non-financial internal control systems could help with this need, the importance and functioning of which are discussed comprehensively and clearly in the article.

Increasing stakeholder expectations (e.g., from employees, investors, or lenders) as well as regulatory obligations (e.g., CSR reporting obligation in the EU as well as the obligation to sustainably align executive board compensation according to ARUG II) force not only an internal conviction of value orientation but also an increased concern with non-financial data. Ehrenberger, Mäder, and Berna state that good corporate governance is value-oriented. Non-financial factors also have a clear financial impact today (e.g., reputation, employer attractiveness, or increase in regulation).

This once again underlines the relevance of value orientation in the entire management. Non-financial data are often more prone to error than financial data, which are easier to standardize, and therefore require a good control system. Even though the topic of non-financial internal control systems – especially in terms of systematics and application – is still in its infancy, at the end of the article, some success factors and thus practice-oriented tips for the implementation of such systems are mentioned.

In Herold and Schlegel's contribution, we also remain in the context of rather structure-based value-oriented corporate management. However, this is already linked to people-oriented leadership (value-oriented personal leadership). The contribution by Herold and Schlegel is about value-oriented compliance, i.e., the necessary integration of an ethical perspective into compliance management systems (CMS) that are often more legal in nature. The original, legal compliance had to evolve. Beyond pure legal compliance, it is becoming increasingly clear that corporate values are effective and thus necessary in the implementation of such CMS. In addition to the need to implement legal requirements, value orientation in the context of compliance also helps to reduce controls and unnecessary bureaucracy (an aspect that is always associated negatively with compliance). Instead of controls and sanctions, value orientation can be based on self-responsibility and trust.

Even with regard to the general legal goal of avoiding liability in the context of compliance, it becomes apparent that values are central to compliance and its requirements. With reference to Carroll's responsibility pyramid, which is clarified in the article, it becomes apparent that values serve as catalysts in the compliance of a company's legal responsibility. Thus, ethical responsibility at the level above in the responsibility pyramid helps to meet legal. An extension of legal compliance to include a value orientation becomes useful, if not necessary. Value-oriented compliance should be seen as a link between integrity management and purely legal compliance. Integrity in this context means an orientation toward existing values and consistent action according to them and thus fits in with our approach to value orientation in this book. In the second part of the article, application-oriented implementation tips are given (e.g., which standards are useful for orientation as well as which aspects need to be considered when integrating integrity into existing CMS).

From the contribution of Lutz and Nummer, you can take a lot for the value-oriented corporate management, for value-oriented personal leadership, and especially for their interaction. This comprehensive text, packed with useful knowledge, helps to understand organizations and to implement value-oriented leadership from this understanding, both organizationally and personally.

From a new view of the concept of work, various new and complex demands on today's work become clear (e.g., sense-making, creation of personal design options, promotion of innovation, health, sustainability, and satisfaction). In order to meet these demands, the paper helps us to gain a new understanding of organization through the concept of organizational behavior. This describes the way individuals and groups act and react in an organization. It is also crucial to consider the recursivity between organization and person, i.e., the behavior of individuals influences the behavior of the entire organization, but also the organizational structures influence the behavior of individuals. In previous leadership approaches, the recursiveness of leadership behavior was usually only partially perceived and thus not holistically.

Organizational behavior is significantly influenced by the fit between person and organization. This is primarily dependent on values at the various levels: personal values, group or team values, leadership values, and corporate values. Dealing with the concept of organizational behavior can help to create a suitable "guardrail system" for value-oriented leadership and to perceive the human side of value creation completely or at all and thus to be able to control it. This can result in a win-win situation for all stakeholders in the company (e.g., identification, satisfaction, productivity, better value creation). In the further course of the article, helpful hints and practical tips for the measurement and analysis of organizational behavior as well as for the creation of this extensive value fit by understanding organizational behavior in the context of value-based leadership are given.

From the Mission Statement to Value-Oriented Corporate Management

Anja Lüthy

Abstract

Conventional mission statements such as "The customer is always king with us!" or "Customers are our focus!" are obsolete. Generations Y and Z, which will make up 75% of employees in German companies in just a few years, think differently. On the one hand, they want to sense a comprehensive employee-oriented corporate and workplace culture when they are looking for a job, and on the other hand, they want to work in a company whose business purpose also appeals to them emotionally. They don't just want to read in a mission statement what visions a company is pursuing. Instead, young people looking at a company as a potential employer want to know:

- Which meaning (= "purpose") the business activity of the company actually pursues.
- Whether work is agile in the sense of "New Work" and whether the work is meaningful.
- How an employee-oriented corporate culture is lived.
- Whether superiors lead and support in a value-oriented, professional, and eye-level manner.
- To what extent flexible working in terms of time and place is possible in the sense of "New Work".

Job seekers also want to know what active employee involvement looks like in achieving company goals.

A. Lüthy (✉)
Berlin, Germany
e-mail: Anja.Luethy@th-brandenburg.de

J. Lange (ed.), *Value-Oriented Leadership in Theory and Practice*,
https://doi.org/10.1007/978-3-662-65883-3_6

Simply presenting a mission statement that describes more of a utopia is no longer enough to inspire young people to join a company. In times of demographic change, which has led to a massive shortage of skilled workers and a veritable "war for talents," companies will only attract the next generation if they first develop a value-oriented corporate management, establish it in the next step, and "live" it in the long term or keep expanding it.

At the end of the chapter, an impressive company example is reported that proves how value-oriented corporate management leads not only to satisfied employees but also to a stable employer brand and economic success.

1 Background: From Mission Statement to Value-Oriented Leadership

Appreciative superiors who empathetically lead and support their employees and continuously ask for improvement requests in the workplace are implicit for younger generations today. Unfortunately, the willingness of supervisors to apply modern leadership methods based on a value- and employee-oriented corporate culture is still not a given in 2020.

This is probably since today the authoritarian post-war generation (the approximately 60–70-year-olds) is still being in charge and the approximately 55-year-old baby boomers (less empathetic digital skeptics) are the decision-makers. Unfortunately, these two generations have not yet realized that the economic success of a company depends to a significant extent on the satisfaction of its employees (Hauser 2008) and that value-oriented corporate management has an extremely positive influence on satisfaction.

Baby boomers grew up in times when so-called mission statements were developed to describe the self-image of a company. Often, mission statements still hang framed on the walls of the company.

Mission statements can be described as follows:

- They are formulated as visions in short sentences.
- They spell out the missions that companies want to pursue.
- They should make it clear to the outside world what a company stands for.
- Their aim is to motivate the workforce to achieve the concisely formulated visions.

Mission statements are rather philosophical and are rarely consistently "lived" or implemented in practice. It is therefore controversial whether mission statements actually lead to positive changes in the company. After all, mission statements often describe an ideal image – almost a utopia – that has too little to do with reality. In addition, mission statements usually lack recommendations for action on how the individual visions can best be implemented sustainably in reality.

Anne Schüller (2020) writes quite drastically in this context in her blog:

> Classic mission statements often sound similar, usually banal, almost always interchangeable and somehow hollow, straight out as if you had used a mission statement generator. They don't celebrate a unique benefit to customers, the marketplace, or the world, but rather a dream of their own greatness and glory. And this is what it sounds like: 'We see ourselves as a market leader with 1-a products.' Or like this: 'We are global leaders with our brands.' Or like this: 'We are the technology pioneer in our industry.'
>
> Common mission statements and the statements associated with them are not only ego-centric, the incredibly special of a company does not come through at all. Rather, it trickles platitudes ('We are customer-oriented'), self-evident statements ('We are reliable') and phrases ('We derive our strength from our employees'). It does not touch. It does not inspire. And it is certainly not internalized.
>
> Ask employees about their company's mission statement and you will get blank stares. With a bit of luck, you might hear: 'I don't remember that, we did it at some point, I think it's on the website.' But what is written there or in the company's glossy image brochures is nothing more than communication prose for the public, which no one internally believes in anyway.
>
> Moreover, all too often the top brass in particular do not act according to the mission statement and values that they have literally 'adopted.' With such a lack of integrity, the hanging up of value posters is pure cynicism. In a rather well-known company in the Düsseldorf area, they call it the 'lying tree' pillar on which photos of executives are hung, who say things like or related to 'mission statement.' (Schüller 2020)

A company that leads in a value-oriented manner first defines and communicates the meaning and purpose of its entrepreneurial existence, the so-called purpose. The entrepreneurial actions of a company whose "purpose" is clear are in turn based on values, attitudes, and positions. These shape the decisions, actions, and behavior of managers and employees. Characteristics of a value-oriented corporate management of companies that have been known for years are, for example, according to the Great Place to Work model (Great Place to Work 2020):

- Credibility, in the sense of authenticity and genuineness.
- Respect, in the sense of lived appreciation.
- Fairness, in the sense of absolute equality for all and without discrimination.
- Team spirit, in the sense of a pronounced "we-feeling".
- Pride, in the sense of identification with the "purpose" of the company.

Value-oriented corporate management provides an organization with a framework and aims to positively shape and influence cooperation within the company. Different structural framework conditions, which are specified by the company management (the owner, the sponsor, the shareholders), also determine which working conditions the employees find or experience in the company. Consequently, value-oriented corporate management is never rigid or static; rather, it is dynamic and continuously evolving.

It is subject to fundamental changes, especially in times of a pandemic and the resulting social, technological, and global challenges. In the wake of the digital transformation and the demands of Generations Y and Z, it is the following working conditions that have come to the fore in recent years because they contribute significantly to an employee-oriented corporate culture. They are shaped by the overriding values of "respect" and "appreciation" for employees:

- Flexibilization of working hours.
- Possibility to work in a home office.
- As much independent work as possible.
- Participation in the achievement of corporate objectives.
- Modern and up-to-date technological equipment at the workplace.
- Extensive digitization of processes.
- Possibility of a balance between work and private life.
- Fair, credible superiors who communicate "at eye level".

It is easy to understand that a "lived" value-oriented corporate management influences the economic success of a company much more intensively than a "lifeless" mission statement that merely describes visions and missions. A culture that is experienced as pleasant by the employees promotes a good working atmosphere and increases the willingness to perform and thus the productivity in the company. A corporate culture that is perceived positively both internally and externally also has a positive effect on the image of the employer brand in the sense of employer branding.

So, Generations Y and Z are rightly looking forward to the fact that representatives of Generation X will soon be entering the boardrooms, the friendly digital experts. These 35- to 45-year-olds, who will be in the front row in 8–10 years at the latest, have understood that value-oriented corporate management is more important than ever for success. Generation X has seen for themselves how the world of work has changed over the last 15 years. Concepts such as "New Work" and modern leadership methods such as "treating employees as internal customers" are familiar to Generation X.

Overall, compared to their predecessor generations, representatives of Generation X are much more successful in looking at jobs and working conditions through the eyes of younger people, entering into dialogue, and continuously working out improvements to working conditions as a team.

The continuous improvement of working conditions must also actually be on the agenda today because of the increasingly dramatic shortage of skilled workers. After all, Generations Y and Z are quite demanding on the one hand and highly sought-after on the labor market on the other. Companies are constantly competing as potential employers and must outdo each other because the number of vacancies exceeds the number of applicants. That is why companies are also communicating increasingly intensively via their career websites how pleasant their corporate culture is and what good working conditions they offer their employees. They even let so-called corporate influencers speak in their social networks, i.e., their own employees who report on their jobs and recommend the company as an employer.

2 What Value-Oriented Corporate Management Comprises and Constitutes

It will certainly take a few more years until representatives of all companies, regardless of the industry they come from, realize that mission statements are "out" and that value-oriented corporate management is a concept for success instead.

However, it is interesting to ask in how many companies the Corona crisis and the associated implementation of the New Work concept (see below) will act as a catalyst for a change in values in companies. Will the lockdown and thousands of employees working "remotely" in home offices lead to a rethink in the direction of New Work and a change in values because top management actually wants change in this time of crisis?

Value-oriented management can only be established if companies know what "purpose" they are pursuing. The term "purpose" is a synonym for "meaning" of entrepreneurial existence and helps both employees and customers to understand what the business philosophy is or what strategic goals the company is basically pursuing. In her blog, Anne Schüller suggests that instead of looking at a mission statement, companies first need to take a close look at their "purpose." According to Schüller (2020), anyone who wants to become fit for the future must therefore start with the meaning and purpose of their company and answer the following questions:

- What is or was the justification of existence of our company in the beginning?
- What are we particularly good at and passionate about?
- What beliefs do we stand for?
- What problems of this world do we solve?
- What values do we create for our customers?
- Which key theme can we use to attract top talents?
- What gives us room for development in future directions?

Only when a company has worked out its DNA or personality can it know which framework conditions are adequate and what value-oriented corporate management can look like.

Basically, value-oriented corporate management today includes the following:

I. Implementation of the "New Work" concept.
II. Establishment of an employee-oriented corporate culture.
III. Management of employees according to the internal customer model.
IV. Use of digital structures and enabling smart working.

I. Implementation of the "New Work" Concept

The first prerequisite for the creation of value-oriented corporate management, which is quite distinct from the philosophy of a static mission statement, is the dynamic concept of "New Work." This concept refers to a new way of working in today's society in the global and digital age. The term "New Work" was coined by the social philosopher and US professor Frithjof Bergmann in the 1970s. The "New Work philosophy" is based on the assumption that previous work systems, such as the division of labor and "working to rule," are outdated.

Frithjof Bergmann argues that our society is changing from an industrial to a knowledge society and therefore the world of work must also adapt (Bergmann 2019). This brings with it a change in values that is characterized by employees working as freely as possible. Outdated classical work structures are transforming in the wake of a new age and giving way to newer more flexible ideas. After all, globalization and digitization bring with them flexibility in terms of time, space, and organization. According to Frithjof Bergmann, future corporate structures will change into the so-called Working World 4.0 and will be oriented toward basic values such as "trust" and "appreciation." In this context, Gründerszene (2020) states:

> The central values of the concept of New Work are independence, freedom and participation in the community. New Work should offer new ways of freedom for creativity and development of one's own personality and thus contribute something really essential and important to the labor market. In this way, real 'freedom of action' is made possible.

Self-determined action is thus at the forefront of "New Work," and old rigid working methods are to be outdated. Ibrahim Evsan (2020) establishes the connection between value-oriented leadership and "New Work" on his New Work Blog:

- New Work is the collective term for forward-looking and meaningful work.
- New Work is not a change program, not a process, but a question of attitude, culture and leadership.
- It is about a modern leadership that is characterized by **eye level** and **appreciation**, by more coaching and less announcements.
- New Work is about giving **confidence** that employees are consciously making good and meaningful decisions.
- Our **employees are our greatest asset** and, in times of scarcity of talent, they are at the heart of everything we do.
- The trend among some executives to currently wear sneakers with their suits and ditch the tie are outward symbols of the changes toward the New Work.

At present, unfortunately, there is still too little understanding among baby boomers in the management ranks that trust, appreciation, respect, and transparency play a significant role in employee management.

Baby boomers even openly admit that they have little desire to "pamper" their younger employees. At the moment, therefore, there seems to be more of a rift running through the generations when it comes to implementing the New Work concept in the sense of a value-oriented corporate culture. In order to prevent this crack from becoming a gap and to ensure that the "New Work concept" can prevail, younger and older employees should take the time to engage in high-frequency dialogue. The content of this regular cross-generational interaction should be any kind of changes that are coming to companies in the coming months and years – in the wake of New Work and value-oriented corporate management. Young people who have grown up digitally are already aware that the following will change in the world of work (Evsan 2020):

- In the future, there will be fewer and fewer hierarchies in companies.
- Home office and associated trust working hours will become increasingly common, and the Corona pandemic from mid-March 2020 has clearly shown that "remote" working is entirely possible for very many companies.
- Value-oriented leadership in the form of digital support and online supervision of employees will become increasingly prevalent and will be a particular challenge in the future.
- The classic "9-to-5 job" on-site at the company will increasingly become outdated, as the ties to fixed working hours and fixed work locations will continue to dissolve.
- The work of the future will be quite flexible in terms of time and place. The boundaries between work and leisure are blurring, workspaces are being relocated, and collaboration is also shifting to virtual space.
- Digitization will lead to a paperless organization with the goal of processing documents regardless of location, as they can be accessed in clouds from anywhere.
- Digitalization will increasingly lead to virtual working worlds that accelerate processes, support people, and free them from routine tasks.

The trust of superiors will be an essential core value in the implementation of "New Work," which must be firmly anchored in an employee-oriented corporate culture. Ultimately, it is not enough to simply invest in new office equipment or approve home office.

A key element in Bergmann's approach (Bergmann 2019) is that employees should do what they "really, really want to do." Employees want a job they want to put their passion into, for the individual well-being of the company and for that of society. But many bosses still have potential in empathizing with their employees' strengths, showing empathy, and implementing latest ideas together. Many supervisors care too much about "packaging" the work and giving their employees a few goodies. That is, of course, far too little.

II. **Establishment of an Employee-Oriented Corporate Culture**

The second important prerequisite for value-oriented corporate management is the development and establishment of a noticeably good corporate culture in the real world of the company. However, this can only be developed and established over several years and not at the push of a button, as the practical example of Upstalsboom shows (Sect. 6.3).

Managers with a tangible employee-oriented attitude (trust, respect, generosity, appreciation) are at the heart of a good corporate culture.

The development of a corporate culture stands and falls with the strategic decision of the board/management to want to become a truly attractive employer.

When companies succeed in becoming a so-called caring company, they demonstrate how important the satisfaction of their employees is to them. Caring companies "take care" of their employees with a wide range of measures, regardless of which occupational group or age group an employee belongs to. Caring companies can be described as follows:

- They offer their employees the opportunity to exercise either at the company's own gym or at a local gym or to participate in online fitness classes.
- They offer their employees healthy food in their on-site canteens.
- They ensure that the employee's mobility is secured and subsidize car sharing or monthly tickets for local public transport.
- They support after-work activities so that teams can meet after work to experience or attend events together.
- It is important to them that employees work at well-equipped (smart) workstations in an appealing environment.
- They offer their employees the opportunity to work from home and provide suitable online tools (e.g., Zoom, MS Teams, Slack, etc.) and adequate work equipment (e.g., a powerful notebook).
- They support the professional and personal development of employees.
- They support flexible working hours and the reconciliation of private and professional life.
- They prove their absolute trust "from above" with transparent communication structures and support communication "at eye level."
- They establish flat hierarchical structures that can be thought of as a triangle, with the top being the top management, the middle being the management, and the bottom being the executive teams working underneath. There should be no more than three hierarchical levels anywhere.

If the framework conditions outlined above have been created and the aforementioned prerequisites are in place, companies can expect to be perceived as value-oriented "caring companies" with which employees:

- Are satisfied.
- Feel proud to work there.
- Identify with the company's goals.
- Experience their work as meaningful.
- Enjoy working as part of a team.

III. **Management of Employees According to the Internal Customer Model**

Value-oriented corporate management can also be recognized by whether a friendly atmosphere prevails in a company overall because the superiors lead well – regardless of whether in the real office on site or in the virtual working world. The quality of leadership is significantly influenced by the *attitude* and *behavior of* the supervisors. Good leadership, which managers can continually demonstrate and shape with their good basic mood in their teams, is the barometer for whether employees feel comfortable accordingly. A good atmosphere is transmitted not only to the willingness of employees to perform but also to the satisfaction of external customers, who in turn become loyal to the company.

Employees leave companies and look for a new job if their superiors do not behave as they would actually like them to. This is also proven by the results of the well-known Gallup studies (2020) every year. Around 75% of employees quit due to the perceived disrespectful and unappreciative behavior of their immediate supervisor.

Employees feel particularly comfortable in their department and in their team when their superiors:

- Behave in a fair and respectful manner.
- Are empathetic and appreciative.
- Communicate with them at eye level.
- Work together with them in a trusting and communicative manner.
- Make decisions transparently and give people a say.

In addition, value-oriented corporate management requires managers to start with themselves and to completely rethink their approach: employees should *no* longer "serve their boss"; instead, managers and employees should serve the customer together.

This approach, known as "The Employee as Internal Customer," was first published by William Deming as early as 1982 (Deming 1982) as part of his TQM research. It involves supervisors viewing their employees as internal customers and their corresponding attitude being shaped by the question "What can I do for you, dear employee, to help you work well at your job?". It is the working conditions that the supervisor can improve to make it easier for employees to do their jobs.

Employees usually behave much better toward external customers and are much more willing to perform or motivated if their superiors have created the best working conditions.

Moreover, according to Evsan (2020), the following are the things that make good leadership in times of digitalization, New Work, value-based management, and an employee-oriented corporate culture:

- As a leader, you should be willing to hand over power to your employees.
- Managers should learn to lead themselves professionally first.
- Properly successful teams create transparency through dialogue and communication throughout the group.

- Meetings, whether online or on-site, should last no longer than 30 min.
- Good leaders in the sense of the New Leadership approach help their employees to discover and develop their strengths.
- Collaboration, community, sustainability, openness and accessibility are the foundation of New Leadership, so supervisors need to make sure everyone feels part of the team and supports each other.

Evsan (2020) offers the following tips to managers in the age of "New Work":

- Trust your employees, delegate responsibility and encourage an autonomous way of working.
- Help employees identify and build on their strengths.
- 'I have a Dream' becomes 'We have a Dream.' In today's world, the sum of talents, knowledge and skills is successfully implemented by many projects. Therefore: Set your own and common goals.
- Rejoice with your employees over goals achieved and praise them for it.

In the past, supervisors sat isolated in their offices; today, "management by walking around" is a common leadership technique. In other words, supervisors regularly walk around the department in a good mood (or hold online meetings in a good mood) and continuously ask their employees (as internal customers) what should be improved in order to implement their ideas together in a timely manner.

Teams work well together when the culture in the company, the behavior of the superiors, and the climate in the team are right. A good team climate has been at the top of the list in empirical surveys for several years (Buxel 2009, 2011, 2013) when young people are asked what is most important to them at work – followed by meaningfulness of the work, respect and empathy of the supervisor, sustainability, and mindfulness.

IV. **Use of Digital Structures and Enabling Smart Working**

Finally, value-oriented corporate management can also be recognized by whether the digital possibilities that are already available to companies today are being used. First, the following must be made clear:

The young people of Generation Z, who will soon be entering the job market, are now around 20 years old. Unlike their parents' generation, they have grown up quite digitally. They were around 7 years old when the first smartphone came on the market in 2007. They have been playing online games since they were 4 years old and chatting with their friends via mobile phone, notebook, or PC since they could write. They have been ordering pizza or new headphones at the click of a mouse since they were teenagers and dictating their checklists into their mobile phones and are delighted when their spoken word is suddenly written on the screen. They are surprised that while you can register at the gym online, you cannot go to the polls online or – at least with the vast majority of city governments – register for your driver's license online. Apps are their constant companions, making their lives much easier.

When these digital experts or Internet "nerds" take up a job, they naturally want to work "smart" there – just as they do in their private lives. They want to use apps and do as much as possible at the click of a mouse or paperless, digitally, and online. In addition, they have no reservations about robots that help them in their daily lives – for example, with vacuuming – or relieve them of monotonous tasks.

For these potential employees who will be entering the job market very soon, companies should already set their course today and create digital structures. In addition to WLAN equipment in every corner of the company, robots, for example, should become increasingly commonplace when it comes to supporting employees. In around 10 years, many processes will certainly be robot-assisted. This is not a threat, but a real assistance.

Young people are not afraid of artificial intelligence and robots, on the contrary. If they must lift a 150-kg patient in a nursing home, for example, they are happy to have a robot do it for them. If they must sort towels into a cupboard, a robot with a gripper arm can do that just as well. Just as helpful is the voice control, which allows patient data to be entered directly into the patient file during the visit.

As far as the technological prerequisites are concerned, this "smart working" is quite possible today and is manageable in terms of costs. Many companies are still hesitant to invest extensively in this area, although it is certainly a mistake not to invest in innovative technologies today. Particularly in times of Corona crisis and in times of demographic change and a shortage of skilled workers, companies in all sectors need to demonstrate to potential applicants that they have their finger on the pulse of the times and provide jobs that are technologically up to date. Those that are already investing in smart working today will certainly have no great difficulty in finding good young staff.

The "war for talents" will only be won by those companies that are aware that young people also want to "find themselves digitally" and work "smart" in their professional lives.

First, however, there must be a change in attitude among those who make decisions today about investing in modern technologies and who sit at the lever that makes "smart working" possible. As long as the conviction prevails that the use of recent technologies does not lead to more facilitation, to faster processes, and to higher employee satisfaction, investments will not be made.

I am firmly convinced that the willingness to work "smart" already exists among the majority of "normal" employees of all occupational and age groups. They have understood that they are relieved when apps, robots, and smart assistants support them, for example.

Teams of all professions should start today to develop a "we-work-smart-strategy" and list how "smart working" will relieve and support them. This strategy can be continued and updated until 2030, when the "digital skeptics" will have retired and will be replaced by "digital experts" who will push "smart working."

In the future, the new generation of managers will hopefully have to credibly demonstrate that they can lead in a value-oriented manner as early as the application process.

Perhaps the product "HiddenCandidates" from a German software company will catch on. This is a candidate platform that brings managers and companies together. Potential executives create their profile with the desired target position at "HiddenCandidates," and from this, an anonymous, authentic personality profile is created in the first step. This is made available to interested companies anonymously at first, but also with the candidate's name after approval by the candidate.

Executives have the opportunity to record a 90-s video introduction and a time-shifted video interview (360 s), which should make the selection process easier for the company. Professional coaches accompany this process on the part of the candidates.

Companies can filter candidates online via a search function, view their anonymous profiles online, and invite them if necessary. In case of interest on the part of the company, the candidate decides for oneself whether the company gets the name or does not suit at all, and he or she wants to remain anonymous.

Since "values" play a key role in the "HiddenCandidates" personality profile, it is a value-oriented form of application and recruiting for candidates and companies.

3 Successfully Implementing Value-Oriented Leadership: Practical Example Upstalsboom

A good practical example of how value-oriented leadership can work over the years and lead to "happy" employees and an economically highly successful company is provided by the Upstalsboom Hotel Group and its owner Bodo Janssen. Schleicher (2020) has summarized the essential contents very well in his blog.

The term Upstalsboom is many centuries old and refers to a meeting place of East Frisian chieftains. The first hotel with this name was opened in the 1970s by the Janssen family. In the meantime, there are more than 10 Upstalsboom hotels and 500 Upstalsboom holiday apartments on the North Sea and Baltic Sea as well as in Berlin with approximately 800 employees.

In 2005, the current managing director Bodo Janssen took over the company from his parents. Upstalsboom doubled its turnover between 2009 and 2019, and Bodo Janssen attributes the growth in turnover to the new value-oriented corporate culture and the resulting increased willingness of the employees to perform.

In 2010, Bodo Janssen noticed during an anonymous employee survey how critically his person – as owner of the hotel group – was perceived by his employees. As a result, he initially attended seminars at Münsterschwarzach Abbey led by Benedictine Father Anselm Grün. For many years, Anselm Grün has been an advocate of value-oriented corporate management in the sense of "values make companies valuable" (Janssen and Grün 2017).

To consistently implement a value-oriented management of all employees, Bodo Janssen set out with his entire company on the so-called Upstalsboom Way.

The aim was to implement a corporate culture in which every employee – from the housekeeper to the hotel manager – can develop their potential and have exceptional job satisfaction. Bodo Janssen is firmly convinced that employees are happy at their respective workplaces when they see the meaning and purpose of their jobs because they can help shape them themselves.

One consequence of employees being "happier" is the company's success, which increases. In addition, the sickness rate decreases. The shortage of skilled workers in the wake of demographic change is no longer a threat if a company becomes an employer brand in the region because of its culture.

Bodo Janssen has managed with his "Silent Revolution" that value-oriented corporate management leads not only to satisfied employees but also to a stable brand as an employer. There are few vacancies in hotels that use the motto "Do you fit in with us?" when recruiting.

In addition, the Upstalsboom Hotel Group has succeeded in communicating its positive image of meaningful work to the outside world in a way that everyone can understand, also via social media activities. Bodo Janssen posts very regularly on Facebook at https://www.facebook.com/bodo.janssen.9 and comments on the actions he implements with his employees.

In a conversation with the author in March 2018, Bodo Janssen explains the ideal image for his hotel chain Upstalsboom, which he leads in the second generation. "I have a vision of happy people." Even if this vision sounds alienating at first, the company has been able to significantly increase the satisfaction of its approximately 800 employees in recent years.

Employee satisfaction has had a positive effect on the recommendation rate for Upstalsboom hotels, which rose to 98%, and turnover doubled within 3 years. But how does the improved attitude to life of the managers become a lived corporate culture?

Together with Oliver Haas, author of the book *Corporate Happiness*, Bodo Janssen implemented a series of measures with the so-called "Corporate Happiness" approach, which changed both the inner attitudes and the behavior of the employees toward each other. In voluntary information events, the workforce learned what this new – previously unknown – topic was all about. At the same time, employees who felt the desire and interest to play an active role were able to register. So-called "Corporate Happiness" officers were to anchor the contents and findings of this approach as multipliers within the company.

Topics such as "own strengths," "energy management," or also "appreciative partnerships" were worked on. In this way, the employees of the Upstalsboom Hotel Group experienced a reflection process that later extended to the working environment and colleague relationships.

Bodo Janssen, for example, reported to the author in March 2018 that appreciation is now not just something that bosses give to employees but also takes place among themselves. Some previously rigid and official relationships even take on playful aspects – even between boss and employee. Something like that lifts the mood considerably.

For Bodo Janssen, it is a matter of the heart that all employees feel good in the company (cf. Janssen 2016). He wishes happiness for everyone. In the past, he used to set the strategy "from the top," but today he actively involves all employees in strategy issues. This allows employees to identify much more with what they are doing.

In 2013, Upstalsboom employees developed 12 guiding values in various workshops and presented them graphically as a tree (Upstalsboom 2020). Each value is understood as a branch (https://www.der-upstalsboom-weg.de/der-upstalsboom-weg/unsere-werte/).

In this way, a new mission statement with 12 values was initially created. A slogan explaining the meaning was developed for each value. Since then, the value tree has been the heart of the corporate culture of the entire Upstalsboom Group.

Four years later, in 2017 (in the spirit of the motto "From a mission statement to value-oriented corporate management"), the 12 values were further developed into so-called Upstalsboomer sense theses. These are 32 theses that serve as in-depth guiding principles for every Upstalsboom employee and are intended to align daily value-oriented behavior.

4 Conclusion

For the year 2030, up to five million vacancies are predicted in Germany that need to be filled. In addition to the three million vacancies that will arise from 2025 onward because of demographic change, because German families will only have around 1.5 children on average, there will also be around three million baby boomers retiring.

It is time for companies to prepare themselves in a timely manner to deal with the massive staff shortage that will hit all industries and all types of businesses hard. Recruiting staff will become one of the most important tasks that companies will have to master in the next 10 years. Unfortunately, many companies have not even realized this yet.

However, before companies can recruit staff, they must become attractive employers for Generations Y and Z, who:

- Work in the sense of "New Work".
- Live an employee-oriented corporate culture.
- Have supervisors who lead professionally, value-oriented, and at eye level.
- Digitize their processes and enable and support smart working.

Employee leadership has already changed completely in the last 10 years and will experience another huge "change" by 2030. Disrespectful behavior, a lack of trust, and too little appreciation for employees are completely "out" and "old school." It drives employees away and doesn't attract applicants. But the strict, less empathetic representatives of the post-war generation will slowly die out, and the empathetic digital experts will take their place.

Generations Y and Z tick digitally. They want to feel the value-oriented corporate management and the employee-oriented corporate culture already digitally on the career pages and take a look at the company during their job search.

In the future, companies will only win the "war for talents" if they manage to credibly communicate their excellent value-oriented corporate personality in the real/analog working world as well as in the digital world and actually live it in everyday working life.

References

Bergmann F (2019) New work new culture: work we want and a culture that strengthens us. John Hunt Publishing, Winchester

Buxel H (2009) Arbeitsplatz Krankenhaus: Der ärztliche Nachwuchs ist unzufrieden. Dtsch Ärztebl 37:A1790–A1793

Buxel H (2011) Was Pflegekräfte unzufrieden macht. Dtsch Ärztebl 17:A946–A948

Buxel H (2013) Arbeitsplatz Krankenhaus: Was Ärzte zufriedener macht. Dtsch Ärztebl 11:A494–A498

Deming W (1982) Out of the crisis. MIT, Cambridge

Evsan I (2020) Blog. https://newworkblog.de/new-work/. Accessed on 05.08.2020

Great Place to work (2020). www.greatplacetowork.de. Accessed on 05.08.2020

Gründerszene (2020). https://www.gruenderszene.de/lexikon/begriffe/new-work?interstitial. Accessed on 06.08.2020

Hauser F (2008) Einsatzbereitschaft wirkt Wunder. EXKLUSIV-STUDIE, Erstmals bewiesen: Unternehmenskultur, Arbeitsqualität und Mitarbeiterengagement befördern nachhaltig den Unternehmenserfolg. Personalwirtschaft 1:22–26

Janssen B (2016) Die stille Revolution: Führen mit Sinn und Menschlichkeit. Ariston, München

Janssen B, Grün A (2017) Stark in stürmischen Zeiten: Die Kunst, sich selbst und andere zu führen. Ariston, Leipzig

Schleicher C (2020). www.co2-positiv.de/werteorientierte-unternehmensführung. Accessed on 13.08.2020

Schüller A (2020) Blog. https://blog.anneschueller.de/purpose-statt-leitbild-wie-sich-unternehmen-in-zukunft-aufstellen-muessen/. Accessed on 05.08.2020

Upstalsboom (2020). https://www.der-upstalsboom-weg.de/der-upstalsboom-weg/unsere-werte/. Accessed on 06.08.2020

Prof. Dr. Anja Lüthy, Dipl.-Psychologin, Dipl.-Kauffrau (FH). Anja Lüthy is a professor with a focus on service management and marketing at the Department of Economics at the Brandenburg University of Applied Sciences. As a sideline, she works as a speaker, trainer, and coach in health and social institutions nationwide. Her topics are corporate culture, intergenerational leadership, employer branding, personnel marketing, online recruiting via smartphone, social media, and apps. More information at www.luethy.de, Twitter @AnjaLuethy

Sustainability in Corporate Governance

Structure and Function of Non-financial Internal Control Systems

Marcus Ehrenberger, Maximilian Mäder, and Johannes Berna

Abstract

Complete and correct data are a central basis for value-oriented management and successful corporate governance. Against this background, non-financial internal control systems have gained in importance for both internal and external stakeholders. To ensure the effectiveness and efficiency of these control systems, procedural and structural success factors must be considered.

1 Non-financial Data Have Financial Significance

The economy is currently in a transformation phase. The EU has presented ambitious plans to achieve climate neutrality by 2050. Despite new problems, such as the Covid-19 pandemic, environmental and social sustainability remain societal megatrends and value drivers for companies. The Green Deal and its associated measures and incentives aim to enable and accelerate this journey (European Commission 2019).

Against this background, environmental and social sustainability are to be understood as values by which companies are currently measured. Non-financial issues such as environmental, social, and employee concerns and compliance have a direct or indirect financial impact via regulations or reputational effects and thus move to the center of companies' management responsibilities. Good corporate governance is therefore value-oriented and

M. Ehrenberger (✉) · M. Mäder · J. Berna
KPMG, Stuttgart, Germany
e-mail: mehrenberger@kpmg.com; mmaeder@kpmg.com; jberna@kpmg.com

J. Lange (ed.), *Value-Oriented Leadership in Theory and Practice*,
https://doi.org/10.1007/978-3-662-65883-3_7

must understand non-financial requirements and consider them in the design of governance structures (Wieland 2014).

The requirements for the governance of sustainability are not new but have gained in importance in recent years. In order to remain competitive in the future, companies must integrate sustainability into their business strategy, back it up with targets and measures, and collect, process, and communicate the relevant data. While accounting-related data is rugged, this is often not the case for non-financial data such as CO_2 emissions, water consumption, and waste production. The processes and structures for collecting, processing, and presenting non-financial data still show various weaknesses compared to the financial area.

An example will illustrate the error-proneness of data collection for a carbon footprint: In practice, Scope 1 and Scope 2 emissions are usually reported. These are direct emissions from the company's own production and indirect emissions resulting from the purchase of energy (World Resources Institute and World Business Council for Sustainable Development 2004). Data collection usually begins with the recording of energy consumption. For this purpose, meters are read and entered into the relevant systems. Sources of error exist in the manual transfer of values into the system. Units can also be forgotten or emissions incorrectly assigned to Scopes 1 and 2. After the values have been recorded, they are converted into greenhouse gases by multiplying them with emission factors. In the process, conversion factors can be confused (such as kilowatts instead of megawatt-hours). Furthermore, incorrect or outdated emission factors can be used. Further sources of error occur when closing data gaps and the final consolidation of the data.

Even if empirical data on the quality of non-financial key figures is lacking, it can be stated with a view to practice: key figures are sometimes incomplete or incorrect. They are also made available with a time lag. The reasons for this are usually unclearly defined responsibilities and processes for data collection and validation, as well as a high degree of manual activity and the use of inconsistent system landscapes (Graff and Hell 2019).

Against this background, non-financial internal control systems (nICS) have become increasingly important for both internal and external stakeholders: an nICS can counteract these sources of error, drawing on a proven system within the company that is already used to ensure complete and accurate financial reporting. In the following section, the relevance for nICS is examined (Sect. 2). Subsequently, fundamental aspects of the structure and function of nICS are presented (Sect. 3). Section 4 provides a summary overview of the structural and organizational success factors of an nICS, followed by an outlook on expected developments (Sect. 5).

2 The Drivers of Non-financial Internal Control Systems

2.1 Regulatory Requirements

2.1.1 CSR Directive Implementation Act

With the CSR Directive Implementation Act (CSR = corporate social responsibility), an obligation to report on sustainability issues has been established in Germany since the 2017 financial year. According to § 289b et seq. HGB (German Commercial Code), capital market-oriented corporations as well as large credit institutions and insurance companies with more than 500 employees and sales revenues >40 million euros or total assets >20 million euros are obliged to publish a non-financial statement (Federal Law Gazette 2017).

In terms of content, companies must report on the topics of environmental concerns, employee concerns, social concerns, respect for human rights, and combating corruption and bribery, among others (cf. § 289c (2) HGB) (Table 1). Pursuant to § 289c (3) and DRS 20.265 (German Accounting Standard), information must be provided on the concepts, measures, objectives, and results pursued in each case. Non-financial data is required for this purpose, such as CO_2 emissions, water consumption, waste production, recyclable materials, accident frequency rates, or the number of supplier audits.

The CSR-RUG (Corporate Social Responsibility Directive Implementation Act) forces companies to determine and communicate non-financial information completely and correctly. This increases the demands on data availability and data quality. In order to comply with the required due diligence and accountability (Section 93 of the German Stock Corporation Act (AktG)), management boards must ensure that the processes and structures through which non-financial data are collected are reliable and resilient. In this sense,

Table 1 Exemplary non-financial data

Issue	Environmental	Employee matters	Human rights	Social issues	Corruption and bribery
Facts	Environmental and climate protection (emissions)	Health, occupational safety	Supply chain, procurement	Social commitment	Compliance
Key figures	CO_2 emissions (Scope 1, 2, 3) NOx emissions (nitrogen oxide) Reduction in electricity consumption	Accident frequency rate Fluctuation rate Proportion of training hours on occupational safety	Number of supplier audits Number of supplier development	Amount of sponsorship expenses and donations Number of projects supported	Number of compliance cases Degree of coverage of compliance management system Number of training hours per employee

control systems must be implemented which consequently do not only focus on financial reporting processes – in short, non-financial internal control systems (nICS).

Against this background, obligations arise for supervisory boards. Pursuant to Section 107 AktG and Section 171 AktG, supervisory boards are responsible for the audit of the non-financial statement in the same way as for the audit of the annual financial statements. For this audit, supervisory boards should monitor the functionality of the data processing procedures and the related effectiveness of the nICS. For this purpose, appropriate documentation, monitoring, and reporting of the nICS are fundamental.

2.1.2 Law on the Implementation of the Second Shareholders' Rights Directive

On 01.01.2020, the Act Implementing the Second Shareholders' Rights Directive (Bundesgesetzblatt 2019) came into force. According to ARUG II (Act Implementing the Second Shareholders' Rights Directive), the remuneration of new or amended management board contracts must be geared toward the "sustainable and long-term development of the company," considering social and ecological criteria.

For capital market-oriented companies, this means that the performance of the management board must also be measured and rewarded with regard to key non-financial, i.e., social and ecological, issues. For this purpose, relevant sustainability KPIs (key performance indicators) must be identified and backed up with concrete targets. According to the current version of the German Corporate Governance Code (Government Commission 2019), the achievement of targets must be traceable. In this sense, quantifiable targets are recommended.

To ensure the reliability and credibility of target achievement and related reporting, companies should implement rugged data collection processes and an nICS. In addition, an external audit at the level of a reasonable assurance is recommended.

2.2 Stakeholder Expectations

Investors and financial institutions play a central role in the transformation to a sustainable economy. The EU Commission is taking this into account with the Sustainable Growth Action Plan (European Commission 2018). The focus here is on environmental sustainability. The Action Plan aims to redirect capital flows toward sustainable investments and mitigate financial risks arising from climate change and the overstepping of planetary boundaries. It also aims to promote transparency and long-termism in financial and economic activity. For example, the introduction of an EU classification system (Green Taxonomy) will provide a uniform definition of which economic activities can be considered sustainable. For the implementation of the measures of the action plan, the EU Commission has secured expert support from the stakeholder forum "Technical Expert Group." In its final report, the Technical Expert Group calls for companies to report publicly on a regular basis on all environmental objectives of the Green Taxonomy (e.g., climate protection, sustainable use and protection of water resources, reduction of pollution). For this purpose, companies need robust non-financial data and thus corresponding processes as well as an nICS.

In addition to civil society stakeholders, such as the "Fridays for Future" movement, economic stakeholders are also reporting demands for transparent non-financial data from companies in order to be able to assess their sustainability performance. The automotive industry is a case in point: German car manufacturers have steadily increased their sustainability ambitions. In order to achieve the goal of climate neutrality, they are increasingly holding their suppliers accountable (Handelsblatt 2019). This is quite logical, insofar as the emissions of the supplier products are included in the emissions of the car manufacturers (Scope 3). From this perspective, the supply chain offers a high potential for CO_2 reduction. Non-compliance can result in painful sanctions for suppliers, up to an exclusion from the supply chain. Against this background, the same applies here: In order to prove compliance, suppliers must implement robust non-financial data and thus corresponding processes and an nICS.

In summary, it can be stated: both regulatory developments and rising stakeholder expectations have significantly increased the relevance of non-financial data for the management of companies. As a result, the requirements for the processes and structures of data collection and processing are also increasing. Transparency, completeness, correctness, and timely availability are criteria against which companies must measure themselves. Up to now, process-related and structural weaknesses have been observed in practice. Processes, control activities, responsibilities, and forms of documentation are not always clearly defined in data collection and communication. A high proportion of manual activities increases the susceptibility to errors. In order to ensure robust data quality, secure processes and an effective nICS must therefore be implemented.

3 The Structure and Function of Non-financial Internal Control Systems

An internal control system (ICS) is defined as the totality of all systematically designed organizational measures and controls in the company to achieve process objectives and to avert damage that may be caused by the company's own personnel or malicious third parties (Institut der Wirtschaftsprüfer e. V. 2006, 2017). This includes the organizational measures and controls in the company to ensure that internal guidelines are adhered to, assets are protected, and corporate goals are achieved. The ICS also helps to create transparency in business processes. The process objectives of an ICS include effectiveness and efficiency as well as reliability of reporting and compliance with laws, regulations, and contracts. An nICS is an internal control system that focuses on non-financial processes and data. In this respect, it is an extension of the classic ICS. The scoping of the ICS is therefore extended to include a new dimension of processes and data. The basic logic and functions of a classic ICS therefore also apply to an nICS.

An appropriate and effectively designed nICS comprises, on the one hand, regulations for *controlling* the company's activities (internal control system) and, on the other hand, regulations for *monitoring* compliance with these regulations (internal monitoring system). Both aspects should be implemented as part of a recurring process among the employees of the business units and among the organizational monitoring bodies.

In order for an nICS to retain its appropriateness and effectiveness in the long term, a systematic approach is required to ensure that processes, risks, and controls are documented and regularly reviewed. The periodic measures required for this can be summarized in an ideal-typical nICS control cycle. The nICS control cycle consists of four phases and is used to identify risks in processes in a structured manner, to develop and review appropriate mitigating control measures, and to prepare the results of the review in a way that is appropriate for the target group. The nICS control cycle can therefore be understood as a continuous process of monitoring and improvement with regard to the appropriateness and effectiveness of the nICS (Fig. 1).

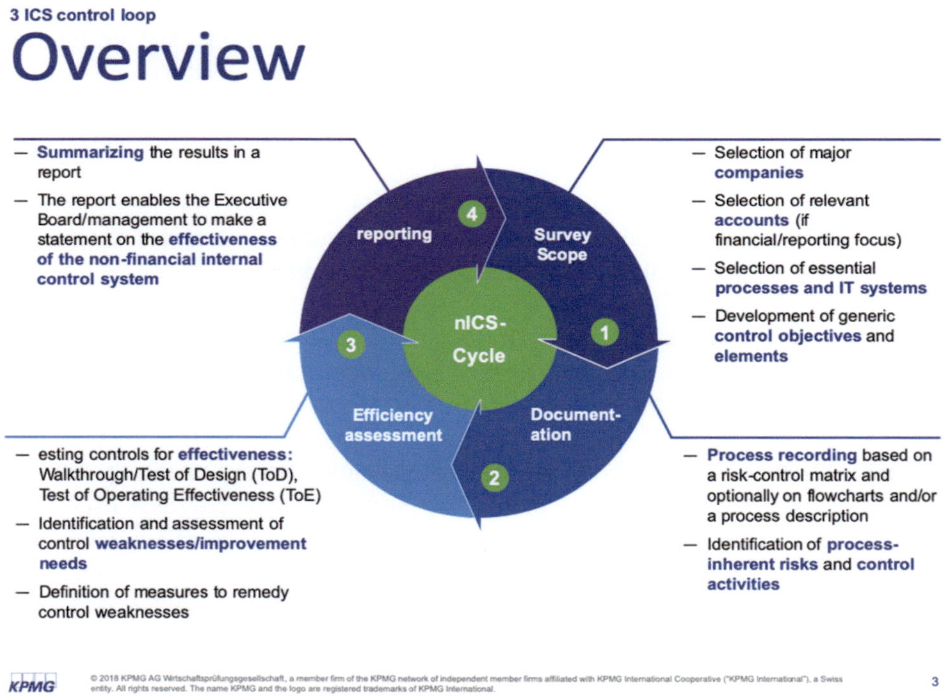

Fig. 1 nICS control loop. (Source: COSO 2009) (Committee of Sponsoring Organizations of the Treadway Commission 2009)

Phase 1: Determination of the Scope of the Survey

In phase 1, the scope of the nICS survey is defined. In practice, this phase is also called "scoping." The process follows a risk-oriented approach, in which it is initially defined to what extent, at which point, and in which way the nICS is to be rolled out. This phase forms the basis for the appropriate and effective implementation of an nICS. In this context, fundamental consideration is given to which business units, business areas, and processes carry significant risks and could thus negatively impact the achievement of the defined corporate objectives (operational business, non-financial reporting, compliance with laws).

Phase 2: Documentation

In the second phase, all relevant processes for the "scope" defined in phase 1 are identified and documented. The documentation at process level is done with the help of process descriptions, guidelines, and process diagrams as well as risk-control matrices.

The process descriptions of the nICS serve to systematically describe the status quo of the non-financial processes in text form. These are mostly recorded and formulated by the central nICS management on the basis of interviews with the process owners of the respective sub-processes.

A risk-control matrix is the central element of an nICS. All identified risks of a process are recorded here and linked to internal controls that are intended to mitigate the respective risk. The risk-control matrix thus serves as standardized documentation focusing on the risks, checkpoints, and controls of the respective processes and business units. It provides the structure by means of which the entire documentation and subsequent effectiveness review can be recorded in an uncomplicated manner throughout the company, usually on an excel basis. The risk-control matrix specified by the central nICS management also contains space for supplementing local risks and controls of the business units. The individual results of the effectiveness review and any measures identified to remedy control weaknesses are also documented in the risk control matrix (phase 3).

Phase 3: Assessment of Adequacy and Effectiveness

In phase 3, the identified controls of the respective process are first checked for their appropriateness in the "test of design." This involves examining the extent to which the implemented control generally meets the control objective. The respective control objective is derived from the identified risk. The effectiveness of the controls is then tested in the "Test of Operating Effectiveness." In this step, the control description is used to validate the extent to which the control has been consistently implemented and documented over time. Measures and clear responsibilities for remediation must be defined for identified control weaknesses.

Phase 4: Reporting The final phase of the nICS control cycle is the reporting of the results of the first three phases in a manner appropriate to the target group. Particular focus is placed on the summary of the results from phase 3. The reporting is intended to enable the executive board/management to make a statement about the general effectiveness of the nICS.

The following "three-lines-of-defense model" forms the regulatory framework for a holistic governance-risk-compliance system (GRC system) to manage corporate risks (Luburic et al. 2015) (Fig. 2). In this model, among other things, the roles and responsibilities of the nICS are embedded as components of the second line of defense in a holistic GRC system. This illustrates which coordination, communication, and impact relationships are necessary between the individual governance elements in order to achieve the defined corporate objectives or to effectively manage the resulting corporate risks.

The first line of defense is the operational corporate level. It consists of the company's operational departments and relates individually to the corporate processes in which corporate risks occur. This line of defense can therefore be understood as a kind of "risk owner" that is responsible for the sustainable implementation of the identified controls for managing corporate risks. In this context, those responsible for the first line of defense must ensure that risk management measures, e.g., the defined controls of the nICS, are actually implemented and enforced.

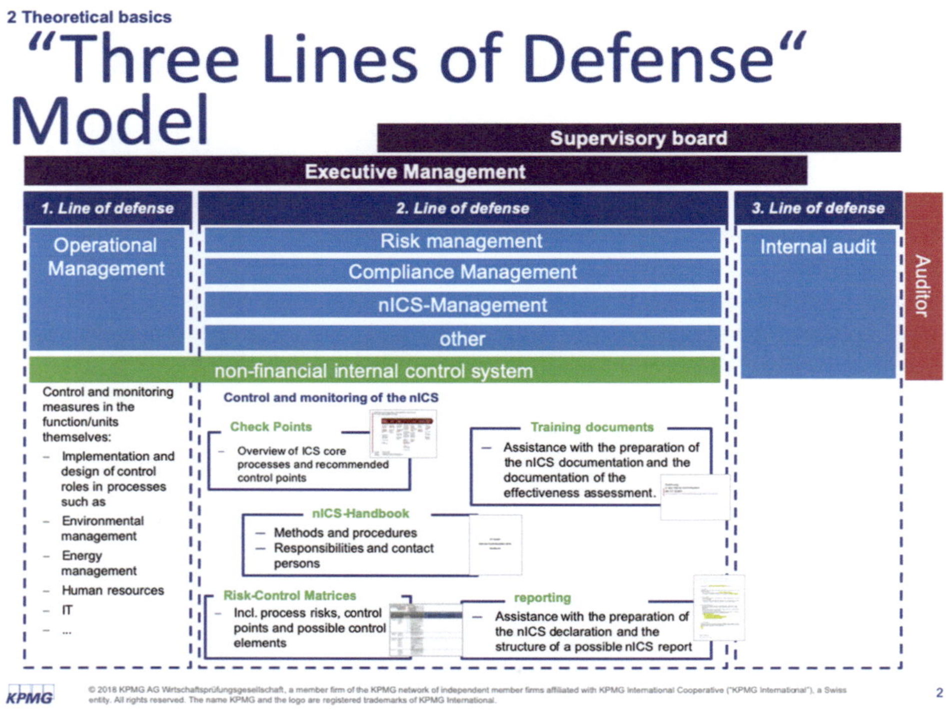

Fig. 2 Three-lines-of-defense model. (Source: IIA 2013)

The second line of defense serves to control and monitor the governance measures of the first line of defense. This includes the definition and implementation of methods, concepts, guidelines, and standardized procedures for risk management. The central nICS management of an organization as part of the second line of defense is thus responsible, for example, for the development of the framework for the nICS including the definition of documentation standards, the implementation of nICS training, and the periodic implementation of the measures from the nICS control loop.

The third line of defense, internal audit, provides an objective and independent auditing and advisory body. In its function as the third line of defense, internal audit supports the company's management and supervisory bodies in regularly assessing the effectiveness of the governance systems. The aim here is to inform the company's management and supervisory bodies as to whether the identified corporate risks are being effectively identified, assessed, and managed.

4 Success Factors for Non-financial Internal Control Systems

The practice of nICS is still in its infancy. Nevertheless, key success factors can be derived from existing experience. These can generally be divided into two areas: The structural area concerns the organizational structure of companies. The procedural area focuses on the process organization (Table 2).

4.1 Process-Related Success Factors

4.1.1 Continuous Improvement

An effective nICS must be critically reviewed and adjusted on a regular basis. The regular execution of the individual phases of the nICS control cycle and the underlying processes is the basis for continuous improvement of the nICS methodology. This agile approach to the phases of scoping, documentation, adequacy and effectiveness assessment, and

Table 2 Success factors for nICS

Processual	Structural
Continuous improvement (control cycle)	Integration into existing corporate governance structures and processes
Bottom-up processes	Cooperation between the first and second lines of defense managers
Process transparency and integration	nICS know-how in the first line of defense
Uniform documentation	Clear communication concept
	Risk-oriented scoping
	Tone from the top

reporting is of great importance because processes and risks are constantly changing. These changes must be considered quickly in an nICS. In this respect, an effective nICS thrives on the findings that are identified as part of the annual control cycle and are subsequently adjusted or improved.

4.1.2 Bottom-Up Processes

The decentralized design of responsibility for risks and controls among those responsible for the first line of defense enables greater motivation and, above all, greater identification with the topic of nICS. However, it should be ensured that there is a clear communication channel for the responsibilities of the first line of defense to the second line of defense. Via this communication channel, process-related improvement potential identified by those responsible for the first line of defense can be passed on to the second line of defense (bottom-up). This increases motivation and acceptance among those responsible for the first line of defense and at the same time improves the quality of the nICS. After all, findings at the operational level are critical for the further development of an nICS.

4.1.3 Process Transparency and Integration

An nICS is always implemented on the basis of the existing operational processes. Conversely, this means that a functioning and, above all, transparent process landscape is of great importance for the successful implementation of an nICS. The more transparently the operational processes are documented and comprehensible in the form of guidelines, process diagrams, or process descriptions, the better an nICS can be based on them. In the optimal state of an nICS, the operational process landscape merges with the nICS. This means that the nICS becomes part of the process documentation and the process activities, e.g., control executions, are directly embedded in the processes. In this sense, there should not be a standard process and an nICS process, but an integrated standard process.

4.1.4 Unified Documentation

Unified documentation of controls using unified tools leads to easier documentation and reduces the susceptibility to errors. In addition, simple and clear tasks create greater acceptance among the executing employees. For the documentation of controls, a central system should be developed in the second line of defense, which is used by the first line of defense. This simplifies the complex task of documentation and also leads to comparability across all company units. In this way, business units that have difficulties with control documentation can be supported by means of exemplary control documentation from other business units.

4.2 Structural Success Factors

4.2.1 Integration into Existing Corporate Governance Structures and Processes

Synergy effects can be exploited by integrating the nICS into existing corporate governance structures and processes. Conceptually, three levels of maturity can be distinguished for this integration (Fig. 3):

1. Sustainability as a patchwork quilt: This level of maturity can currently be observed in a large number of companies. Sustainability processes are usually not adequately documented. Process standardization and harmonization is only taking place to a limited extent. Controls are not consistently identified, implemented, or documented. Non-financial data is largely recorded manually. A structured nICS does not exist.
2. Sustainability in the silo view: This maturity level is characterized by increasing standardization. For example, there are standardized processes for data collection, processing, and communication, which are formalized in unified process descriptions and risk-control matrices. Relevant controls are implemented and documented but are not integrated into the existing ICS organization.

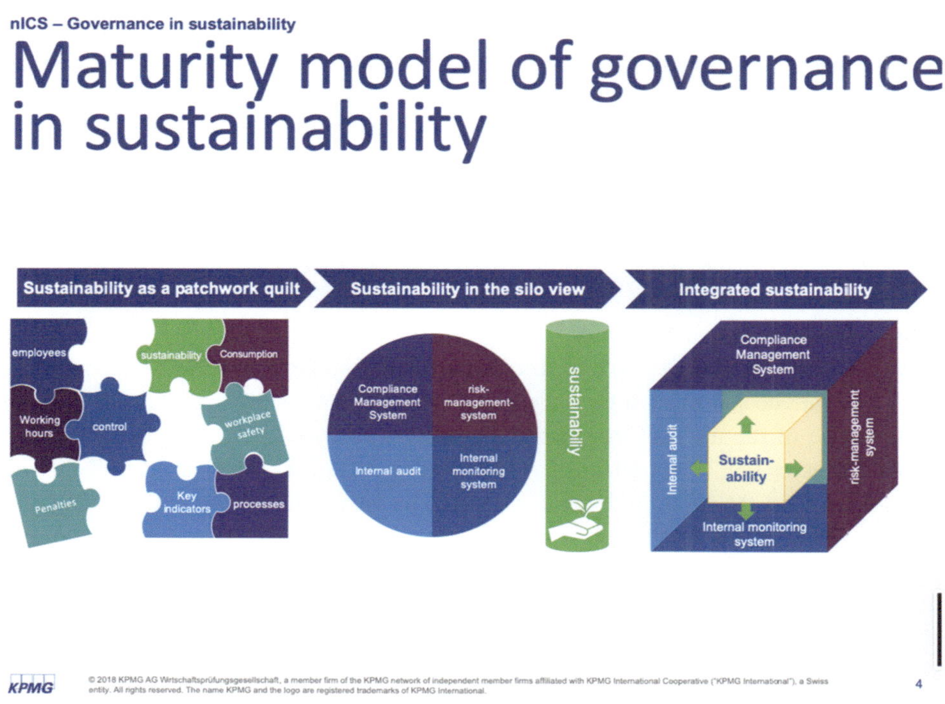

Fig. 3 Maturity model of sustainability governance

3. Integrated sustainability: Processes for non-financial data are integrated into existing elements of corporate governance, i.e., risk management, compliance management, internal audit, and the classic ICS. This promotes a holistic perspective on risks and improved process transparency and data quality. It also reduces duplication of effort and structures.

4.2.2 Cooperation Between the First and Second Lines of Defense Managers

Through interdisciplinary cooperation between the first and second lines of defense and the associated exchange of knowledge, operational issues and problems can be solved efficiently within the framework of an nICS and improved accordingly in the nICS methodology. This contributes significantly to an effectively designed nICS. By integrating responsibilities from both lines of defense into decision-making processes, the nICS can be precisely adapted to local and operational circumstances, and risk management can be made even more effective.

In this context, it must be ensured that the responsibilities for both lines of defense are clearly defined. A common and unified understanding of the distribution of roles forms the basis for successful cooperation between the two lines of defense.

4.2.3 nICS Know-How in the First Line of Defense

A sound knowledge of the nICS methodology among those responsible in the first line of defense ensures successful implementation of the nICS. Generally, the topic-specific knowledge around the nICS methodology is located in the second line of defense, as it is at this point that the methodology is conceptually developed. This knowledge must be passed on to the first line of defense via specific training and workshops. The more understanding there is of the nICS methodology in the first line of defense, the more appropriate and effective the operational design of the nICS will be. Continuous nICS knowledge building and knowledge sharing should therefore be the goal of any nICS organization.

4.2.4 Risk-Oriented Scoping

Risk-based scoping is critical to the effectiveness of and employee's identification with an nICS. Relevant decisions must be made in the first phase of an nICS project. The focus is on the scope of the nICS: Through which business units will the nICS be rolled out? Which processes will be included and which will be excluded? Which risks in these processes are part of the scope and which are not? The answer to these questions should be based on a risk-oriented approach. This ensures that the material risks are identified with regard to non-financial reporting and mitigated by appropriate controls. This approach limits the scope of the nICS to the material issues. The rule is often that less is more. If this is not successful and employees cannot understand the purpose of the requirements and controls, an nICS becomes wastepaper: controls are then carried out as an obligation and not for reasons of advantage. The potential of an nICS thus remains unused.

4.2.5 Tone from the Top

A clear commitment to the nICS on the part of the management level through active exemplification of the components of the nICS methodology and through active communication leads to a deep anchoring of the nICS in the corporate culture. The relevance of the management culture is often underestimated. Yet it is of fundamental importance for the successful implementation of an nICS. It is important to note that the term "management level" does not only refer to top management in the sense of the executive board/management. All management levels down to the operational processes of the individual business units must be considered. The higher the prioritization and recognition of this topic at the management level, the better the results of the nICS will be.

5 Outlook

The topic of nICS will continue to gain importance in the coming years. Motivated by regulatory developments and stakeholder expectations, companies will increasingly professionalize their non-financial reporting and related systems. nICS will play a central role in this process. As with any new development, improved processes and structures must emerge for nICS through the trial-and-error principle. A "one-size-fits-all solution" does not exist. It is important to avoid duplicate structures and duplicate efforts. Non-financial aspects and financial aspects must be integrated and designed according to the company's individual needs. If ICS are not designed individually for each company, they lose their effectiveness and their internal acceptance. Employees quickly recognize when controls are only carried out for the sake of control and do not provide any additional process security or other added value. When designing an nICS, process-related and structural success factors should therefore be considered. At the procedural level, it must be ensured that an nICS runs through a recurring regular process and is thereby continuously improved. In order to create the necessary process-related transparency, the developed nICS methodology must be consistently and unifiedly documented. On a structural level, it is recommended that an nICS be embedded in existing structures and not designed as a silo function. In addition, structural conditions must be created for cooperative collaboration between the operational level (first line of defense) of the nICS and the nICS methodology department (second line of defense). A clear definition of responsibilities is important for this. Of key importance is the "Tone from the Top": without a clearly exemplified and clearly communicated endorsing attitude of the management toward the nICS, an adequate and effective implementation is not likely. If the success factors are considered and interlock, nICS will make a significant contribution to the quality and reliability of non-financial data and processes and successfully accompany companies into a sustainable economy.

References

Bundesgesetzblatt (2017) Gesetz zur Stärkung der nichtfinanziellen Berichterstattung der Unternehmen in ihren Lage- und Konzernlageberichten (Jahrgang 2017, 18.04.2017). Bundesgesetzbl Teil I(Nr.20):802–814

Bundesgesetzblatt (2019) Gesetz zur Umsetzung der zweiten Aktionärsrechterichtlinie (Jahrgang 2019, 19.12.2019). Bundesgesetzbl Teil I(Nr. 50):2637–2651

Committee of Sponsoring Organizations of the Treadway Commission (2009) Internal control – integrated framework, guidance on monitoring internal control systems – introduction, 2009

European Commission (2018) Aktionsplan: Finanzierung nachhaltigen Wachstums (08.03.2018). https://ec.europa.eu/transparency/regdoc/rep/1/2018/DE/COM-2018-97-F1-DE-MAIN-PART-1.PDF. Accessed on 23.04.2020

European Commission (2019) Communication from the commission to the European Parliament, the European Council, the Council, the European Economic and Social Committee and the Committee of the Regions: the European Green Deal (11.12.2019). https://ec.europa.eu/info/sites/info/files/european-green-deal-communication_en.pdf. Accessed on 22.04.2020

Graff A, Hell C (2019) Mehr Sicherheit für die Nachhaltigkeitsleistung. CGO Gov Mag 07:68–71

Handelsblatt (2019) VW erlässt Vorgaben für Nachhaltigkeit bei Zulieferern (25.05.2019). https://www.handelsblatt.com/unternehmen/industrie/autobauer-vw-erlaesst-vorgaben-fuer-nachhaltigkeit-bei-zulieferern/24382258.html?ticket=ST-779839-SOGQnxAbWBhGXP4AiFTA-ap5. Accessed on 23.04.2020

Institut der Wirtschaftsprüfer e. V (2006) Feststellung und Beurteilung von Fehlerrisiken und Reaktionen des Abschlussprüfers auf die beurteilten Fehlerrisiken. Wirtschaftsprüf 2006(IDW PS 261):1433–1445

Institut der Wirtschaftsprüfer e. V (2017) (Hrsg) Feststellung und Beurteilung von Fehlerrisiken und Reaktionen des Abschlussprüfers auf die beurteilten Fehlerrisiken. IDW-Fachnachr 2017(IDW PS 261 n.F.):Tz. 20

Luburic R, Perovic M, Sekulovic R (2015) Quality management in terms of strengthening the "three lines of defence" in risk management – process approach. Int J Qual Res 9(2):243–250

Regierungskommission (2019) Deutscher Corporate Governance Kodex (16.12.2019). https://www.dcgk.de//files/dcgk/usercontent/de/download/kodex/191216_Deutscher_Corporate_Governance_Kodex.pdf. Accessed on 23.04.2020

The Institute of Internal Auditors (2013) The three lines of defense in effective risk management and control, IIA Position Paper, January 2013

Wieland J (2014) Normativity and governance. In: Governance ethics: global value creation, economic organization and normativity. Springer, Berlin, 27–42

World Resources Institute and World Business Council for Sustainable Development (2004) The greenhouse gas protocol. A corporate accounting and reporting standard (03.2004). https://ghgprotocol.org/sites/default/files/standards/ghg-protocol-revised.pdf. Accessed on 23.04.2020

Dr. Marcus Ehrenberger is a manager in the Sustainability Services division at KPMG AG Wirtschaftsprüfungsgesellschaft. His focus is on auditing and consulting in the area of sustainable business models and sustainability governance. He is also a lecturer in sustainable corporate governance at the University of Tübingen.

Maximilian Mäder, Manager in Corporate Governance Services, has been with KPMG AG Wirtschaftsprüfungsgesellschaft since 2014. His work focuses on advising and auditing companies in the area of internal control systems. During this time, he has been involved in the implementation and auditing of internal control systems in numerous national and international projects. In particular, he has advised companies on the implementation and auditing of internal control systems, which are subject to a US Department of Justice monitorship for violations of the Foreign Corrupt Practices Act (FCPA). He also specializes in the design and delivery of internal control training. Currently, he is also a lecturer at the Nürtingen-Geislingen University of Applied Sciences in the field of corporate governance.

Johannes Berna, Senior Associate in Corporate Governance Services, joined KPMG AG Wirtschaftsprüfungsgesellschaft in 2017 with a focus on Internal Control Systems and Internal Audit. During his time at KPMG, Johannes Berna advised and supported numerous nationally and internationally operating companies in the implementation and effectiveness testing of internal control systems in various business processes as well as the conception of training courses on the topic of ICS for various target groups and experience levels.

Value-Based Compliance: Integrating Integrity and Compliance Management

Timo Herold and Florentin Schlegel

Abstract

This chapter describes the integration of the ethical perspective (integrity) into the often legally shaped compliance management system of companies. As a basis, the term compliance is first briefly explained, and the discourse between compliance as a standards-based management approach and integrity as a value-based approach is addressed. Subsequently, it will be discussed how both can be integrated within the framework of a system, which instruments and methods can be used for this purpose, and what added value a corresponding combination of the approaches offers.

1 Origin Compliance

> *Culpability generally will be determined by the steps taken by the organization prior to the offense to prevent and detect criminal conduct, the level and extent of involvement in or tolerance of the offense by certain personnel, and the organization's actions after an offense has been committed.* (U.S. Sentencing Commission 1991, p. 347)

This short paragraph from the US Federal Sentencing Guidelines of 1991 is an essential milestone for the emergence of compliance programs in companies. It defines that the amount of the penalty for companies convicted in court can be reduced under certain conditions. Accordingly, a reduced sentence is possible if, among other things, a company can credibly demonstrate that it had already implemented structures and processes that support

T. Herold • F. Schlegel (✉)
Forchtenberg, Germany

J. Lange (ed.), *Value-Oriented Leadership in Theory and Practice*,
https://doi.org/10.1007/978-3-662-65883-3_8

the prevention of criminal acts prior to the offence (Ferrell et al. 1998). Today, this is generally referred to as compliance.

Media scandals such as the one surrounding the bribery of Japanese government officials by an aircraft manufacturer in the early 1970s (Hishikawa 2003) and numerous cases of corruption and insider trading in the US financial industry highlighted the need for stricter measures to prevent such and similar crimes. For example, the US Foreign Corrupt Practices Act of 1977 prohibits payments to foreign officials in connection with business relationships (U.S. Department of Justice 2017). To bring about sustained behavioral change, the deterrent effect of fines has been enhanced by the aforementioned promotion of preventive measures in the Federal Sentencing Guidelines. The Guidelines allow for reduced penalties for all those among the defendant companies that had implemented and communicated to employees' internal regulations to prevent violations of the law. These measures were originally intended to specifically combat corruption and insider trading, but quickly spilled over into other jurisdictions and regions outside the USA.

Today, compliance is a topic that no major company can ignore. Important internationally standardized requirements can be found in the legal regulations of the Foreign Corrupt Practices Act, the US Federal Sentencing Guidelines, and the Sarbanes-Oxley Act (Engelhart 2012).

In Germany, the voluntary German Corporate Governance Code defines that the management board "shall ensure compliance with statutory provisions and internal guidelines and [...] shall work towards their observance within the company (compliance)" (Government Commission 2019, p. 4). Here, a development in the understanding of compliance becomes apparent: Compliance is expanded from the original pure adherence to legal provisions to include adherence to internal guidelines. This example alone makes it clear that compliance is therefore not definitively and unchangeably defined but is subject to constant further development. From a purely legal perspective, compliance is successively expanding with new case law, such as around the topics of data protection or technical compliance. In the discourse on the actual effectiveness of compliance in day-to-day business, a company's values and principles have emerged as essential. The extent to which compliance requirements are actually adhered to and practiced is particularly important from the perspective of evaluating compliance systems, which is why value-based compliance approaches are becoming increasingly important. Integrity, moral conduct, as well as values and principles of the corporate culture are increasingly coming to the fore (Konstanz Institute for Corporate Governance 2017). What this development means for the concept of compliance and how compliance and integrity can be distinguished are explained in the following section.

2 Distinction Between Compliance and Integrity

In fact, the discourse around the distinction between compliance and integrity is not new. As early as 1994, Lynn Paine stated that norms, values, and attitudes of the corporate culture are essential for explaining corporate misconduct (Paine 1994). As a rule, individual "rogue employees" (Paine 1994, p. 106) are not responsible for the misconduct; rather, it is based on systematic causes in the corporate culture. Based on the insight that corporate culture is essential for the prevention of corporate misconduct, the question arises as to which measures can be used to effectively influence it. This is precisely where the discourse on the distinction between compliance and integrity comes in.

The original concept of compliance focuses on adherence to legal requirements. In the context of the Federal Sentencing Guidelines, the goal of this legalistic approach is clear: compliance programs are implemented in companies in order to reduce potential penalties due to illegal actions and to avoid liability of governing bodies. While these programs per se include the prevention of criminal acts, the focus is clearly on the avoidance of penalties and liabilities, on the reduction of external sanctions.

With this narrow definition of the term compliance, one also speaks of legal compliance (Bussmann et al. 2013, p. 28). Compliance programs that are developed and implemented on the basis of this legalistic approach often focus on monitoring and controlling employees and threatening them with sanctions (Paine 1994, p. 111). Employees are forced to act dutifully. They do what they have to do; otherwise, they are punished. Purely extrinsic incentives in the form of threats of external sanctions for transgression are prevalent. Individuals' behavior is shaped by norms, which usually impose constraints on them.

Another approach to preventing white-collar crime is integrity management. In this context, integrity means that an individual is guided by the values and principles he or she has set and acts consistently with them (Grüninger et al. 2015, p. 6). Orientation to values and principles that the individual recognizes as right for one is key here. The guidelines are not adhered to out of fear of external sanction, but out of an inner conviction of their correctness. The self-responsibility of the individual is emphasized. His behavior is shaped by values which give him orientation in his decision-making.

In the corporate context, values and principles also have a significant influence on the actions of employees. In this respect, a corporate culture characterized by integrity requires a conscious commitment to self-imposed basic moral values and principles and consistent action in accordance with these values and principles. The exact definition of individual values should not be regarded as final and unchangeable. On the contrary, it is precisely the active reflection of personal attitudes and the resulting actions that is also essential in the corporate context. This is the only way to ensure ongoing recognition of the correctness of values and principles and thus intrinsic motivation. In contrast to standards-based legal compliance, value-based integrity management therefore does not aim to avoid external sanctions, but to promote ethical decision-making. In addition, it is important to shape the moral core values in line with the corporate identity, as otherwise contradictions arising in everyday actions would undermine the authenticity and thus the effectiveness of integrity management (Grüninger et al. 2015, p. 14).

Orientation in the definition of these basic moral values and principles is basically provided by social and cultural norms and moral concepts. Somewhat more concrete are, for example, the principles of the UN Global Compact or the OECD Guidelines for Multinational Enterprises. Existing standards also provide guidance on specific issues, such as the National Action Plan for Business and Human Rights, in relation to human rights across the supply chain. Integrity management is particularly important in areas that are not legally clear or are handled differently in different countries. If there are no legal regulations at all, the orientation of one's own actions to self-imposed values is all the more important.

Table 8.1 provides an overview of the distinction between compliance and integrity.

In summary, legal compliance is based on extrinsic motivation with the goal of avoiding sanctions. Integrity management emphasizes the individual's responsibility, requires active reflection on the company's values and principles, and thus focuses intrinsic motivation to act in accordance with these guidelines, which are perceived as correct. Thielemann sums up as follows: "From an organizational point of view, integrity [...] means opening the organization to ethical insights, while compliance means closing the organization to ethically misguided courses of action" (Thielemann 2005, p. 37).

The CSR pyramid in Fig. 8.1 by Carroll offers a clear way of illustrating the different objectives of compliance and integrity management. Legal compliance is classified at the level of legal responsibility and describes minimum legal requirements. Integrity management or social compliance is classified at the level of ethical responsibility and reflects the expectations of employees and society.

This orientation of compliance in the sense of integrity management has become increasingly important in companies in recent years (Frankenberger 2018, p. 9). As a result, compliance has expanded to the level of the ethical responsibility of the company, which, however, is not least due to the transformation of so-called soft law into new legislation, as can be seen in the example of CSR reporting (Schulz 2018, p. 1283). In corporate implementation, however, the tension between standards-based and value-based approaches remains, as these are often established separately in the company, with different management tools, and in different areas (Kleinfeld and Martens 2018, p. 4). It is therefore necessary to examine whether it is possible to integrate standards-based legal

Table 8.1 Overview of the differences between compliance and integrity

	Compliance	Integrity
Approach	Standards	Values
Destination	Avoidance of external sanctions, exemption of the institutions from liability	Promotion of ethical decisions, integral behavior of the company
Motivation	Extrinsic	Intrinsic
Culture	Control	Self-responsibility

Source: Based on Schluchter and Levi (2013, p. 414) and Grüninger et al. (2015, p. 9)

Fig. 8.1 CSR pyramid. (Source: Based on Carroll 2016, p. 3)

compliance with value-based social compliance or integrity management and how this can be designed. Before discussing the integration of the two approaches, it is worth taking a look at the main systems for managing compliance requirements.

3 Compliance Management System

Various standards and frameworks have emerged in recent years for the development of compliance management systems (CMS). In this section, three standards relevant in the German and international context will be presented as examples, and it will be discussed whether these standards are generally suitable for depicting value-oriented social compliance. For this purpose, the audit standard 980 "Principles of Proper Auditing of Compliance Management Systems" of the Institute of German Certified Public Accountants (IDW PS 980), which is established in Germany and used by many companies as a basis, is presented first. Furthermore, the international standard ISO 19600 "Compliance Management Systems – Guidelines" is considered. Subsequently, the Guidance Document "Evaluation of Corporate Compliance Programs" of the US Department of Justice – Criminal Division is included in the analysis.

3.1 IDW Ps 980

In the German context, IDW PS 980 is of particular importance for the actual design of compliance management systems. On the one hand, orientation toward the auditing standard offers the advantage of a structure that has already been tested in practice and can be adapted to individual needs. On the other hand, many companies already aim at a later audit by an auditing company in the phases of development and implementation of the compliance management system, which is why the early orientation toward the auditing standard makes sense in these cases. The seven basic elements of IDW PS 980 provide a quick overview of its key points (Fig. 8.2):

Fig. 8.2 Basic elements of IDW PS 980. (Source: Own representation based on IDW 2011)

1. Compliance culture.
2. Compliance goals.
3. Compliance risks.
4. Compliance program.
5. Compliance organization.
6. Compliance communication.
7. Compliance monitoring and improvement (IDW 2011).

IDW PS 980 understands compliance management as a holistic system for ensuring compliance with statutory and self-imposed regulations. It thus clearly goes beyond a purely legalistic understanding of compliance. Specifically, the auditing standard mentions the "organization of compliance with voluntary commitments (e.g., the principles of the United Nations Global Compact)" (IDW 2011, p. 18), i.e., the basic moral values in integrity management, as a possible focal point.

In addition, the basic element compliance culture clearly illustrates the importance of integrity within the compliance management system. The compliance culture is determined, among other things, by a "lived set of values," "communicated principles of conduct," and "the integrity, responsible and value-oriented conduct of the members of management" (IDW 2011, p. 21).

Consequently, it is clear that integrity as an essential element of IDW PS 980 is already a component of the compliance management systems in practice and their audit.

3.2 ISO 19600

Just like IDW PS 980, ISO 19600 provides orientation for companies through the harmonization and standardization of CMS. In addition, ISO 19600 in particular enables international benchmarking of different CMS and reduces hurdles in the implementation of global compliance management systems due to its worldwide significance.

A CMS according to ISO 19600 is based on the following five pillars:

1. Assessment of compliance risks.
2. Leadership.
3. Systemic management and control measures.
4. Training and communication.
5. Monitoring, internal audits, and response (Jonas 2015).

In this abbreviated presentation, the importance of integrity in the context of ISO 19600 is not immediately as obvious as in the case of IDW PS 980, but integrity is nevertheless essential above all for the points of leadership as well as training and communication: In the shaping of corporate culture, basic moral values and voluntary commitments through internal regulations are important building blocks for ISO 19600. In addition, ethical aspects of entrepreneurial action and integrity codes are components of ISO 19600 due to their increasing importance (Bleker and Hortensius 2014, pp. 2–3). The focus is on legal compliance, but integrity and probity, i.e., appropriate conduct independent of legal regulations, are essential criteria of corporate governance according to ISO 19600.

Here, too, it should be noted that ISO 19600 is suitable for mapping social compliance.

3.3 DOJ Guidance for Compliance

Like the two frameworks mentioned above, the "Evaluation of Corporate Compliance Programs Guidance Document (DOJ Guidance)" of the US Department of Justice provides guidance on evaluating the design and effectiveness of compliance management systems. A revised version of the DOJ Guidance was published in April 2019. Due to the extraterritorial effect of US criminal law, the DOJ Guidance is also highly relevant for companies outside the USA (Federmann et al. 2019, p. 268).

The guidelines provide concrete orientation for the implementation of effective compliance management systems on the basis of the following three questions, each with a different focus:

1. Design question: Is the company's compliance program adequately designed?
   - Risk assessment.
   - Policies and procedures.
   - Training and communication.
   - Confidential reporting and investigation processes.
   - Third-party review.
   - Mergers and acquisitions (M&A).
2. Implementation question: Is the company's compliance program being implemented effectively?
   - Commitment of senior and middle management.
   - Autonomy and resources.
   - Incentives and disciplinary measures.
3. Effectiveness question: Does the company's compliance program work in practice?
   - Continuous improvement, regular testing, and review.
   - Investigation of wrongdoing.
   - Investigating compliance incidents (U.S. Department of Justice 2019a, b).

The DOJ Guidance thus provides orientation for a broad spectrum of thematic focal points, repeatedly emphasizing the high importance of integrity within the compliance management system: With respect to policies and procedures, the establishment of core moral values is called for (U.S. Department of Justice 2019a, b, p. 3). In the context of training and communication, companies that offer ethical guidance to employees are cited as best practices (U.S. Department of Justice 2019a, b, p. 4). On the topic of third-party review, the question asks whether and to what extent a company incentivizes moral behavior by third parties (U.S. Department of Justice 2019a, b, p. 8). Senior and middle management are again required to actively promote a corporate culture based on moral values (U.S. Department of Justice 2019a, b, p. 9). Consequently, company-internal incentive systems for moral behavior should also be implemented (U.S. Department of Justice 2019a, b, p. 13).

The DOJ Guidance thus also underscores the importance of integrity in compliance management systems. Depending on the level of development of the CMS, it provides guidance for the effective implementation of compliance and integrity.

Thus, all of the three essential standards discussed for building compliance management systems call for integrity to be addressed in the context of compliance management. How the tension between standards-based and value-based approaches can be resolved in practice is discussed in the next section.

4 Integration of Compliance and Integrity

Compliance management systems of a modern nature not only are, as described above, designed for a purely standards-based approach but are also suitable for, or even require, a value-based approach.

This is particularly the case because questions of what is good and permissible in a complex and globalized world cannot be answered solely by implementing laws in the form of standards-based regulations. Rather, the application of laws in corporate decision-making situations requires interpretation and ethical reflection. In addition, in a complex world with different stakeholders, mere adherence to rules is not enough to ensure the sustainable success of a company.

The question now is how an integrative approach of standards and value orientation can succeed and thus the integration of compliance and integrity.

4.1 Anchoring Integrity as a Compliance Goal

The starting point here is the objectives (according to IDW PS 980) or the scope (according to ISO 19600) on which the CMS is based by the company management. For this purpose, it is necessary that, in addition to compliance with the law and the liability of the executive bodies, the ethical responsibility of the company for society is included and emphasized. Which integrity and compliance goals are pursued requires individual consideration for each company and depends on the company's goals and business model. Here, each company must ask itself what additional responsibility it assumes in addition to pure compliance with the law. To this end, it can, for example, identify and prioritize the additional requirements of the stakeholder groups within the framework of a stakeholder dialogue. This prioritization of different requirements and which ones are ultimately pursued is necessary due to scarce resources. For this reason, a company should primarily pursue the stakeholder requirements or goals that meet the following criteria:

- **Influenceability**: The requirements or objectives must be closely linked to the company's business activities. This means that the company has the opportunity to exert influence and can assume responsibility.
- **Resource availability**: The company has the necessary resources and possibilities to achieve the requirements and goals and can actually assume the responsibility.

This responsibility must be defined as a management task (Wieland 2010, p. 88). It can find influence in the CMS in the form of voluntary commitments and codified ethical principles, which are anchored within the framework of codes of conduct or ethics.

The objectives of the CMS are thus no longer solely compliance with the law and liability avoidance for the company's executive bodies, but rather the fulfillment of social responsibility and the requirements of the stakeholders. An example of this can be a responsible handling of personal data that goes beyond what is legally permitted and subjects every new data processing not only to a risk assessment but also to an ethical discourse.

4.2 Integrity as a Component of the Compliance Culture

An essential step is to anchor these goals in the compliance culture. The decisive factor here is the role of management, i.e., that compliance is understood as a management task and is included in the processes and decisions in the company. Compliance can therefore not be the responsibility of a department that sets rules and monitors compliance (Frankenberger 2018, p. 28). Integrity is based on the ethical orientation and intrinsically motivated self-commitment and self-control of the individual. Morally correct behavior and personal responsibility, which are based on ethical reflection, are supported in this process. The participation of employees in the process of value creation and culture building is elementary here for the creation of a culture of trust that enables the assumption of responsibility, the free expression of opinion, a critical attitude, and the possibility of discourse between stakeholders (Kunze 2008, p. 123). Thus, while the classic legal compliance approach is more of a culture of control, in the context of social compliance, which is based on integrity, it is a culture of trust in the individual's ability to make decisions. This culture must be exemplified by managers and supported by the other measures in the CMS so that it becomes a lived culture of responsibility in which every individual has an awareness of compliance and integrity in their everyday work.

4.3 Designing the Compliance Program from an Integrity Perspective

To promote and establish such a compliance culture of trust, the compliance program and its measures must be set up in a value-oriented manner. An essential component here is the organization and the policy landscape with clear tasks, competencies, and responsibilities as well as corresponding rules of conduct. To ensure a compliance culture of integrity, these must be geared toward individual responsibility and thus be based as general guardrails, in particular on principles such as integrity, fairness, and ethics (Roth 2012, p. 63). Here, the legal guidelines in the form of codified internal standards are the supplement to these principles for specific application. This requires a different approach to the design of guidelines than the mere establishment of rules based on the content of legal requirements. The focus of a guideline must be on the clear allocation of responsibility, the motivation of the person responsible to behave in accordance with standards and values, and the empowerment of the person responsible to interpret and apply specific rules in ambiguous situations (Schulz 2018, p. 1284).

Other measures within the framework of the compliance program must also be designed accordingly in order to promote value orientation. In addition to the sanction mechanisms that often exist for non-compliance, a company should set appropriate incentives for more integrity-oriented behavior. Dilemmas between financial targets and compliance as well as one-sided incentives based on economic aspects must be avoided if legal, moral, and economic requirements are not in harmony (Fürst 2014, p. 665). One possibility is, for example, the inclusion of compliance in the target agreement and a financial reward for behavior with integrity in such conflict situations (Schulz 2018, p. 1284). Integrity should also be considered accordingly in personnel selection and promotions, as this is where the foundation is laid for individuals to behave with integrity, and managers in particular have a major influence on the compliance culture. In particular, no employees with negative or conspicuous behavior should be promoted to a management position (Haag and Jantz 2019, p. 2).

4.4 Communication as a Key Factor

Compliance communication is an elementary component of establishing a value-oriented compliance culture, and the communication of values plays a decisive role in this. It has the task of linking the value culture of the company, the individual value attitudes of managers and employees, and the standards-based regulatory systems into a common mechanism of action (Rademacher and Möhrle 2014). Due to the complexity of the subject matter, this cannot be seen independently of the expansion of knowledge and competence (Frankenberger 2018, p. 28). On the one hand, it is necessary to impart the appropriate knowledge about the desired norms and values, and on the other hand, competencies in application and ethical reflection in conflict situations must be considered. For the transfer of knowledge, it is crucial in this context that the contents of the communication are prepared in a comprehensible and addressee-appropriate manner, for example, in the form of training courses, and that the values associated with the rules are explained in order to increase acceptance and provide orientation for the employees (Schulz 2018, p. 1287). Building on this, communication must impart the action competence and problem-solving ability to apply this knowledge in different situations and to reflect ethically on issues in a self-responsible manner. This is particularly important due to the fact that all gray areas and contingencies can never be covered by the existing rules and regulations in the company (Frankenberger 2018, p. 33). Moreover, this is crucial for the application of norms and values, as only internalized values have an influence on the decisions and behavior of individuals (Erpenbeck and Sauter 2018, p. 84).

The form in which knowledge and competence are imparted is also of importance. Since integrity is based on individual responsibility and participation in creating the values and culture, the formats must also enable this. That is why communication should not be exclusively through one-way channels such as training courses, but should focus on joint workshops, coaching sessions, or intranet forums that enable dialogue and discourse (Frankenberger 2018, p. 47).

5 Added Value Through an Integrative Approach to Integrity and Compliance

As shown in the previous section, compliance and integrity can be linked and mapped in a system. Compliance management systems can serve as a starting point for this, which must be expanded and supplemented in individual elements. The question now is why companies should do this and what added value this brings.

First of all, increasing the effectiveness of compliance management is a decisive factor here. Rules, controls, and sanctions do not in themselves lead to a change in behavior and internalization of values. However, this is crucial to the success of compliance because at the end of the day, it is the decisions of individuals that lead to violations (Erpenbeck and Sauter 2018, pp. 79–80). Studies have shown that the control or risk of misconduct being detected has less of an impact on behavior than the realization that this behavior contradicts one's own values and those of the environment (Kennecke et al. 2014, p. 235). For this reason, the complement of a norm-based compliance toward a value-based compliance based on integrity is necessary, as compliance is otherwise ethically blind and disoriented. Of course, however, an integrity-focused approach should also be complemented by legal compliance, as otherwise one would be relying purely on ethical reflection, without any control. This can also be explained by looking at the fraud triangle, which describes the main incentives for white-collar crime. These are:

- The *opportunity to* commit a criminal act, e.g., through control gaps.
- The *motivation to* do so, e.g., for their own lack of money or to achieve goals.

- The *justification of* the act, for example, by the inner attitude "I deserved it".

As can be seen from this, standards-based systems mainly focus their control on opportunity and value-based systems in particular on motivation and justification through the communication of corresponding values and the establishment of incentive mechanisms (Grüninger 2010, p. 44). This shows that white-collar crime can only be effectively prevented through value-based compliance.

Value-based compliance, i.e., the integration of compliance and integrity, means opening up the organization to ethical values and self-responsibility and closing down failed courses of action through rule-based controls (Thielemann 2005, pp. 36–37).

At the same time, a combination of approaches can refute the accusation of disproportionate bureaucracy, which is often countered by compliance management systems that are strictly geared toward adherence to laws. In order to ensure compliance, increasingly detailed regulations and finer-meshed controls must be established as the complexity of regulation in the company increases, which in turn leads to little acceptance and thus to circumvention strategies among employees (Wieland 2008, pp. 156–157). The conscious interplay of norms and values makes it possible to limit regulations and controls to the necessary extent and to supplement this with individual responsibility. Complete coverage of all transactions by appropriate controls is neither possible nor desirable (Wieland 2008, p. 165).

It also increases employees' identification with compliance, as it introduces guiding principles and values that are crucial for motivating human action.

Another aspect that makes an integrative approach useful, if not necessary, is the complexity, both of the requirements and of the companies themselves. A standards-based approach can never be able to secure all possible requirements in all possible decision-making situations through appropriate rules and controls. At the same time, the requirements are also only partially regulated by laws, and these vary or even contradict each other across countries, especially in the case of internationally active companies. The instruments of integrity management are therefore required here in order to identify and systematically record the requirements that are socially desirable. Likewise, ethical/moral reflection is necessary in order to perceive the responsibility that the company wishes to assume in the case of differing or diametrically opposed regulations and requirements (Straubhaar and Schellinger 2019, p. 23). An example already mentioned above is the protection of personal data, for which there is no unified framework internationally and the regulations of individual countries differ greatly. For companies, in addition to legal compliance, there is also the need to reflect on the handling of data in an ethical manner and to implement data responsibility as part of a voluntary commitment in compliance management. This can be applied to many different compliance areas.

Another advantage of the combination and integrated handling of compliance and integrity is economic efficiency. Compliance management systems can be made more efficient by optimizing regulation and control, since integrity complements them accordingly. In addition, an integrated approach can save resources and avoid redundancies. Thus, an integrative approach increases not only the effectiveness but also the economic efficiency of the overall system.

Integrity and compliance are therefore not incompatible management approaches; on the contrary, an integration of both approaches is possible and makes sense. They complement each other in many issues and, in their synergy, lead to better results than if they were taken individually. The core question of value-oriented compliance is: How much regulation and control are necessary to allow sufficient ethical room for maneuver for self-responsibility?

References

Bleker S, Hortensius D (2014) ISO 19600: the development of a global standard on compliance management. Bus Compl 2:1–12

Bussmann KD, Nestler C, Salvenmoser S (2013) Wirtschaftskriminalität und Unternehmenskultur. VERLAG, Frankfurt am Main

Carroll AB (2016) Carroll's pyramid of CSR: taking another look. Int J Corp Soc Res. https://doi.org/10.1186/s40991-016-0004-6

Engelhart M (2012) Sanktionierung von Unternehmen und Compliance. Duncker & Humblot, Berlin

Erpenbeck J, Sauter W (2018) Wertungen, Werte – Das Fieldbook für ein erfolgreiches Wertemanagement. Springer, Berlin/Heidelberg

Federmann B, Gnändiger JH, Scheben B (2019) Orientierungsleitfaden von DOJ und OFAC. Zur Bewertung von Corporate Compliance-Management-Systemen. ZRFC 6(19):267–275

Ferrell OC, LeClair DT, Ferrell L (1998) The federal sentencing guidelines for organizations: a framework for ethical compliance. J Bus Ethics 17:353–363

Frankenberger S (2018) Kontrolle als Kultur? Compliance und compliance – Kommunikation aus systemischer Perspektive. Technische Universität Kaiserslautern, Masterarbeit

Fürst M (2014) Grundprinzipien und Gestaltungsmerkmale eines verhaltensbasierten, anreizsensitiven Intergritätsmanagements. In: Wieland J, Steinmeyer R, Grüninger S (Hrsg) Handbuch Compliance-Management: Konzeptionelle Grundlagen, praktische Erfolgsfaktoren, globale Herausforderungen, 2. Aufl. Erich Schmidt, Berlin, S 643–S 675

Grüninger S (2010) Werteorientiertes compliance management system. In: Wieland J, Steinmeyer R, Grüninger S (eds) Handbuch compliance-management. Erich Schmidt, Berlin

Grüninger S, Schöttl L, Wieland J (2015) Unternehmensintegrität & Compliance-Was wirklich wichtig ist. https://www.dnwe.de/inhalte/fci-news/FCI_Unternehmensintegritaet_Compliance-Was_wirklich_wichtig_ist.pdf. Accessed on 08.04.2020

Haag O, Jantz M (2019) Compliance im Personalwesen. Compliance-Berater 5:1–4

Hishikawa M (2003) The FCPA: an outgrowth of corporate scandals. https://archive.is/20030710132138/http://www.dbtrade.com/publications/the_fcpa.htm. Accessed on 13.04.2020

IDW (2011) IDW PS 980: Grundsätze ordnungsmäßiger Prüfung von Compliance Management Systemen

Jonas P (2015) Die wichtigsten Inhalte der ISO 19600 für Ihr Unternehmen. Lexis Nexis. https://www.lexisnexis.de/blog/compliance/iso-19600. Accessed on 24.04.2020

Kennecke S, Frey D, Kaschube J (2014) Organisationspsychologische Aspekte der Compliance. In: Schettgen-Sarcher W, Bachmann S, Schettgen P (Hrsg) Compliance Officer: Das Augsburger Qualifizierungsmodell. Springer Gabler, Wiesbaden, S 221–258

Kleinfeld A, Martens A (2018) CSR und Compliance im Kontext ihrer Bedeutungsentwicklung. In: Kleinfeld A, Martens A (Hrsg) CSR und Compliance – Synergien nutze durch ein integriertes Management. Gabler, Berlin, S 3–33

Konstanz Institut für Corporate Governance (2017) Compliance Essentials. Was aus der Perspektive von Justiz, Verbänden und Unternehmen wirklich zählt. https://www.htwg-konstanz.de/fileadmin/pub/ou/kicg/Compliance_Essentials.pdf. Accessed on 18.04.2020

Kunze M (2008) Unternehmensethik und Wertemanagement in Familien- und Mittelstandsunternehmen. Projektorientierte Analyse, Gestaltung und Integration von Werten und Normen. Gabler, Wiesbaden

Paine LS (1994) Managing for organizational integrity. Harv Bus Rev 72(2):106–117

Rademacher L, Möhrle H (2014) Compliance Kommunikation: Säule der Corporate Governance. In: Zerfaß A, Piwinger M (Hrsg) Handbuch Unternehmenskommunikation. Gabler, Wiesbaden, S 1253–1268

Regierungskommission (2019) Deutscher Corporate Governance Kodex. https://dcgk.de//files/dcgk/usercontent/de/download/kodex/191216_Deutscher_Corporate_Governance_Kodex.pdf. Accessed on 21.04.2020

Roth M (2012) Der compliance officer und seine Instrumente. In: Lengwiler C, Nadig L, Pedergnana M (Hrsg) Management in der Finanzbranche – Finanzmanagement im Unternehmen. IFZ – Hochschule Luzern, Luzern

Schluchter A, Levi M (2013) Compliance & Integrity – Strategien für konformes Verhalten in Unternehmen. In: Kuhn A, Margot P, Aebi MF, Schwarzenegger C, Jositsch D, Donatsch A (Hrsg) Kriminologie, Kriminalpolitik und Strafrecht aus internationaler Perspektive. Stämpfli, Bern, S 411–423

Schulz M (2018) Compliance-Management im Unternehmen – Wirksamkeitsfaktor „Compliance-Kultur". Betriebs-Berater 23:1283–1287

Straubhaar A, Schellinger J (2019) Ethik in international tätigen Unternehmen. In: Tokarski KO, Schellinger J, Berchthold P (Hrsg) Nachhaltige Unternehmensführung: Herausforderungen und Beispiele aus der Praxis. Gabler, Wiesbaden, S 13–55

Thielemann U (2005) Compliance und Integrity-Zwei Seiten ethisch integrierter Unternehmenssteuerung. Lektionen aus dem Compliance-Management einer Großbank. ZfWU 6(1):31–45

U.S. Department of Justice (2017) Foreign corrupt practices act. https://www.justice.gov/criminal-fraud/foreign-corrupt-practices-act. Accessed on 19.04.2020

U.S. Department of Justice (2019a) Evaluation of corporate compliance programs. https://www.justice.gov/criminal-fraud/page/file/937501/download. Accessed on 10.04.2020

U.S. Department of Justice (2019b) Guidance document: evaluation of corporate compliance programs. https://www.justice.gov/criminal-fraud/page/file/937501/download. Accessed on 10.04.2020

U.S. Sentencing Commission (1991) Federal sentencing guidelines. CHAPTER EIGHT: sentencing of organizations. https://www.ussc.gov/sites/default/files/pdf/guidelines-manual/1991/manual-pdf/1991_Guidelines_Manual_Full.pdf. Accessed on 13.04.2020

Wieland J (2008) Die Kunst der Compliance. In: Löhr A, Burkatzki E (Hrsg) Wirtschaftskriminalität und Ethik. Rainer Hampp, München, S 155–170

Wieland J (2010) Verantwortungsvolle Unternehmensführung. In: Hardtke A, Kleinfeld A (Hrsg) Gesellschaftliche Verantwortung von Unternehmen – von der Idee der Corporate Social Responsibility zur erfolgreichen Umsetzung. Gabler, Wiesbaden, S 87–102

Timo Herold joined KPMG AG Wirtschaftsprüfungsgesellschaft in 2018 as a Senior Manager in the Corporate Governance Services department. The focus of his work is advising and auditing companies in the areas of compliance and risk management. From 2013 to 2018, he held a position of responsibility in the automotive industry, where he was responsible for various governance topics. Prior to that, he worked as a consultant at KPMG, where he was particularly involved in projects for the implementation of internal control systems and compliance management systems. He studied at the University of Ulm, where he was involved in academic research on the topic of business ethics, particularly in the context of globalization. In the course of this work, he published several articles on ethical codes in a globalized economy.

Florentin Schlegel joined KPMG AG Wirtschaftsprüfung sgesellschaft in 2019 as a Senior Associate in the Corporate Governance Services department. He focuses on the development, implementation, and audit of compliance management systems of listed companies. Furthermore, he supports companies in identifying and managing risks as well as discovering and realizing opportunities. He studied at the Vienna University of Economics and Business Administration and the University of Mannheim, focusing on management, business ethics, corporate law, and philosophy. Among other things, during his work at the Chair of Corporate Social Responsibility at the University of Mannheim, he contributed to the preparation and publication of several articles in renowned journals.

Organizational Behavior and Values as Principles of Integrated, Value-Driven Leadership

Hans-Jürgen Lutz and Daniel Nummer

Abstract

Industry and Work 4.0, New Work, digital transformation, etc. not only are the new buzzwords from the industrial and service sectors but also mean, in general, a social change that affects the entire breadth of the economy and the workforce. For companies, this means that a dynamic adaptation of organizational structures and leadership behavior becomes necessary. "Organizational behavior" is the application of knowledge about how individuals and groups in an organization act and react, thereby achieving the highest quality of performance and dominant satisfaction. This requires a deeper and objective insight into the workforce, the values of individuals and the organization, and the current and future relevant leadership behaviors. The objective is to combine a novel organizational diagnostic system to adapt behavior based on integrated, value-driven leadership.

H.-J. Lutz
Institut für Wirtschaftsethik, Wertemanagement & Compliance, Knowledge Foundation @ Reutlingen University, Reutlingen, Germany
e-mail: hjl@iwwc.de

D. Nummer (✉)
PREDICTAME GmbH, Nieder-Olm, Germany
e-mail: mail@predictame.com

J. Lange (ed.), *Value-Oriented Leadership in Theory and Practice*,
https://doi.org/10.1007/978-3-662-65883-3_9

1 The Importance of "Organizational Behavior" in a Digital World of Work

1.1 The New World of Work and Its Influence on Organizational Structures

The world of work is in a state of almost epochal upheaval. A new understanding of work is creating new challenges and new opportunities. The "brave new world of work" causes uncertainty in equal measure as it fascinates. The structural change in the world of work is accelerating worldwide and heralding an era of new work organization.

New technological processes, digitalization and further globalization, as well as demographic change and constantly changing values are drastically changing the world of work. What and, above all, how we will work in the future concern us all. This change should not alter the basic understanding of good work. The work of the future must also serve society as a whole in a way that creates value and prosperity and is socially balanced. At the same time, it must offer each individual personal and entrepreneurial creative competencies and promote innovation, health, sustainability, and satisfaction (Robbins and Judge 2010).

Increasingly, higher-level competencies are required that can be applied across disciplines in a wide range of professions and fields of activity. Thus, in addition to competencies in the context of automation, planning activities, organization, interpersonal skills, and timely communication, creativity, abstract, networked and cross-thematic thinking, analytical skills, etc. are becoming increasingly important (Fleig 2010).

In the context of cultural history, work and organizational structure have always been re-evaluated in regular cycles, and until now, management structures have seen little added value in including the personal feelings of the individual in the evaluation. The vast majority of jobs are still very much defined in terms of instructions, so that independent thinking or even creative solution finding is still severely suppressed sometimes. However, at a time when the interfaces with customers and clients are becoming larger as ever, when finding solutions to challenges quickly is in demand and required, it is important to create structures that consist of dynamic networks of experts. At the same time, management must allow decision-making to take place where it actually makes sense and is in the interest of value creation – and in most cases, this is not just the management, which sometimes has to act at a great distance from the actual value-creating processes.

In view of the changing requirements for value-creating work, it is now necessary to say goodbye to the old traditional organizational structures, because these serve only one purpose on the basis of "Taylorism" – "self-preservation." The times when there was too little of everything are over. In the future, it will be all the more important to think and act within a holistic framework. This requires significantly more intellectual flexibility and will make the classic target orientations of companies in terms of KPIs (key performance indicators) much more complex. The organizational structures that are supposedly already "agile" are intended to promote further productivity gains, among other things, but are currently still virtually unchanged at their core in many industries (Baker 2019). Current growth of industries is therefore largely passively explained by consumer behavior rather than by sustainable and meaningful content.

The social development and the younger Generations X to Z now provide for a new consideration of the term "work." With the increasing relevance of the category "the meaning" and the growing tendency to be able to realize oneself personally in one's job, the current definition of the term "work" points far beyond the previously valid regulations in the everyday life of most companies. If you want to find meaning in your daily activities, you have to ask yourself to which parts you find yourself in the value chain and in which context this is done for the benefit of your personal and social understanding of values. Since the desire for individual realization will become ever greater in the future, companies should address as quickly as possible how they can recognize the abilities and competencies, the needs and values, and the interests and personality traits of their employees and use them as effectively as possible. In any case, companies do not gain the information they need for this through CVs that are read out and assessed by software, but through the earliest possible, objective, and continuous exchange (Robbins and Judge 2010).

In the future, many companies will be more careful with their most valuable resources, people and knowledge, and will place more emphasis on looking at actual "organizational behavior" (Baker 2019). They will incorporate the ideas, personality, behavior, interests, and experience of each individual into processes, product developments, and projects, thereby fundamentally changing the substantive aspects of work structures and design. Organizational behavior, that is, the application of knowledge about how individuals and groups feel, act, and react in terms of their fit in an organization, represents a valuable resource through which the highest quality of performance becomes attainable, because "people are replaceable – personalities are not."

1.2 The Basics of "Organizational Behavior"

According to Robbins and Judge (2010), organizational behavior examines the influence and impact that individuals, groups, and organizational structures have on behavior within the organization in order to apply this knowledge to improve the effectiveness of an organization. In today's business world, systematic analysis of organizational behavior should be an essential tool for managing effective teams and help understand and predict human behavior in an organization. It examines how organizations can be structured more profitably and how internal and external events affect organizations.

One of the main goals of organizational behavior is to vitalize a value-added, holistic organizational structure and to develop a better conceptualization of the interplay in organizations. As a multidisciplinary field, "organizational behavior" has been influenced by developments in a number of related disciplines, such as sociology, psychology, medicine, and economics, as well as by the experience of practitioners.

The roots of studies in the field of "organizational behavior" go back primarily to the social and cultural changes during the Industrial Revolution, a time when new forms of organization (see "Taylorism") were also introduced. Today, it is a normative and applied science that takes a holistic approach to organizational development and structuring.

Measuring and identifying the drivers and barriers in a company has become significantly more important in recent years (Brief and Weiss 2002; Robbins and Judge 2010). Due to societal change, increasing digitalization and globalization, as well as the constant change in the understanding of values and against the background of an increasing tendency toward individualization, companies have to master to adapt to the rapidly changing external conditions. All organizations and groups experience the direct relationship between job satisfaction and performance on a daily basis. To maximize the performance of people within a system or group, it is important to develop optimal interpersonal chemistry in dynamic networks (Kristof-Brown et al. 2005).

The purpose of organizational behavior is to gain a better understanding of the factors that influence the dynamics of individuals and groups in an organizational setting. Thinking pragmatically and in terms of everyday life, it is about the fit between people and their work environment (Baker 2019). This understanding can then be used to help individuals, groups, and the organizations they belong to become more efficient and effective. Much of the assessment and identification of organizational behavior ultimately aims to provide management and human resource professionals with the information and tools they need to select, train, and empower employees in ways that maximize benefits for both the individual and the organization (Brief and Weiss 2002; Robbins and Judge 2010).

Analyzing and recognizing organizational behavior enables companies to make use of previously unrecognized or insufficiently identified capacities. In this context, the measurement methods do not consider the classic elements of corporate management, i.e., turnover, costs, profit, etc., but focus more on the fit between people, task, and environment, i.e., the "human side" of the organizational structure. The widely used financial metrics or KPIs (key performance indicators) largely refer to defined projects and their execution or to the measurement of "financial strength" – i.e., a situational determination to determine "past success." The elements of organizational behavior, on the other hand, focus on the measurement of "facilitating and hindering behavior" of individuals and describe the interaction of organizational parts. In terms of the desired definition of goals (e.g., fostering innovation, process improvement, etc.), comparative studies thus provide clear measurement points that allow for deliberate, objective, and, most importantly, continuous management of the organization. They do not reduce business success to metrics that can in part be strongly influenced subjectively but provide information on an "internal" assessment and evaluation of the success factors that are relevant now and in the future. In this way, the identification of organizational behavior promotes both a functioning value system, innovative strength, meaningful process design, as well as communication, reflective leadership behavior, and solution and change competence within the organization.

Organizational behavior is an interdisciplinary field of study. One of the main reasons for this interdisciplinary approach is that the field of organizational behavior encompasses multiple levels of analysis necessary to understand behavior within organizations because people never act in isolation. That is, workers influence their environment and are also influenced by their environment. Within the procedures for determining organizational behavior, there are few absolute truths, which is related to the "contingency variables" among other things. Thus, many of the results collected describe situational characteristics or situational variables that function between independent and dependent factors. As an example, it is generally more important for the man to earn more money than the woman.

However, the relevant levels of an organizational assessment (Fig. 1), among others, could be adapted as follows (Kristof-Brown et al. 2005). It is a model and an abstraction of a reality perceived from different perspectives.

Explanation of Fig. 1: Job Fit: personal perception (fit to the requirement, values, personality, needs, competencies, etc.). Team Fit: perception of cooperation in a group (behavior patterns, communication patterns, exchange, etc.). Supervisor Fit: perception of leadership behavior (leadership style vs. productivity). Organization Fit: perception of fit with the organization (values, cultural attributes, norms, etc.)

At the individual level of analysis, organizational behavior includes, but is not limited to, the study of demand and individual fit, competencies, perception, creativity, motivation, personality-related traits, facilitative behavior, and hindering behavior. At this level of analysis, organizational behavior draws heavily on psychology, engineering, and medicine (Brief and Weiss 2002; Robbins and Judge 2010).

At the team level of analysis, organizational behavior includes studies of group dynamics, intra- and inter-group conflict and cohesion, interpersonal communication, networks,

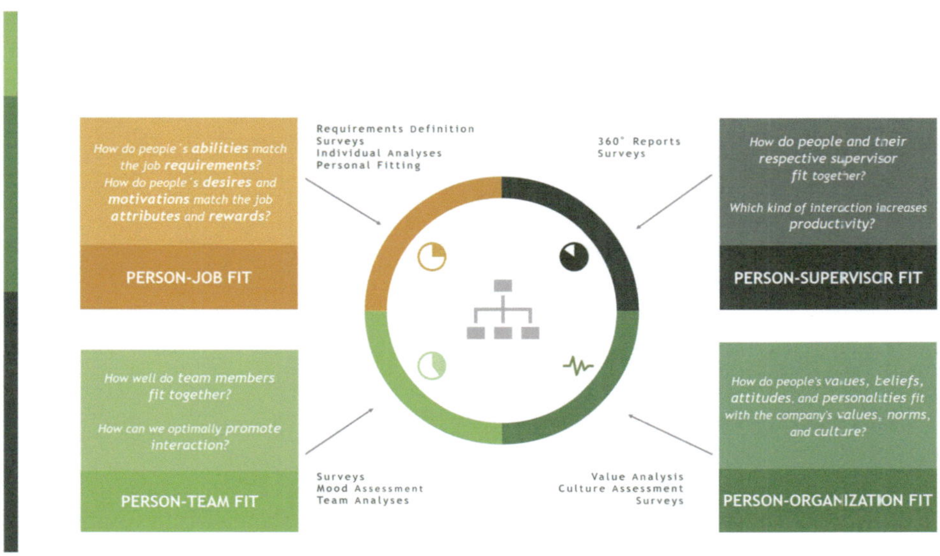

Fig. 1 Simplified representation of the relevant subject areas for assessing the fit in the holistic organizational approach

and roles. At this level of analysis, organizational behavior draws most readily on the sociological and social psychological sciences (Kristof-Brown et al. 2005).

At the supervisor level, the main focus is on identifying the actual perceived leadership behavior, as well as the evaluation of possible effects on employee motivation, delegation, information behavior, promotion, and mutual understanding. The effects on the management of business processes are also assessed (Kim and Kim 2013).

At the organizational level, studies of organizational culture, organizational structure, inter-organizational collaboration, values, process control, and external environmental factors are combined. At this level of analysis, organizational behavior draws on anthropology and political science (Kristof-Brown et al. 2005).

What all approaches have in common is that they view organizations to a large extent as complex, dynamic entities with a mixed socioeconomic character. They are intended to approximately explain the purpose, emergence, and functioning of organizations and to positively influence the design of interfaces between areas of responsibility along value creation processes based on the division of labor. The following explanations are based on the hypothesis that the evaluation of the "fit" (to the requirements of the work, the group orientation in the team, the leadership behavior, as well as the organizational values or the "culture") can be regarded as a sufficient methodology, in the attempt to describe the "reality" more closely and objectively, and thereby profitable behavior can be promoted.

1.3 The Objective of Organizational Behavior

The organizations in which people work affect their thoughts, feelings, and actions. These thoughts, feelings, and actions in turn affect the organization itself. Organizational behavior examines the mechanisms that govern these interactions and seeks to identify and promote those behaviors and fits that are conducive to organizational survival and effectiveness.

1. Job satisfaction.
2. Finding the "right" people.
3. Organizational culture.
4. Leadership and conflict resolution.
5. Understanding employees better.
6. Understand how to develop "good" leaders.
7. Understand what a "good team" is and how to develop it.
8. Higher productivity.

These eight exemplary organizational behavior objectives show that this is concerned with people within the organization, how they interact, how satisfied they are, how motivated they are, and how they can be improved in a way that allows for the highest productivity. The underlying mechanisms directly or indirectly influence the business metrics. In a business context, these are productivity, value added, profit, costs, turnover, absenteeism, labor turnover, commitment, and (job) satisfaction. These are the factors that could be influenced by some behavior and which in turn should themselves be influenced positively in terms of the organizational purpose. Influence can be exerted on four levels (see Fig. 1) and includes, at the individual level, personal fit to the requirement, competencies, and needs. On the team level, it is about the evaluation of the cooperation, i.e., interaction, communication, and behavior patterns, among other things. In addition to leadership behavior at level 3, identification with the values, norms, and requirements of the organization at level 4 is also important within this model (Brief and Weiss 2002).

People seek satisfaction at every stage of their lives. From the satisfaction of their basic needs, such as hunger, thirst, rest, and social interaction, the community today has, in addition, its own standard of goals and fulfillment that can, or should, be more or less achieved by individuals. One element of fulfillment and personal goal attainment is securing a "good" job, preferably with good pay and hopefully with high job satisfaction. However, there are no set and formal guidelines on how to manage work to motivate individuals to achieve personal job satisfaction or organizational goals. Rather, it is a very complex "ecosystem" that is influenced by a wide variety of facets of the person themselves and the environment (Baker 2019). At the same time, it is also a very dynamic system of interaction, so that the objective cannot be to try to define this system in a universal and all-encompassing scientific way. It is therefore about approaching perceived reality from different perspectives (Robbins and Judge 2010). The more we understand how and why certain groups work successfully and satisfactorily on defined tasks, the more these impulses and impressions can be used to help other individuals and groups develop as well based on these experiential insights. Based on the exploration and learning of organizational behavior, individuals and groups can be assisted in practicing positive work attitudes toward their own task and professional responsibilities. Likewise, barriers or also drivers in the personal fit to the requirement or also in the interaction to other group members or a certain leadership behavior can be recognized and adapted in the best possible way.

In everyday life, all organizations and groups experience the direct relationship between job satisfaction and performance. In order to maximize the performance of members of a system, it is important to develop optimal interpersonal chemistry. There is growing evidence that teaching and implementing soft skills should be given a higher priority in the educational and organizational training process, but at the same time soft skills should only ever complement hard skills, not replace them (Brief and Weiss 2002).

However, the determination of organizational behavior also has limitations. It always reflects only a part of the "lived organization" and cannot avoid conflicts, frustration, misunderstandings, or communication weaknesses, but it can weaken their negative effects. Recognizing one's own organizational behavior opens up a defined path toward "improvement" based on human perceptions from the organizational structure itself. However, it does not claim to be the absolute solution to all problems and should always be considered as a complementary approach that can adequately but not comprehensively describe the real situation. Thus, the results and resulting proposed actions should always be understood and applied in the context of the situation and reality.

2 The Evaluation of Organizational Behavior and Its Importance for Effectiveness

If employees feel emotionally attached to their employer and identify with their task, their team, and the company's management behavior, then they also have a personal interest in the company doing well – the company's interests thus become their own. As a rule, these employees also express positive opinions about their employer, show a high level of motivation and willingness to perform, and enjoy their work. All this has an impact on productivity, customer service, turnover, innovative capacity, and the company's image (Brief and Weiss 2002).

A company that wants to work effectively and "agilely" (in the sense of "change-competent") should also pay increased attention to various elements of "fit" within organizational behavior.

1. A good fit between applicant or employee and job (requirements), for example, is an important prerequisite not only for the recruitment of new employees but also for the successful integration of employees into the company and the continued high level of motivation and satisfaction in the existing organization.
2. The constant evaluation of the perceived leadership behavior and its fit to the goal orientation and team constellation ensures a reliable honest exchange between supervisor and employees.
3. A good fit of individual team members to each other (caveat: fit here does not mean "identical opinions and roles"!) ensures a shared relationship of trust and more pronounced interaction and willingness to perform.
4. Last but not least, the fit of the employees to the organizational values and norms is important.

But how can a company or institution make such assessments in an existing organizational system? How can these findings be profited from?

2.1 How Companies and Groups Benefit from Organizational Behavior

An organization or group benefits in five keyways when leaders have a strong foundation in organizational behavior (Kristof-Brown et al. 2005):

1. The organization is given a frame of reference that clarifies the interplay between profit, value creation, productivity, and human resources.
2. Managers understand the organizational impact of individual and group behaviors and receive suggestions for action that can promote satisfaction, productivity, and health.
3. The organization becomes more effective in motivating employees and increases trust between management and teams.
4. Managers can better assess and control employee behavior and reduce intentions to quit.

5. The organization is able to make optimal use of human resources and to match the requirements for successful task performance with the personal characteristics of the employees.

Of course, the demands on the management level are very high based on the dynamics and fast-moving routine business. Not all leadership roles are the same. "Managers," "leaders," and "expert chiefs" differ in their abilities, and different personality traits are attached to each, each of which can be situationally conducive or obstructive. This has a not inconsiderable influence on the entire organization.

All too often, executives are used more as "managers" than as "leaders" in operations. Classically, management sets the order, structure, and direction. Then "work packages" are formulated which are to be implemented in the management cascade. Unfortunately, the evaluation of a successful implementation is too often based only on the key figures for a project or an internal order – in other words, retrospectively. Thus, there is a danger that teams inevitably prioritize their respective defined goals, interfaces are insufficiently clarified, and the holistic value creation process "limps" at various transitions. In such a structure, there is often a lack of motivation to coordinate the content of things, there can be little authentic leadership behavior in order to secure one's own position in the hierarchy, and this in turn leads to less identification of the individual with the company and generates a higher degree of dissatisfaction.

An organization that is successful in the long term has a very good and, above all, continuous understanding of its own behavior and its own value system. Conducting a company survey once a year and offering firmly structured, partly rigid training content for the various management levels are not enough to form a living, change-competent organization. Here, a regular "pulse check" is much more effective in order to be able to adjust during the year.

2.2 The Introduction of a Holistic Control System: The "Human Side of Business"

In the routine, managers and teams are often heavily utilized. The "scales" tip more and more in the direction of the operational implementation obligation instead of in the direction of the "leadership competencies" that will be needed more in the future. Individual needs, strengths and weaknesses, interests, personal characteristics and skills, competencies, and potential, for example, are insufficiently, if at all, used to guide the organization or teams. The assessment of these characteristics depends too much on the individual constitution or assessment of the respective leader. Moreover, the majority of leaders in an organization reveal widely divergent skills and leadership styles. A "guardrail system" for understanding situational leadership and appropriately supportive behavior would be useful, since employees will usually follow not just one leader on their career path but several and will inevitably make comparisons. An objective evaluation of such facets costs time, which is usually not available or invested – a dilemma situation.

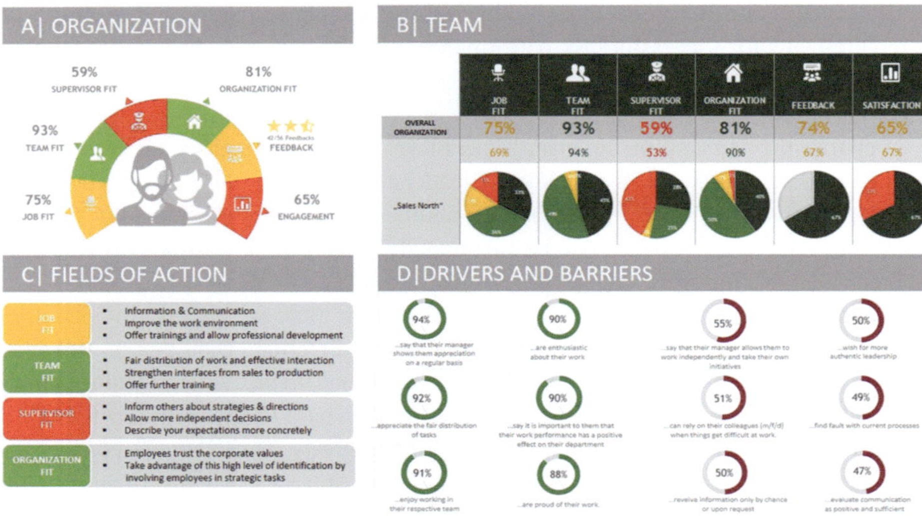

Fig. 2 Schematic representation of the primary results from the organizational assessment

A way out of this situation could be shown by the foundations of organizational behavior. In today's world, a digital control system for assessing the fit in organizational behavior can be implemented relatively pragmatically and anonymously (considering the specifications of a works council) in companies of any size (see Fig. 2). The process is based on regular surveys or analyses assigned to managers and employees. Through their assessments and responses, the system creates a "helicopter perspective" on the organization. It continuously reflects the "people side of the business," so to speak. By constantly surveying the impulses and characteristics in the organizational parts, the organization receives a frame of reference that clarifies the interaction of profit, value creation, productivity, and human resources. At the same time, the results and suggestions from the system remain primarily independent of the "filter function of the managers."

Such a procedure can also be carried out very "quietly," i.e., no IT connections, interfaces, or other technical integration processes are necessary that could potentially disrupt routine business. The procedure continuously identifies selected relevant facets of the "real perceived working environment" (employees' view), can query and perceive as well as structure the impulses from the workforce, shows the needs of the individual teams, and presents them comparatively. In addition, the software also surveys, among other things, the perceived leadership behavior. In this way, all levels of the organization benefit from greater transparency within the group and from team-specific suggestions for action. These can be implemented by the team itself, by, or better, with the manager or a trained expert/coach. Both the result and the suggested action are generated from 1. an algorithm that puts the different measurements in context with each other and evaluates them and 2.

an expert human assessment of the situation (based on existing results and their long-term development and in relation to accepted leadership practices, mentoring, and coaching). The software thus enables the promising combination of objective assessment and subjective human experience in routine.

In doing so, no intervention of the organization itself is necessary to control the system. Therefore, no working time is lost, and the system becomes a kind of "virtual organizational monitoring," which indicates at predefined intervals how the strengths could be strengthened and how the weaknesses could be made insignificant. The approach analyzes the four dimensions "job fit," "team fit," "supervisor fit," and "organization fit" mentioned in Sect. 1.2.

Explanation of Fig. 2: **A** Presentation of the organization-wide comparative study on employee feedback and satisfaction, as well as on perceptions of fit with the job, teamwork, leadership behavior, and the values and norms of the organization. **B** Presentation of a specifically selected team in the organization from A. **C** Suggestions and recommended actions for further work on the identified issues at the team level. **D** Presentation of the highest and lowest ratings at individual team level.

As a basis and methodological framework, the system makes use of a battery of predefined or organization-specific analyses and surveys. Following the results of a study by Kristof-Brown et al. (2005), this instrument can be used to approximately examine the fit of individuals with the variables of the professional environment on the four levels. The anonymity of the respondents is preserved at all times, as the results are only ever evaluated up to the team level.

The advantage: The company gains a more objective and continuous insight into the drivers and barriers of the organization and benefits from team- and organization-specific suggestions for action. The time required to conduct the analyses and surveys is usually between 60 and 180 min per year and employee. The aim is to promote satisfied and productive interaction and to strengthen understanding and trust between management and employees.

By means of an individually adaptable reporting structure, the organization is given the opportunity to flexibly compare different parts of the organization or to get a picture of the strongest or weakest characteristics.

The results are based on a defined procedural structure (see Fig. 3).

Explanation of Fig. 3: Specific coaching elements can optionally support or accelerate the implementation and optimization processes. The regular re-evaluation serves the quality assurance of the processes and forms the starting point for further optimization.

1. **"Surface sensing":** A real anonymous mood picture of the overall organization as well as the individual teams in different functions is collected by digital survey. The results include the perception of one's own fit to the requirements ("job fit") as well as the definition of the actual requirements, the cooperation in the team ("team fit"), the leadership behavior ("supervisor fit"), and the identification with the company values and standards ("organization fit"). At the same time, impulses from the workforce are requested, and barriers and drivers in everyday life, in communication, or in specific

Fig. 3 Schematic representation of the typical procedure for determining organizational perception over a calendar year

processes are identified. Included team-specific suggestions for action support the managers in implementing the first defined obvious fields of action as effectively as possible.

2. **Implementation phase:** Work on the results, possibly with coaching support.
3. **"Pulse sensing":** The fields of action that have emerged from 1. are tracked via a 1–2 min pulse survey. In this way, organizations receive a respective "fever curve" which continuously describes the implementation in the teams and which can be supported by coaching aspects.
4. **"Depth sensing":** Depending on the characteristics in the organizational parts, analytical methods are applied in the areas of "job fit," "teamwork," "leadership competence," or "value management" (see Fig. 4).

Explanation of Fig. 4: Analyses are selected and used on a situation-specific basis. In each case, this is only an approximation to the perceptions in the organizational structure.

In addition to the "real perceptions" from the staff's point of view, the evaluations also obtain further information on barriers and drivers in the organization and are to be understood as a continuous process. It aims to motivate the organization to continuously develop and to mediate between management and employees at an early stage. Due to the variety of variables and the complexity of the interaction, it is not possible to realistically depict all aspects of the organization, but the procedure increases the sensitivity for communal interaction, for conducive and harmful behavior, as well as for value-oriented cooperation. The effects, despite their variance depending on the selected methodology, can be summarized as follows (Kristof-Brown et al. 2005):

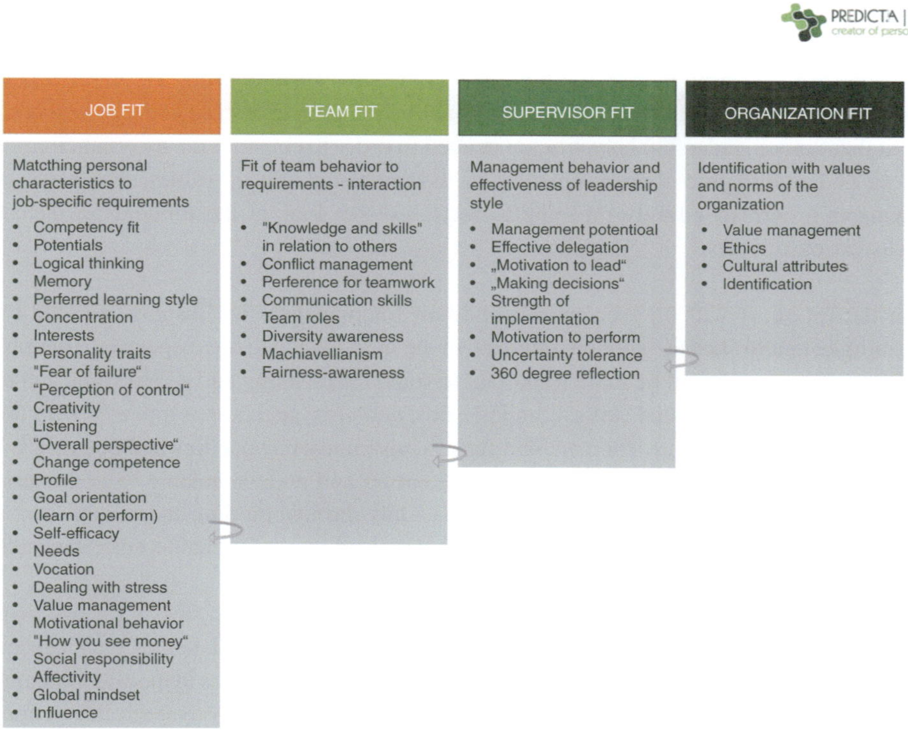

Fig. 4 Overview of the further in-depth analyses for the concretization of individual or organizational behaviors

At the company level, "organization fit" satisfaction is increased by 44%, commitment by 51%, and performance by 7%; in addition, intentions to quit are reduced by −35% and resignations by −14%. The results also show a similar picture at the other levels of organizational behavior: satisfaction (team +31%, supervisor +44%, job +56%), commitment (team +19%, supervisor +9%, job +47%), and performance (team +19%, supervisor +18%, job +20%).

2.3 Modernization of Leadership as a Necessity for Effective Organizational Management

Numerous companies are embarking on the journey into the new world of work, promising to boost their performance and innovative strength as well as improve the productivity and health of their employees. The potential of new forms of work is indeed huge: a study on the effectiveness of new forms of work found a possible increase in employee productivity of up to 35% (Bruch and Schuler 2016). However, only a few companies succeed in doing this.

Leadership is gaining immense importance in the new world of work. However, a new focus and accentuation of important facets of organizational coexistence and a corresponding vitalization of leadership behavior are needed in order to consider the external circumstances of demographic change, changes in the understanding of values, and ways of working in a correspondingly meaningful way. A closer look at the influencing factors reveals various drivers:

1. In the future, it will be even more important for managers to "inspire," to lead by example, and to show a "genuine interest" in the individual and the respective strengths and weaknesses. It will be more important to stand for meaning and added value and to try to bring the individual skills, competencies, and also weaknesses into a fit with the requirements and the environment and thus to raise unused capacities and potentials.
2. It will be about "living" and keeping alive a strong and understandable value system. The focus will be on mutual support and trust. Only through binding and reliable cooperation will strong relationships be created, which in turn will enable empowerment and personal development.
3. The leader of tomorrow should behave authentically and offer employees or process owners a helpful and meaningful scope of action. Fewer "individual heroes" are needed because these will no longer be able to keep up with all the challenges in the areas of communication, appreciation, process planning, and leadership in a highly dynamic interaction.
4. To do this, a manager must develop very fine antennas of perception in order to recognize competencies, interests, needs, and personal characteristics and to be able to use them optimally or use systems that support this. Finally, it is also about finding people who show the highest degree of "fit" to the requirements and the environment.

Organizational structures are on the verge of a massive upheaval that will offer us and the working world a multitude of new opportunities to work in a more satisfied, value-adding, healthier, and more productive way. The effects have been proven in empirical studies. The Hays HR Report (Eilers et al. 2015), for example, makes it clear that the following three biggest challenges, of all things, can become the "eye of the needle" for a new leadership and a change toward a new working world: (1) no time for leadership, (2) the difficulty of letting go and granting room for maneuver, and (3) the move from presence-based to results-based control. The resulting consequences are severe for employee motivation and perceived employer attractiveness (Bruch et al. 2015).

By applying the described organizational diagnosis model, companies could objectively identify possible internal barriers much more quickly, increase productivity and satisfaction, and thus support management levels and employees above all in the long term to work effectively and add value. This results in an organizational cycle that can increase sales and profits and reduce costs. In the course of globalization and digitalization, a change in values is taking place within society. As described earlier, this is evident in the workplace, among other places. The value attribution of flexibility, independent action, self-realization, and work-life balance have increased significantly. In earlier times, there was also significantly less individual room for maneuver. Accordingly, employees' expectations of the company are changing in the direction of value-oriented, meaningful work. The procedures described in Sect. 2 can support the identification of the status quo and provide the basis for optimized value-oriented leadership behavior.

3 Optimize Leadership Behavior Through Integrated and Value-Driven Leadership

3.1 Needs and Values and Their Role in Value-Driven Leadership

Dealing with values plays a decisive role not only in our everyday professional life. Each individual is strongly influenced by the personal development, based on one's upbringing and further education. If we go back to the Latin origin of the term value, then "valere" means to be worth something, healthy, and strong. Accordingly, values determine what we consider important and what gives us meaning for our lives. In this context, they not only serve as a point of orientation but also help to guide decisions and the associated behavior as a kind of guardrail, in order to describe corridors or boundaries (Krumm 2016).

The determination and importance of values for people are of course also shaped by the social environment. Peter Wippermann and Jens Krüger have been publishing the so-called German Values Index every 2 years since 2009, based on the recording of 15 fundamental values in German-speaking social media. The Values Index actually stands for the importance and relevance among German-speaking consumers and is intended to help companies with their values-oriented communication strategies, but these empirical studies very clearly show the change in values in our society over time (Wippermann and Krüger 2020). They also show that certain topics are discussed and evaluated differently between Generation Y and the older generations.

The change of values as well as the change of the meaning of defined values over time in society is under the influence of the socioeconomic and political conditions of the respective environment of the people. This, of course, also determines the selection and meaning of values for the human individual. Therefore, for the determination and application of the values in the management of people, it is very important to note that it is always only a snapshot. Thus, the determination of values cannot be a one-time measure, but should be subject to regular verification.

The process of identifying and measuring organizational behavior described in Sect. 2 identifies, among other things, the needs of individual organizational parts and in the aggregate of an overall organization. If values are seen as the derivation of needs, then the next step in changing organizational behavior is to identify values. The challenge here is to identify and determine the relevant values for the respective organization from a variety of several hundred values in the German-speaking world alone (Girbig 2014).

The discourse toward determining a set of values that is valid for all is a crucial step in changing organizational behavior. This important discussion can be more objective, focused, and effective if it can be built on the data of "identifying and measuring" as described in Sect. 2. For the discussion of the identified variety of values, Wieland's (2004) value quadrilateral is still an effective method for structuring before selecting a limited number of values to be applied later, by differentiating between performance, communication, cooperation, and moral values. It also helps afterward to define the set of values valid for the organization, so that a certain balance can be established between the different quadrants of values. Finally, the discourse should lead to the consensus of the most important values to be considered as the "value set" of an organization. In order to make the implementation and application within the framework of value-driven leadership effective and thus be able to positively change organizational behavior, the number of identified values should, if possible, be kept more manageable so that targeted integration in the interaction between manager and employee can be made more feasible.

The discourse to determine values should encompass the entirety of the organization ("organization fit"), i.e., beyond the discussion within individual organizational units ("team fit") with their respective managers ("supervisor fit"). Leadership and conflict resolution, as described in Sect. 1.3, is one of the critical goals in organizational behavior in order to initiate and also target change within it. If the values derived from identified and measured needs and other organizational characteristics are to be the basis of value-driven leadership, intensive engagement with them is an important step in change. The challenge here is to find a consensus between the values of the employee, the leader, and the organization (Krumm 2016). Value-driven leadership and the associated change in organizational behavior can only work if a consensus on this is reached as far as possible. For this purpose, the procedure described in Sect. 2 appears to be an ideal, unproblematic, and, above all, anonymous approach to analysis. Finally, after the common set of values has been determined, the discussion about the contents and thus the definition of the values follows. The understanding of the meaning created in this way is an essential building block in the application of value-driven leadership.

In the interaction with the employee, the manager will be judged by whether the jointly defined values will be recognizable and comprehensible in his leadership behavior. For their part, however, the manager should refer to the agreed values when working with the employee, such as in constant exchanges and not just in half-yearly or year-end meetings. This also creates a connection between the manager and the employee, which builds on the discourse to determine the value set.

The change in organizational behavior can then, as described in Sect. 2, be monitored, among other things, by the degree of satisfaction of needs within the organization at regular intervals (through the appropriate implementation of "pulse surveys" within the software) and thus reflects the influence of value-driven leadership in the change.

The integration of values into everyday management is also very often associated with the concept of value management and thus in the derivation of the value manager. The definition of the "American Management Association" describes management as "getting things done through other people" (Holzbauer 2000). However, if one uses the concept of value work (Girbig 2014) and associated with it, that of the "value worker," a completely different dimension of consideration emerges. Aristotle used work in the sense of "doing, creating, effecting." In a figurative sense, the value worker therefore not only exemplifies the values, but through his value-driven leadership creates the space within the organization for them to be lived.

If recognized and measured organizational behavior is to be changed through value-driven leadership, this can only be successful through consistent value work.

3.2 The Competence-Motivation and Crisis-Pressure Model Specific to Each Organizational Unit

The second step of change, after determining a common set of values, in value-driven leadership in organizational behavior is first not about the leader themselves, but about the employees.

The diversity of employees in their specific area of impact and influence ("job fit"), as well as the respective management situation, plays a decisive role here (Krumm 2016). An important distinguishing feature is the individual competence profile for each employee, which can be subdivided into five specific competencies (Fleig 2010):

- Action competence.
- Expertise.
- Methodological competence.
- Social competence.
- Self-competence.

The competence profile is important for the manager in that it allows him to assess and evaluate what individual prerequisites the employee has to fulfil agreed objectives and meet the requirements of his position. The method of recognizing and measuring organizational behavior described in Sect. 2 offers important insights in this respect, as even before a position is filled, the requirements for the job holder can first be defined through analysis and the fit (Frey and Schmalzried 2013) of the respective candidate to this can be checked. This approach even offers a higher resilience of the definition because the requirements can be based on the analysis, objectively carried out not only by the direct supervisor but also by team members, HR experts, or other people. If this measurement is carried out for already existing organizational units, it can be used to check to what extent the individual persons with their individual competence profiles, or as a unit in the team, are suitable for the requirements of the whole. In value-driven leadership, this is an important indicator in order to be able to specifically approach a change to a desired organizational behavior.

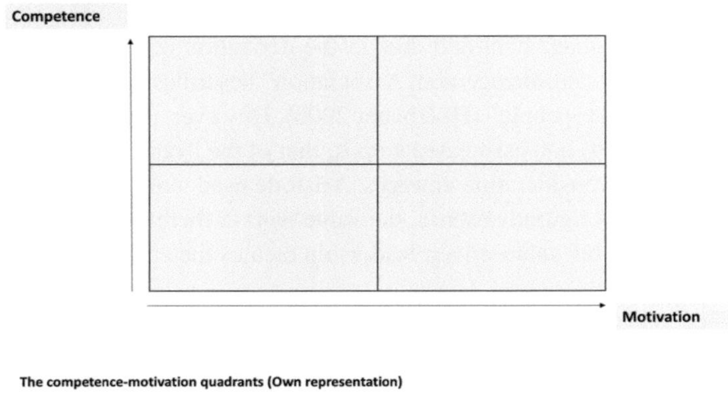

Fig. 5 The competence-motivation quadrants

The second important distinguishing characteristic of the employee is his motivation, whereby a distinction is made between extrinsic and intrinsic motivation (Frey and Schmalzried 2013). Extrinsic motivation includes the monetary reward systems that appeal to the employee more on the rational level. In intrinsic motivation, the values discussed in the chapter play a significant role as they make an important contribution to the employee's motivation.

The competence-motivation quadrants shown in Fig. 5 support the value-driven manager in picking up the employee individually and, based on this, specifically using his or her leadership possibilities. For example, a highly motivated and competent employee requires different support than one who is competent but not sufficiently motivated or one who has room for improvement in his competence profile but is highly motivated. It should always be kept in mind that especially in the case of motivation, the value work of the manager can have a great influence.

The crisis-pressure quadrants shown in Fig. 6 are an important element for value-driven leadership in assessing the specific leadership situation in each case. In a difficult crisis situation with the corresponding high pressure on the organization, leadership must be different than in non-crisis situations with low pressure. In any case, a common set of values between the manager and the employee plays an important role, as this can better ensure mutual understanding in the interaction.

The respective competence profile and motivation of the employee as well as the corresponding specific situation determine the value-driven leadership behavior and thus consequently the organizational behavior.

How the manager can act in it is described in the following section.

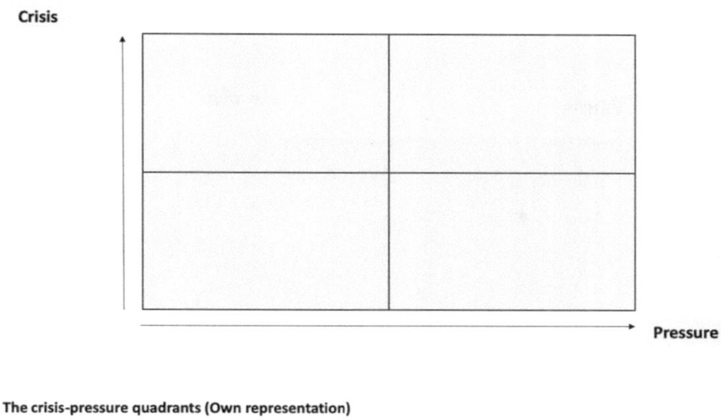

Fig. 6 The crisis-pressure quadrants

4 The Implementation of a Leadership Concept and Employee and Situation-Specific Recommendations for Action Based on a Value Orientation

If change is to be brought about in organizational behavior through leadership and conflict resolution, this must be clearly anchored in the manager's remit, and at the same time, the mechanisms of value-driven leadership must be internalized (Banke and Lutz 2018). Even if one knows how to apply the models of competence-motivation and crisis-pressure quadrants described in Sect. 3, it can be stated that there is no such thing as the "one right leadership style" (Frey and Schmalzried 2013; Krumm 2016). In the interaction between employee and manager, it is not only the differences between the management situation and the employee that must be considered but also those of the manager himself.

Numerous publications on the most diverse leadership styles can be found in the literature. The first studies on leadership behavior can be traced back to Kurt Lewin from 1939, who defined three typical leadership styles (Bartscher 2018):

1. Authoritarian: the supervisor decides and controls. The employee executes.
2. Democratic: the employee is involved in decision-making processes, and external control is partially replaced by self-control.
3. Laissez-faire: the decision is up to the employee or group.

A far more nuanced look at the application in management of control and involvement of the employee was published by Robert Tannenbaum and Warren H. Schmidt in the Harvard Business Manager in 1958, incidentally one of the most reprinted articles in that journal since its initial publication, which only underscores the timeliness of the content (Tannenbaum and Schmidt 2019).

Tannenbaum and Schmidt describe in a model the extent to which a superior's influence changes and thus also his leadership and communication behavior (see Fig. 7). At the same

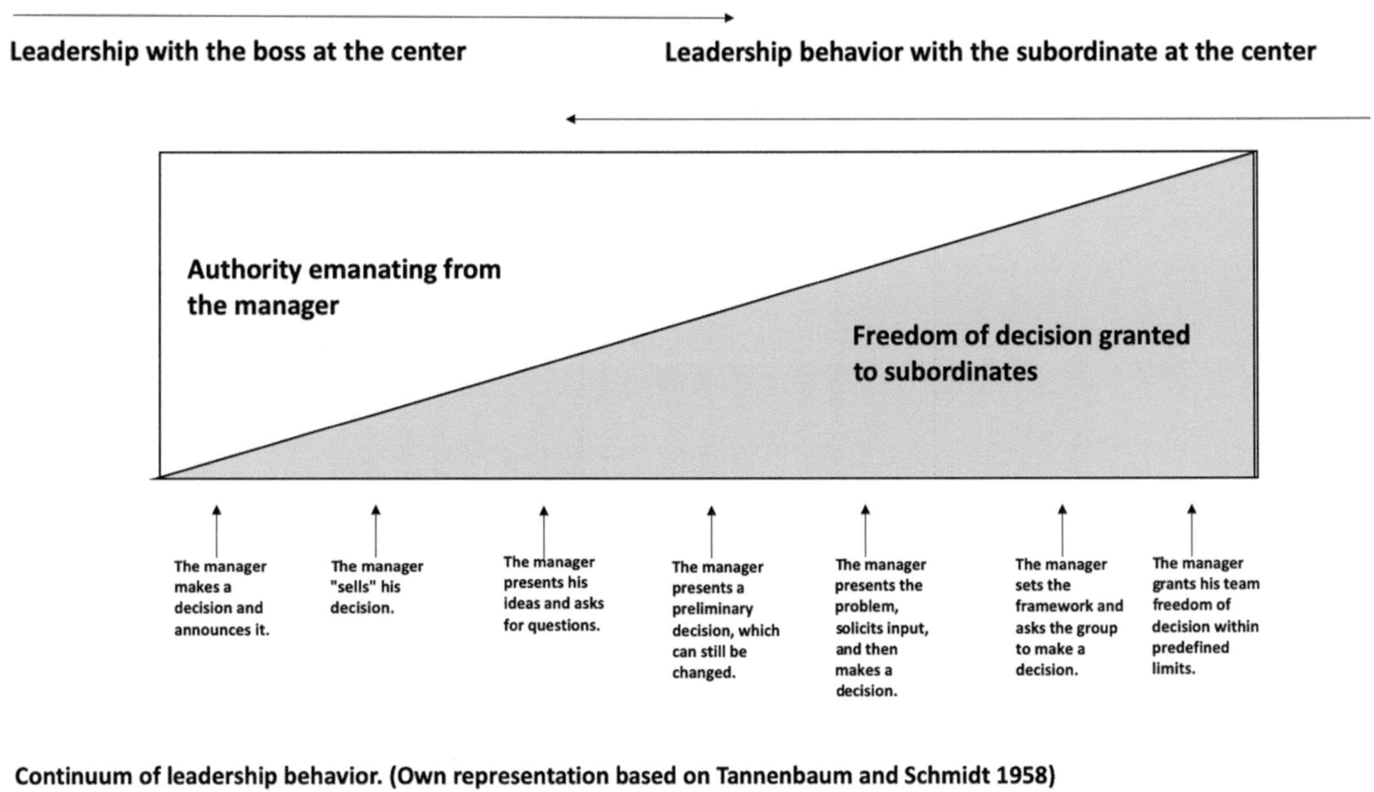

Fig. 7 The continuum of leadership behavior. (Own representation based on Tannenbaum and Schmidt 2019)

time, it shows how the employee's or group's freedom of action changes, and with it the freedom of decision granted.

For value-driven leadership in the sense of organizational behavior and its change, the following prerequisites are decisive:

1. A set of values derived from the needs of the group and jointly defined.
2. A classification of the individual competence-motivation determination of the employee (see Fig. 5).
3. A specific assessment of the respective leadership situation (see Fig. 6).

Daniel Goleman developed a leadership model in which the respective leadership situation can be linked to the appropriate leadership style (Goleman et al. 2003). On the one hand, the dissonant leadership styles are there to restrict the employee's scope for decision-making in crisis situations or to achieve ambitious goals or to almost exclude it in the case of the commanding leadership style (see Fig. 8). Applied in the right leadership situation, they are very powerful and effective and are supported by the employee, as they provide security in difficult situations. However, if the leadership situation no longer fits the dissonant approach, this can very quickly have a negative effect on the climate in the organization. Therefore, in value-driven leadership, a continuous alignment of the existing situation must be carried out.

The so-called resonant leadership styles automatically go hand in hand with an extended freedom of decision for the employee, up to the democratic leadership style, where from the viewpoint of the leadership continuum according to Tannenbaum and Schmidt, the authority emanating from the manager is reduced to the bare minimum (see Fig. 9). In value-driven leadership, it is precisely here that the value set of the respective organization is an important factor, as this provides a basis for the interaction between manager and employee and can also be used in the feedback on leadership situations. Organizational behavior can only be changed through leadership if not only positive but also negative

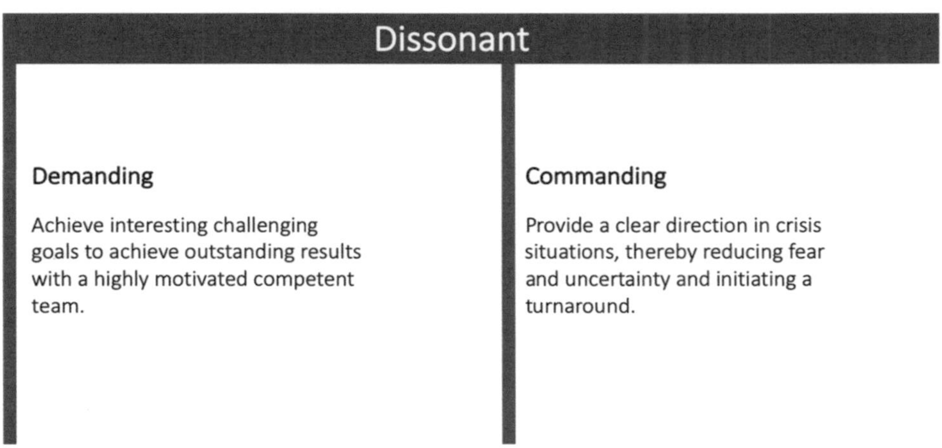

Fig. 8 Dissonant leadership styles. (Own representation based on Goleman et al. 2003)

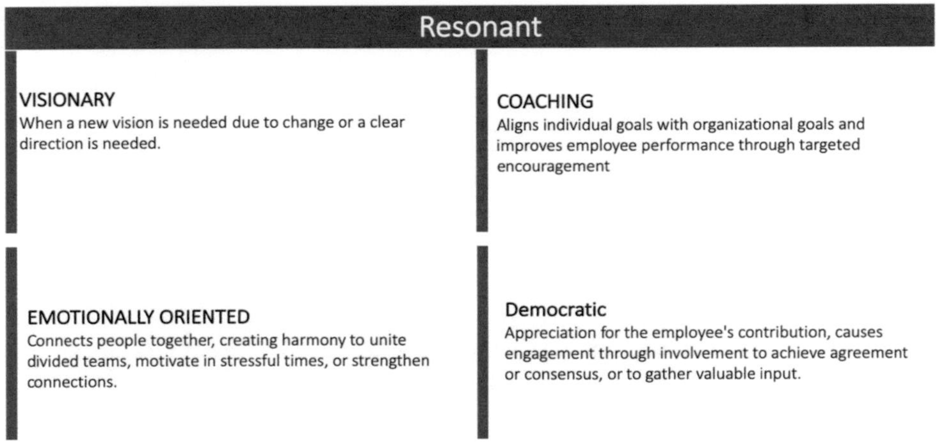

Resonant leadership styles. (own representation based on Goleman et al. 2003).

Fig. 9 Resonant leadership styles. (Own representation based on Goleman et al. 2003)

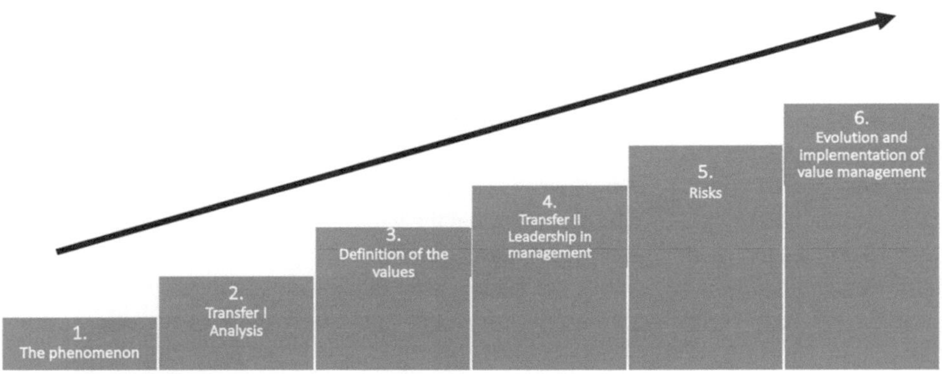

Fig. 10 Six-step model for value management

value experiences are taken up and clarified in discourse (Girbig 2014). In any case, it is recommended to integrate the value set into the target agreement of the managers. This not only clarifies the importance of values in leadership but also offers the opportunity to discuss positive as well as negative value experiences in the appraisal interviews.

The definition of values and the change and further development of leadership behavior are modules 3 and 4 of a step-by-step approach of a six-step model (Fig. 10), which can be chosen as an approach to be able to consistently and fundamentally change value management in an organization (Banke and Lutz 2018).

5 Conclusion

Changing ways of working based on societal change offers some opportunities for employers. If these newly discovered capacities are used and promoted in a constructive way, a new, more value-creating work environment could develop from this. It is now up to management, human resources, and organizational development, as well as executives, to shape the right framework for value-based work and thus lay a foundation for sustainable economic growth. They should start early, because people will increasingly pay attention to the cultural orientation of an organization and use it as a basis for deciding for or against a potential employer. One way to accomplish this is illustrated here. It is about objectively assessing status based on the impetus from the organization, i.e., organizational behavior and subsequent work on value-driven leadership. This holistic approach enables the measurement and recognition of individual organizational characteristics and promotes value creation from within. Consequently, actions become authentic and comprehensible and ensure better cooperation between managers and employees.

The organization is provided with a frame of reference that clarifies the interplay between values, profit, value creation, productivity, and human resources.

References

Baker WE (2019) Emotional energy, relational energy, and organizational energy: toward a multi-level model. Annu Rev Organ Psychol Organ Behav 6:373–395

Banke B, Lutz HJ (2018) Sechs Schritte zur Schulung von CSR- und wertegesteuertem Management. CSR und Compliance, Kleinfeld A, Martens A. Springer Gabler, Berlin

Bartscher T (2018) Revision von autoritärer Führungsstil. https://wirtschaftslexikon.gabler.de/definition/autoritaerer-fuehrungsstil-27693/version-251337. Accessed on 17.04.2020

Brief AP, Weiss HM (2002) Organizational behavior: affect in the workplace. Annu Rev Psychol 53:279–307

Bruch H, Schuler A (2016) Mehr Energie für den Neustart. Harv Bus Manag, Sonderheft, pp 42–49

Bruch H, Fischer J, Färber J (2015) Arbeitgeberattraktivität von innen betrachtet – eine Geschlechter- und Generationenfrage. Top Job-Trendstudie. https://montua-partner.de/wp-content/uploads/2015/08/2015_Trendstudie_Arbeitgeberattraktivitaet.pdf. Accessed on 17.04.2020

Eilers S, Möckel K, Rump J, Schnabel F (2015) HR report 2014/2015. Schwerpunkt Führung. Hays, Mannheim

Fleig J (2010) Mitarbeiterkompetenz und Kompetenzprofile. b-wise GmbH, Karlsruhe

Frey D, Schmalzried L (2013) Philosophie der Führung. Springer, Berlin

Girbig K (2014) Wertemanagement. Springer Gabler, Berlin

Goleman D, Boyatzis R, McKee A (2003) Emotionale Führung. Ullstein, München

Holzbauer U (2000) Management. Friedrich Kiehl, Herne

Kim TY, Kim M (2013) Leaders' moral competence and employee outcomes: the effects of psychological empowerment and person-supervisor fit. J Bus Ethics 112:155–166

Kristof-Brown A, Zimmerman RD, Johnson E (2005) Consequences of individual's fit at work: a meta-analysis of person-job, person-organization, person-group, and person-supervisor fit. Pers Psychol 58(2):281–342

Krumm R (2016) Werteorientiertes Führen. Gabal, Offenbach
Robbins SP, Judge TA (2010) Organizational behavior, Edition 01. Pearson Education Limited. Prentice Hall, New York Public Library
Tannenbaum R, Schmidt HW (2019) Harv Bus Manag Spezial 1:78, Hamburg
Wieland J (2004) Handbuch Wertemanagement. Murmann, Hamburg
Wippermann J, Krüger P (2020) Werte Index 2020. Deutscher Fachverlag GmbH, Frankfurt am Main

Dr. Hans-Jürgen Lutz is in charge of the Institute for Business Ethics, Value Management, and Compliance (IWWC) at the Knowledge Foundation@Reutlingen University. After completing a degree in natural sciences and a subsequent doctorate, he began his professional career in industry in 1987. Among other things, as CEO and Managing Director in Italy, he was also responsible for the entire business in Southern Europe of a corporate division. This stage of his career in particular has had a strong influence on his understanding of value-driven management. Leadership has always played a central role for him. Parallel to his professional activities, he has been a lecturer and instructor at renowned institutions such as the ESB Reutlingen or the University of St. Gallen since 2003. Since 2014, he has been in charge of the Institute for Business Ethics, Value Management, and Compliance (IWWC), where he focuses on value management. His many years of experience in industry help him to combine scientific principles with a practical background.

Dr. rer. Nat. Daniel Nummer has been working on the topics of organizational behavior and control in corporate structures for over 13 years. He is the founder and managing director of PREDICTA|ME GmbH. Prior to that, he worked for more than 12 years in internationally overarching responsibilities for listed companies in the diagnostics and pharmaceutical industries. He started his scientific-analytical career at the German Cancer Research Center, DKFZ, Heidelberg, in the field of tumor immunology.

The focus of his current work is the analysis of the connection between people, task, and environment in changing organizational structures, in particular the development of holistic people analytics and consulting structures for the management in companies to increase job satisfaction and corporate value creation.

Part III

Practical Thinking

Covid-19 Sharpens the Eye for Values

Günther Wagner

Abstract

At the time I agreed to contribute to this book, *Value-Based Leadership*, I had no idea how much the world and world events could change in a short period of time. With Covid-19, the entire world was forced to regroup. To what extent the associated changes and new priorities will actually take root in a sustainable way, possibly reshaping the value framework of the economy, remains to be seen. But one thing is certain; the measures taken to contain the spread of Covid-19 have been so severe that world affairs and the economy will have to deal with the consequences and potential upheavals for some time to come. What this can mean in concrete terms for the future of the economy, in what way the economy and economy-driving values are called into question by Covid-19, and in what way the values of companies lose their power and relevance, that is what I would like to put up for discussion in my contribution, to analyze and reflect on the values of the economy from a new perspective.

At the time I agreed to contribute to this book, I had no idea how much the world and world events can change in a short period of time, and certain values become the measure of all things in a short period of time, such as the value of life – not that this value and the values associated with it, such as health, social responsibility, cooperation, safety, helpfulness, compassion, fairness, etc., should not have been a top priority before the crisis, but with the Corona crisis, the value associated with life became seemingly the whole world's

G. Wagner (✉)
Günther Wagner Unternehmensberatung, Salzburg, Austria
e-mail: guenther@wagner-consulting.eu

J. Lange (ed.), *Value-Oriented Leadership in Theory and Practice*,
https://doi.org/10.1007/978-3-662-65883-3_10

top priority again, and with the emergence of the Covid-19 virus, the value of life seems to have been brought back to the attention of the entire world.

Within a very short period of time, everything had to be done to protect lives, especially the lives of impaired people, the elderly, or people with pre-existing conditions – and that meant implementing a global lockdown, shutting down the economy completely except for a few industries.

The value of life was above all.

Values of business, such as career, status, profit, stakeholder orientation, and power, were socially put on hold from 1 day to the next, lost the big stage of attention, and had to give way from 1 day to the next to the value of preserving life at any cost, whatever the cost.

Now I don't want to criticize this in any way, but some questions came to my mind with this sudden value hype for life and the worldwide set lockdowns associated with it:

- Why was life brought into such absolute focus with the appearance of the Covid-19 virus, when even before Covid-19 other life events and global developments, which were also not necessarily favorable, were affecting the lives of many people in an extremely unfavorable way and will continue to do so, such as environmental pollution, which claims millions of lives every year?
- Likewise, every year people die much earlier than they should because of smoking. Why does no one worldwide ban smoking and shut down the production of cigarettes?
- Tens of thousands of people still die of hunger every year, which is also a plight that should be solved immediately, if the value of preserving life is really so important. Why don't we try to organize the world economy in solidarity so that this deplorable state of affairs can be remedied?

With Covid-19, you make an urgent appeal for solidarity, therefore shutting down the economy to protect life, and with other actions around the world, also with high death rates, you don't – what's the difference?

- Why is it that with Covid-19 the value of life is suddenly considered to be unrestricted and above everything and covers the whole world, and before that with environmental pollution, poverty, smoking, etc., the value of life was and still is not apparently the supreme goal, the supreme value, after which the world and the world economy try to orientate itself?

What I am currently forced to understand in relation to my questions is that some values seem to have no stringent constant in the life of societies, as well as of individuals, but are more a hype that suddenly gains relevance through an event. In this respect, the modern media landscape may certainly have an even more rapid and pervasive influence on position, strengthen or weaken values accordingly. In the case of Covid-19, there was no medium that did not inform about it and influence streams of people in this respect – whether positively or negatively is not the point to be discussed at this point, but rather how quickly values become stronger or do not seem relevant due to an appropriate media preparation.

So, when we talk about values, I think we first need to consider whether a particular value is just hype; whether it is a value that has been appropriately well positioned by the media, by education, by politics, and by business; or whether it is actually a deep human need that is constant beyond any hype.

I would like to explain what I mean by this with a less dramatic example, such as poverty, environmental sins, smoking, etc.

Austria prided itself on being a country of culture. But with Covid-19, there was hardly anything left of the value of culture in Austria – on the contrary, in the fight against the consequences of the lockdown, culture was ignored, was, as it seemed, not bothered to find adequate support. It may be true that culture cannot directly save lives in crises, but to then let this value almost disappear overnight is also questionable, when many livelihoods are losing their basis of existence as a result of inadequately thought-out lockdowns or inadequate measures in dealing with the lockdowns. The value of preserving life is not in question, but what about all the other values that keep a society, the economy alive – are they then obsolete from 1 day to the next, no longer important, no longer relevant to life?

It seems that the current situation with values is the same as with other issues, such as the environment, scarcity of resources, aging, and migration – people do not see through the complexity; they do not recognize the mutually stabilizing network of different values, the associated goals and ways of acting. With Covid-19, many are falling into the complexity trap with consequences that will occupy us for a long time to come.

One value alone may be important, right, to justify certain ways of acting. However, no value exists on its own, but lives in conjunction with other values – in a value culture, in a colorful, mutually inspiring, but also in a mutually testing cooperation. And it is precisely this kind of consciously lived culture of values that creates a milieu that increases the ability to find above-average solutions to problems (Schaller 2020) – and in times of crisis in particular, this is an elixir of survival whose value can hardly be surpassed.

If we think about this statement explicitly for companies in the current Corona crisis, a consciously lived culture of values can support companies in times of crisis and generate solutions that are relevant to their survival. The currently helpful values, which were supposedly praised as important and relevant in connection with digitalization even before the Corona crisis, include the dismantling of rigid structures in the direction of more personal responsibility and self-regulation, more agility, more networking and more empathy, more cooperation, fairness, and environmental awareness. At the same time, with firmly anchored value cultures, the danger can be contained that the increase in self-regulation may cause subsystems to become independent and develop their own goals, which may subsequently contradict corporate goals (Schaller 2020).

A consciously lived, colorful culture of values counteracts the problem that one holds individual values disproportionately high, which then possibly ends in dogmatism – to the extent that one simply blindly follows a singularly hyped value without any ifs and buts. If one considers values to be relevant and important, then values must also be critically examined and possibly questioned here and there with regard to the implementation of values and adapted accordingly – which is only possible, however, if values are not played off against each other, but rather discussed about in an open and appreciative manner.

If one simply affirms values because that is what many are doing at the moment, then these are often not values that many are reflecting on, but guidelines that one considers to be quite good at the moment. But such guidelines quickly lose their power and also their significance. Values are emotionally deeply anchored, show considerably more staying power, but, as already mentioned, with the danger of tipping over into dogma, which can easily mutate into a set of rules, which one must subsequently try to enforce with a lot of effort and strength in order to keep it going. If values have to be ordered, then the values have lost their sense, their meaning, and also their power or had never been really deeply anchored by a broad crowd – which should also critically be thought. A society with a well-anchored culture of values is able to use values as a solvent in a mindful, reflective way, appropriate to the respective situation and challenge. But this is precisely what no longer seems to be coherent and feasible in a fast-moving age. At the same time, it is apparent that almost all companies above a certain size refer to values.

Etymologically, the Germany term for "economize" even includes the meaning "to create value," which has only recently been reduced to the pure economic basis (Schaller 2020). Studies clearly show that three quarters of top managers believe that corporate values will actually become more important in the future.

Alberto Alemanno, author, political activist, and named a Young Global Leader by the World Economic Forum in 2015 and Global Clinical Professor of Law at New York University School of Law, lists ten personality traits or value-related competencies that are highly relevant for leaders in the future (Alemanno 2017):

- Compassion and emotional intelligence.
- Integrity and openness.
- Fairness and inclusion.
- Competence and consideration of (interdisciplinary) data.
- Consistency and modesty.

But without the third eye, without a guardian, without competent alertness, it becomes extremely difficult to keep values or value abuse in a healthy measure:

> According to Alemanno, competent vigilance is an instance within oneself and at the same time outside oneself that is able to protect society and oneself from social as well as from one's own extremes. Only when such an instance keeps an eye on the doings, the follies and excesses, can something emerge globally that actually serves the common good for once. (Alemanno 2017)

It is possible, however, that you dismiss the apparent rise of values as mere gobbledygook, as a current highly hyped marketing gimmick, which now in this chapter in this book on values from my side is only aimed at setting myself apart from other consultants and influencers in the hot competition for the best strategies in the battle for survival and recognition. If that were actually the case, however, I would approach the value perspective very differently.

Be that as it may, I can only tell you at this point that, due to the outbreak of the Covid-19 virus, the measures associated with it, and the highly complex intertwined challenges and consequences, I see the power of reflective consciousness in conjunction with values as the strongest force for really getting to grips with the not exactly favorable economic as well as social situation.

In my opinion, only with a trained consciousness and a consciously lived value culture can so much resilience, innovative spirit, intuitive knowledge, and courage be built up in connection with the grasp of highly complex processes such as the worldwide rapid restructuring of the global economy after and with Covid-19, in order to be able to participate as a healthy shaper of the future, to generate a new future with and after Covid-19.

Matthias Horx, futurologist, writes that the Covid crisis is a special moment for humanity and can influence the future of this planet in a far-reaching way. Now doors are open for new spaces of possibility. It is the time of "Manything goes" (Zukunftsinstitut GmbH 2020) – and values are the driving force. Values provide orientation, form the basis of cooperation, ensure cohesion, and specify goals (Heimsoeth 2019).

This seems to be so easy and simple, so normal, that most of you might think you know it anyway and are therefore convinced that what you are doing is right, is based on values, and therefore has enough power to lead the company successfully through the challenges of the twenty-first century, namely, climate change, overpopulation, resource shortages, and the Corona crisis.

If this is the case, then it will not be difficult for you to spontaneously select your ten most important values for your life or for your successful professional work from the following values (Fig. 1):

Let's get even more specific now: Which four values are most relevant in relation to the ten values that you have just found to be currently shaping your everyday work and life?

1.
2.
3.
4.

Are your personal values compatible with the values of your company and do they form a stable value culture?

- If so, in what ways does this manifest itself?
- If no, in what way does this hinder and hindered you in your work – in the Corona crisis or also in terms of environmental awareness in your company, in terms of adequate use of resources, etc.?

Most of the time, however, we don't really recognize the potential associated with values, even though many talk about them, but there are a lack of trust and a lack of anchoring some values in the flesh. We are, whether we like it or not, very much taken over by technically rational, professional knowledge, and we have lost the resource of values, which

Recognition	Health	Wealth
Education	Sociability	Quiet
Gratitude	Helpfulness	Frugality
Discipline / Willpower	Individuality	Self-esteem
Friendship	Integrity	Status
Honesty	Career	Security
Diligence	Competence	Spirituality
Family Sense	Creativity	Beauty
Fitness	Power	Faithful
Free time	Courage / Courage	Reliability
Peace	Nature	Trust
Pleasure	Sense of order	Restraint
Sense of Justice	Sense of duty	

Fig. 1 Values – an overview

drives each and every one of us every day and mobilizes strength, as a strength-giving anchor.

It may be that now, in the face of the profound confrontation with the pandemic caused by the Covid-19 virus, things are a little different, and many in the business world are becoming aware that it was not exclusively the value of financial profits, the focus on constant growth, that made a company ambitious, but that other forces led the company to success – an inspired idea, a profound concern – and each concern is based on personal values, a personal driving force, on very concrete motives in life.

But there is another important aspect in the mechanism of action of the values, which is however even less often consciously addressed than the values themselves – and exactly this is also currently much more evident in the Corona crisis than before.

When working with values, one must also face the polarity or the dilemmas in relation to the values – in other words: understand values as a pair of poles and thus as a dilemma. That is why it is so important to talk about a culture of values and less about individual values.

What I mean by this is that every value, every motive becomes a vice when it is lived too one-sidedly, when it is unilaterally elevated to a dogma. Excessive discipline, for example, makes us compulsive, cold, and sad. We lose warmth of heart, empathy, and love of life. At the same time, a lack of discipline throws us into chaos (Gassert 2013). Analogously, this can be played out with other pole pairs with consequences and implications that are extremely rarely considered in everyday work, but which now become all the more obvious in a crisis (Fig. 2).

People tried to protect lives at all costs during the Covid crisis. This value was above everything at the beginning of the Corona period, but what this value also entails as a

Fig. 2 Values – pole pairs

Change	Continuity
Innovation	Quality
Flexibility	Consequence
Competitiveness	social responsibility
Environmental awareness	Profit orientation
Shareholder orientation	Stakeholder orientation
Harmony	confrontational joy
Order	Freedom
Hierarchy	Self-organisation
Management system	Self-responsibility
Team orientation	individual development
Competition	Cooperation

consequence only became apparent later. This is not to say that the value of protecting life is wrong, but upholding values has consequences at other levels, which leads us into dilemmas that could have unpleasant consequences at other levels. For example, if consistency (in the sense of impact) is made an important value in the organization, then the positive countervalue of flexibility is put on the sidelines. However, consistency and flexibility form a polar pair of values. Consistency is not valuable without flexibility, not promising success, and vice versa. For a certain period of time, the main focus can be placed on consistency, but in the long term, these values consistency and flexibility can only be effective as a pole pair promising success (Wallner and Völkl 2018).

At this point, you may also find it interesting to revisit the ten or four personal important values you have identified and add the pole pairs.

Your four most important current values are counterparts to your values:

1.
2.
3.
4.

- Do you have a hard time finding the pole pairs for your values?
- Do you even feel a little reluctance to add possible pole pairs to your values?
- Are you trying to keep pole pairs out of your environment or even stall them as not being right?

If this is the case, then this is a completely normal human reaction, but it requires more attentiveness in order to avoid falling into the value-related traps. Most management systems are still too often one-sidedly oriented toward values, often even only as a marketing instrument, hyping those values that are capable of demonstrating the measurability of profitability and success at the respective moment, not paying attention to the dilemmas with values (Loll 2010). But this is precisely the Achilles heel of many companies – the place where companies are vulnerable and can be brought down. The VW diesel scandal is a good example of this. VW's diesel scandal shows that the value of honesty didn't seem to be well embedded in a healthy set of values, and therefore people could agree to the installation of manipulated software across multiple layers seemingly without hesitation. But such an abusive approach to values takes its revenge – in times of global interconnectedness, perhaps even more quickly than before.

The great challenge for many companies is currently to get back on track with the often no longer noticeable concern, the values (Plötzeneder and Gehrer 2014). Currently, in the Corona period, this is perhaps even a strategy that is essential for survival, because many companies were and perhaps still are so severely affected by the Corona measures that they have to reorient themselves as a company anyway.

What I mean by the subtle power of values, a healthy culture of values, can perhaps be made more comprehensible with an example of "The Archer."

I would like to invite you now to let rise in you the idea that you are now a master of archery. The framework of values forms your bow. Your strategies, your ideas, and your decisions are your arrows which you seek to hit right into your targets.

As a master of archery, you know exactly how to hold the bow, how much you need to tighten the bow in any given weather condition, wind, sun, or rain, in order to hit the arrows into the target in the best possible way. At the same time, you know how to hold your arrow, depending on the bow, the tension, and the distance from the target, in order to shoot the arrows in the best possible way. And you know your target very well. You are one with your target to be able to hit your bow and arrows right into the heart of the target (Senger 2020).

This sounds somehow plausible, perhaps even so simple that one thinks everyone knows this and acts accordingly. But I fear that too many fail to recognize one or the other aspect of dealing with values, with goals, and with strategies – especially the basic prerequisite, a mentally open, reflected basic attitude toward the values, the strategies, and the goals, as well as an awareness of the external influences, the environment, which influence both the basic mental attitude, the mindfulness, and concretely the values, the bow, the strategies, the arrows, and the goal.

Certainly, there are enough companies that consciously deal with the bow, i.e., values, the arrow, the strategy, and the goal, that are moved by values, and that seek to manage challenges and goals and have the necessary basic mental attitude, including the mindful guardian. But nevertheless, there is no denying that many decisions are made without consideration of the arc, without consideration of the values, and without consideration of the elusive modes of action. Perhaps it is not so much the values themselves that are lacking, the knowledge of the existence of the arc, but much more the resolute awareness, among other things also the courage to take the arc really intentionally in the hand with the conviction of wanting to enrich the world with something that seems to be really important and right, to make the standards underlying the values transparent, and to address them openly.

Please do not misunderstand me; it is not about morality, but about awareness. In my opinion, awareness is clearly more necessary in order not to fall by the wayside in the future in the global economic competition and in the race with environmental challenges. Bernd Ankenbrand, professor of economy of sense, is even convinced that the question of values will become a key resource for companies and managers in the future (EY 2019).

In this respect, HR has a key role to play in determining the extent to which a given value base can be promoted in the company in the future – which is tantamount to long-term implementation. However, studies show that in practice the topic of values is accorded significantly less importance in personnel interviews than the other more performance-related assessment criteria (Schaller 2020) – it may be that Corona has changed this view. However, this would still have to be analyzed and compared with the checks before Corona.

Be that as it may, the value of preserving life at all costs in 2020 has forced the world and the global economy in a short period of time to change courses of action and strategies, to realign, to cooperate and communicate in new ways, to face fears, and at the same time not to get lost in fears in order to rethink the future. What the world should learn from Covid-19 is the picture of a healthy future – healthy in terms of coronavirus, healthy in terms of environmental stress, healthy in terms of poverty, healthy in terms of resource constraints, and many other things. Business has an essential role to play in this, and business, every single business, should be aware of this – not as a burden, as a constraint, but as a role model, as a driver of innovation as masters of archery, shaping the twenty-first century in a particularly wise, sensitive, and sustainable way.

References

Alemanno A (2017) A 10-point guide to responsible leadership in the age of populism. https://www.weforum.org/agenda/2017/01/a-10-point-guide-to-responsible-leadership-in-the-age-of-populism/. Accessed on 09.09.2020

EY Deutschland (2019) Nur wer Sinn stiftet, kann auch Wert schöpfen. https://www.ey.com/de_at/purpose/nur-wer-sinn-stiftet-kann-auch-wert-schoepfen. Accessed on 04.04.2017

Gassert M (2013) Alles ist schwer, bevor es leicht wird. Mit dem Wissen der Shaolin zu mehr Disziplin und Willenskraft. München. Random House ebook, Pos. 132 von 3621

Heimsoeth A (2019) Herausforderung Change: Wie werteorientierte Führung weiterhelfen kann. https://antje-heimsoeth.com/herausforderung-change-wie-werteorientierte-fuehrung-weiterhelfen-kann/. Accessed on 07.02.2020

Loll AC (2010) Ohne plan geht's Auch. Frankfurter Allgemeine. http://www.faz.net/aktuell/beruf-chance/arbeitswelt/zielvereinbarungen-ohne-plan-geht-s-auch-11039847.html. Accessed on 11.09.2019

Plötzeneder T, Gehrer C (2014) Das große Anliegen. Große Anliegen zielen auf großen Nutzen ab, auf grundlegende Veränderungen. Steinverlag, Bad Traunstein

Schaller PD (2020) Management und Führung – erfolgreicher durch Werte!? https://www.yumpu.com/de/document/view/5162237/erfolgreicher-durch-werte-org-portalorg. Accessed on 07.02.2020

Senger T (2020) Mindset – Trendbegriff oder Schlüssel zum Erfolg? https://gobran.de/mindset-trendbegriff-oder-schlussel-zum-erfolg/. Accessed on 14.05.2019

Wallner HP, Völkl K (2018) Die Erfolgsprinzipien der Führung: Auf die richtigen Werte kommt es an. https://berufebilder.de/erfolgsprinzipien-fuehrung-richtigen-werte-kommt/#werte-bringen-polaritaet. Accessed on 17.03.2015

Zukunftsinstitut GmbH (2020) Internationale Gesellschaft für Zukunfts- und Trendberatung. https://www.zukunftsinstitut.de/fileadmin/user_upload/Whitepaper-Die_Wirtschaft_nach_Corona.pdf. Accessed on 21.04.2020

Günther Wagner has been active as a leadership coach, management consultant, speaker, and lateral thinker since 2011. Before that, he was an officer in the German Air Force for many years and later a sales manager for international insurance companies. Out of personal concern, he took a look beyond his own nose and became effective as a board member of "Human Helping Humans" in 2004 with the tsunami relief. His life was and is characterized by transformation processes. His expertise is based on a very multi-layered work and life experience. Starting with leadership training, change management, conflict management, systemic organizational development and consulting, evolution management, up to longer study stays in Asia. There he deepened his mindfulness practice and expanded his knowledge of Aikido. It is said of him that he dares to look beyond the mainstream and brings processes to bear differently. He deliberately takes detours to inspire just such an edge to success. His core themes are leadership in highly complex times, World of Work 4.0, the related education that needs to be realigned, and closely related to these topics, discretely addressing the broad resistances to change that are often difficult to access. Degrees: Dipl.-Ing. (FH) Electronics/Electrical Engineering, Officer College of the LSK/LV Kamenz, MBA, Systemic Organizational Development and Consulting, University of Augsburg/UCD Michael Smurfit School of Business Dublin.

Making a Difference in the Workplace: Why My Employees No Longer Give Their Heads to the Gatekeeper

Stephanie Bräuer

Abstract

As a manager, I see it as my responsibility to create a framework that provides my employees with security and orientation in terms of their behavior. In order to be able to assume this responsibility, I act according to certain values and give them a high priority every day. Meaningfulness, co-determination, and team spirit are particularly important to me personally. But what happens if these values are not shared by your own employees right from the start? Setbacks and conflicts in the team are inevitable. I have found for myself that time and patience are just as relevant as continuity and discipline. I can already see the improvement in the motivation and cooperation of my team due to the changed values. However, this change in values is not yet complete. There are still some challenges to overcome.

1 Initial Situation of My Department

My company is in the food industry; our site produces delicacies. Logistics, my department, is an internal service provider for the production department at the factory site and for central distribution. Production orders are planned. The required materials are planned, delivered, stored, and made available. Finished products are picked, stored, and shipped. Utilizing production lines and keeping line personnel busy is the number one goal in the factory to keep volume output high and costs low. As a result, much of my team's work is influenced from outside the department. The day-to-day operations have the highest

S. Bräuer (✉)
Berlin, Germany

J. Lange (ed.), *Value-Oriented Leadership in Theory and Practice*,
https://doi.org/10.1007/978-3-662-65883-3_11

priority. The daily routine is characterized by urgent tasks and thus short communication channels, frequent coordination, and quick decisions within and between departments. There is a large proportion of short-term troubleshooting. This is reflected in a high speed in the processing of daily issues and a certain stress level for the employees. Tasks are largely operational and not very strategic. Projects are short to medium term instead of long term.

Before I started as Head of Department, my department consisted of about two thirds industrial and one third commercial employees. Just under 85% were men; 15% were women. The average age was just under 45. In summary, then, this was a department that was structurally composed of rather male, rather older, rather fewer academic employees. This structure supported the prevailing culture. I never met my predecessor as Head of Department personally. My knowledge of him and his management style comes from personal conversations with employees. This logistics manager was in office for many years and had a strong influence on the department. I found hierarchical structures where decisions were made by authority. Discussions about decision-making were rare. Employees were required to carry out instructions. Independent thinking was not encouraged and sometimes even rejected. The employees lacked the overall view in the processing of their subtasks. They were rarely provided with the necessary information. The identification with their own tasks was relatively low. The employees worked for the most part as individuals and not as a team. Teamwork was not a priority and was therefore not developed further. The statement that employees should give their heads to the gatekeeper when they enter the factory dates from this time. My impression was that the employees at that time were not completely happy with the prevailing culture. However, they had accepted it and adapted.

2 My Prioritized Values

As a graduate, I had the choice at the time, greatly simplified, whether to pursue a professional or managerial career. I chose the latter with the awareness that my character traits, my attitude, and my values were essential for this. These were shaped by my environment. Firstly, they originated in my family upbringing. They were formed and learned through my education, at school and university, and further honed by companies in which I worked. When I took my first position after graduation at my company's headquarters, a new management team had just formed: characters with a modern understanding of corporate culture and people management. Values and culture were redefined and lived out internally and externally in different ways. Ties were banned and the form of address was introduced. Various working forums were founded, and decisions were worked out by employees. As assistant to the management, I was more closely involved in this change in values than almost anyone else. Elsewhere in the company, especially in the geographically distant production sites, the new values did not take hold at all or only very slowly. I, on the other hand, had already completely internalized them and was experienced in implementing them. I had the great opportunity to learn from the members of the management team the leadership skills that I could identify with and that I would later apply myself. For me, strong reflection led the way, and I had a concrete picture of what values I wanted to represent as a leader. I believe that values and culture make a difference, as they are instrumental in motivating employees and thereby making them more efficient and effective. Motivation of employees depends on more factors than just salary. Personally, I wouldn't go to work if I didn't get paid. But equally, I wouldn't stay with a company if there wasn't more to it than just the pay. We spend a lot of time at work and with colleagues, so we need a structure of team spirit. As a manager, I see it as my job to create this framework in order to provide security and orientation. Values are subjective and therefore there is no "one right" way. Meaningfulness, co-determination, and team spirit are particularly important to me personally.

2.1 Sense

Every person needs a purpose to strive for. For some, this is the upbringing of children and for others a charitable association or career. Meaning is subjective and therefore multifaceted. Even our actions, every action, in my opinion, requires meaning for us to be willing to perform them. This is just as true for everyday work: without meaning, meaninglessness ensues. There is a lack of identification and ultimately passion and motivation. As a leader, I have the opportunity to give my employees the information they need to see the big picture and the overarching benefit. An example: For the task processing of the material planners in my department, it is not relevant to know the product that is being manufactured. They schedule the materials that are on their requirements lists. However, if I share with them product placements in grocery stores or campaign concepts from our marketing department, this information leads them to better identify with their task. For example, they realize that a custom-made raw product with long delivery times and special storage conditions is the reason why a product sells well. Especially when it comes to the work area of the employees themselves, timely transparency about backgrounds, decisions, and changes is indispensable. Intransparency and withholding information, on the other hand, can lead to demotivation for the same reason.

2.2 Co-determination

For me, involving employees in management decisions is central. I let those have their say who ultimately have to implement a decision that has been made – regardless of their role or hierarchical level. In order to achieve the appropriate participation from my employees, it is relevant how open I am toward my team. Only if my behavior is perceived as honest and authentic will my team be willing to participate. This includes explaining decisions and actions taken to my team in a transparent manner. I therefore always allow discussions to take place on an equal footing and convey the security that everyone is allowed to disagree with me if one disagrees. I see it as my job to keep my team well informed so that all the necessary data is available for decision-making. When possible, I involve multiple decision alternatives that can then be evaluated together to ultimately make a final decision. For example, we discussed several alternatives for a layout of multiple freezer cells, all of which had different advantages and disadvantages. In areas where all the alternatives are comparable for me, I take the opportunity to opt out of the decision completely, like when choosing office furniture or signage in the warehouse. For me, it's important that ideas for decision options are not exclusively designed by me. Therefore, I encourage and even actively solicit suggestions and ideas from my team. To create an environment in which employees think about new ideas, I always approach new thoughts with an open mind, evaluating them objectively and fairly in terms of their implementation. In this way, I create an environment in which others enjoy thinking about new ideas and present them without hesitation to the team and to me as a manager. I encourage employees to be courageous and try things out. Furthermore, for me, co-determination goes hand in hand with taking responsibility. Anyone who has actively participated in a decision also bears the consequences, both positive and negative. The greater the co-determination, the greater the acceptance of responsibility. Some employees want to have not only a say but also an area in which they can make their own decisions. They are responsible for this area and act relatively freely here. This is the case, for example, with the material planners, who have divided the materials required for production among themselves into product groups and are responsible for these areas independently.

2.3 Team Spirit

For me, writing individual employees in the same box in an organizational chart does not create a team. What counts for me is the awareness that the team is more valuable than each individual on one's own. In my opinion, no one can be successful if their own performance is good but team performance is not. Shared tasks promote collaboration on collective goals. But it takes more than just a substantive connection. Leaders and team members learn what behavior is appropriate in the work environment and adapt accordingly. However, they are still themselves, even during working hours. This means that the personal character of each employee has an impact on how they work together. In my opinion, leaders and team members represent more than just their job titles through their individual personalities. To me, an authentic person appears stable, credible, and comprehensible in his or her actions. I have made the experience that this facilitates cooperation. For me, this includes not only the use of strengths but also the concession of weaknesses. Knowing the personality of the others and their strengths and weaknesses and giving them a place in the structure of the team are a central factor of teamwork, in my opinion. For example, when it comes to finding out all the risks of a project in advance, the pessimist in the team helps me. That's why feedback on behavior is just as important to me as feedback on technical issues. Every employee has different wishes, needs, and fears; it differs from others and therefore needs individual attention. For example, certain appreciation for one person is not automatically for another. One employee may feel valued when one can personally present project results to the top boss. Another employee finds this rather unpleasant and coercive.

3 Our Path to a Change in Values

When I took over the management of logistics at my company's Berlin production site, I didn't fit the usual profile of a logistics manager. I am a woman and young and have an intensive academic background, little operational expertise, and hardly any management experience. I still remember my inaugural speech as a newly appointed logistics manager: "I am not the expert in all the areas that belong to our team, you are. And I'm not stepping up to tell you how to do your job, I'm stepping up to work with you to find the ways." No one came up to me to congratulate me on the new job, to shake my hand, to tell me they were looking forward to working with me. Very few employees seemed happy about the decision that had been made. Getting me as the new head was seen as weakening the department, as I didn't meet any of the obvious relevant criteria. There was also the point that I worked differently with the employees than they were used to. There are two incidents in particular that stick in my mind. There was a co-worker with whom I had been on first-name terms for months before I became logistics manager. Suddenly he asked me to address one other formally again. I approached him about it and he explained that I was now his manager and he didn't want to be on a first-name basis with me anymore. Another employee came up to me relieved and assured me that decisions were much easier now. I asked him why. He told me that he and I had discussed decisions a lot before. But now that I was logistics manager, I would just decide as his manager, which would make everything easier. For the two employees, their attitude seemed self-evident; I, on the other hand, did not feel comfortable in this value context and did not think it was right.

At the time, my values fitted into the corporate culture exemplified by the Head Office. However, they did not fit into the corporate culture that prevailed at the location and not always with the personal values of my new employees. I have a modern understanding of leadership, completely contrary to the traditional structures that had prevailed up to then. My company had made it possible for me to take the job and had thus consciously made a concession to me and my value structure. This strengthened me to implement my values even against resistance in my department. In order to be able to take on this responsibility, I gave my values a high priority every day. At the time, no one, including me, could grasp it completely, but a culture and value change had begun that would not be easy for anyone, my team, or me.

3.1 Enable Meaningfulness

In order to give my team an overall picture in the context of their tasks, I always try to transparently map and communicate everything from the beginning (background, origin) to the end (result). For me, it was undisputed from the beginning that this would mean added value for everyone. However, the practice was different. Many employees could not independently categorize the information provided and felt overwhelmed. More context was needed to understand the original information. Some information was already outdated shortly after it was shared and needed to be refreshed, such as which days and shifts the factory planned to schedule special production. Particularly important or urgent information was lost in the shuffle. It was not always clear what was a task and what was pure information. Demotivation arose even faster if I informed late or even forgot to do so than it was the case before. I was often unsure when to share confidential information with my team, for example, in the context of reduced hours, so they were informed either too early or too late. In some places, certain information were considered too much, such as automatic unit failure notifications in the cold store, and in others too little, such as the timing of repairs to those units. But the most difficult thing for me was that some employees had no interest in or need for certain content at all and felt unnecessarily distracted and overwhelmed with information.

I still believe in sense-making and continue to share information with my team. However, I now understand how to differentiate. When I share information, I also provide context where I feel it is necessary. This way, I don't overwhelm the recipients and avoid extra consultation loops. Information that I expect to change again, I no longer give out in a timely manner. I wait for adjustments and only communicate final input. I send content to smaller distribution circles, pre-selecting recipients. In order to define more clearly what are concrete tasks and what are pure information, I consistently use the designation "for information" in the first place in emails if it is purely informative content.

Through these adjustments to my information flow, my employees now feel sufficiently informed, but at the same time do not feel overwhelmed or demotivated in the processing and implementation of the information. By sharing the background and the end result transparently, I have noticed that my employees' interest in their tasks has increased and that they know the meaning of their actions.

3.2 Promoting Co-determination

In my ideal picture, a constructive discussion in the team leads to a joint solution. My experience is that the offer of co-determination is often understood as an offer to take over the decision. The employees claim that they can wish what the final result looks like because they are the ones affected. If the final decision goes against their wishes, there are great resentment and accusations of not having been consulted. In the example already mentioned concerning the various alternatives for a layout of several deep-freeze rooms, the advantages and disadvantages also include aspects of fire protection, occupational safety, hygiene guidelines, and the traffic concept. These are outside the decision-making powers of my department, but it is imperative that they are included in the decision. Therefore, I not only explain these influencing factors to my employees but also define them as cornerstones that cannot be changed. In this way, I set a decision-making framework in which only the variables that can be influenced can be discussed. Other examples of co-determination are holding team meetings (time, length, location) or defining information flows (team members, medium, content).

New ideas do not automatically lead to support from the team, as change is often initially rejected out of human nature, as it is associated with uncertainty. To create an environment where new ideas are generated, I reverse certain perspectives. Two statements I have often heard on my team are "It's always been this way" and "It can't work." These are phrases that have come up often in my company and have been judged as traditional. Yet, these two phrases speak to two essential factors: change and feasibility. I prefer the positive phrases "What has changed?" or "What are the new conditions?" and "How could it work?" or "What does it take?". The change in language makes a difference in employee attitudes.

Areas of responsibility clearly defined by the company and by me as a manager ensure that employees have certain duties in this area, but also certain rights. I show my employees the goal; where possible, I let them define the way to get there themselves. If my department is given a task, it usually goes to the appropriate technical team or expert. If I receive a task for my department, I forward it for team action or refer the sender directly to the appropriate person. This means that I expect everyone in their area of responsibility to be proactive and not wait for me to delegate and set tasks. Only when I am needed in the solution finding process do I get involved. For example, if my department's production planning department receives an additional demand request from sales, my team independently checks the feasibility and consequences without being asked. For the final planning decision, I am involved by my employees if necessary. As a consequence of the areas of responsibility, issues are dealt without my direct knowledge, and I am not always able to give an opinion when an issue requires my input. Therefore, I have moved to being copied or briefed on relevant issues when emails are sent. This provides an assurance to my employees that they are acting within my knowledge. This is the case, for example, when materials are transferred from one warehouse to another.

I introduced new software (video conferencing, chat, call tracking) and hardware (tablets, laptops, company mobile phone) in my team to make flexible working (including home office) possible. For many, this was both a previously unknown freedom and a strong vote of confidence. However, precisely because home office was previously unknown to my team, rights were overstepped within the scope of the given freedom. For example, on-site appointments were cancelled without consulting me, citing home office as the reason, or the ability to work (availability and system access) at home was not ensured. Therefore, we have jointly defined rules in the team with regard to absences (hardware and software, availability, substitution, calendar transparency home office, illness, and vacation), to which everyone must adhere. Home office, for example, can only be used if all systems can also be operated from home and telephone forwarding has been set up. Home office, like any other absence, is entered by everyone for the team in the Outlook calendar. This creates clear expectations of behavior, as is also the case with a professional job.

In my opinion, co-determination and the assumption of responsibility are characterized by freedoms and limits as well as rights and duties. It is still a sensitive and difficult topic for my team. Through the standards and rules that we have introduced together in my department, I have noticed that it has become easier for the employees to classify and adapt themselves and their behavior.

3.3 Awakening Team Spirit

At our production site, there are commercial and industrial employees: two groups that, in my experience, don't want to feel like one team by definition. And then in these two groups, there are again smaller, social constructs that separate themselves from each other. At least that's how I found it in my department. My goal was to form a team out of all the small groups and individuals, professionally and emotionally. In the department, however, rejection was practiced at every opportunity, and distance was created. Therefore, I first began to break down and redefine designations and then fill them with life. For collaboration and data exchange, there is now a single shared drive "Logistics," in which the specialist sub-departments and their topics can be found. There are email distribution lists and messenger groups by department and a common one for all. The participants for meetings are selected based on the topic, depending on their area of responsibility.

Another issue is the distribution of tasks. I regularly re-evaluate the workload of each individual and redistribute it within the department if necessary. In holiday or sickness situations, everyone is called upon, not just the direct replacement. When necessary, everyone who can helps, not just those whose job description it is. It is important to me to be approachable by all. My schedule is unlocked to the extent that everyone on my team can see when I am in which appointment. On the one hand, this increases the basis of trust, and on the other hand, my team can reach me in necessary cases or know when I am available. Personally, although there is still a group leader level, I communicate intensively with all employees in my department. In doing so, I take care not to undermine my group leaders and coordinate closely with them. Although I was initially the link between the groupings, I make a point of ensuring that these links also take place without me. I observe this and specifically point it out to my team when necessary. Prior to my time as logistics manager, there was a logistics manager's office along with an anteroom. In my opinion, my team and I needed more proximity to each other and another meeting room. So, the former logistics manager's office was converted into a four-person office and the anteroom into a meeting room. I'm often out and about in the factory during the day and rather seldom at my workplace. I'm always sitting where I'm needed, where I need someone to sit, or where a seat is free (which is always the case due to vacation, home office, and illness). If I'm speaking confidentially or on the phone, I go to one of the meeting rooms.

As already mentioned, common team rules were defined in the team, which are essential for the cooperation. These apply to my team as well as to me. Calendar maintenance (entry of professional and private unavailabilities as well as making absences known) and appointment culture (no appointment without prompt reaction, notification of delays) are just a few of them. Team rules mean, among other things, that habits are redefined, a process that does not always go smoothly. It happens more often, for example, that appointments are responded to with a cancellation without giving a reason. For the sender, it is uncertain whether the appointment was just not sustainable in terms of time or whether a general attendance is not reasonable. It is therefore often necessary for me to remind people to follow the defined rules. Over time, my team has realized the benefits of these and uses them for their own work. As a result, adherence to the rules is becoming more and more routine. I have come to realize that how we communicate and act has a huge impact on how well or poorly we work together and therefore on the motivation, productivity, and effectiveness of a collaboration. Therefore, I place a high priority on this issue when providing feedback to my employees. I also proactively approach my team on a regular basis and ask for feedback on me and my behavior. This is a challenging process that is not yet working to my satisfaction. Very few employees are used to giving feedback to their own manager and often shy away from it. Honesty and openness are not always given directly. I also encourage my team to give each other feedback. Only through mutual reflection is it possible to optimize the team. Conflicts among each other do occur. In order to reduce tensions, I moderate appointments for cooperation with individual team members. In these meetings, the focus is on the way of working together, not on the content.

During my time at the company headquarters, I organized many employee events and experienced how small and big ideas were implemented. These were often heartfelt gestures, and money always played a subordinate role. The aim was always to create a team spirit and to enrich everyday working life in one place or another. We do this in the commercial team by having a regular breakfast. If I want to introduce a standard of team spirit, it helps me to get people excited about my idea and use them as additional multipliers. With one member of my team, we co-founded a company running group that meets regularly during lunch to run. This group in turn took part in a company run, and other people from the factory were inspired to do so. I also bought a soccer table and organized a soccer championship to coincide with the World Cup. Afterward, the table could still be used during the breaks. Every year in December, I do an Advent calendar event where each participating employee contributes a gift and receives another in return on a certain day. Such events help to bring the company and the employees closer together. However, it is important not to create any coercion. Every employee is different and not everyone enjoys the same things. For example, some are more sociable or sporty than others.

From my experience, being intentional about my team's needs, creating equity, and focusing on how I work together have really helped build team spirit in my department. I see more efficient and effective teamwork than was previously the case. The employees also say they feel more comfortable in the new team structure and are more motivated to tackle tasks together.

4 My Conclusion and Outlook

In retrospect, I see the biggest challenge of my value-oriented people management as being that values and culture in general are often still given very low priority, both by one's own team and by other departments. The connection between values and employee performance is often not known. Since values are not measurable, their positive influence is rarely present. In my experience, a value orientation is only accepted by the management level if the performance of the team concerned is good or even only if there is proof of success that the value orientation is correct. Another challenge for me is the issue of time. Especially when values of different parties were far apart from the beginning, change needs time and patience of the manager. Not all employees will adapt at the same speed and not always in the same direction, so conflict occurs along the way. This is only natural, and I try not to let it demotivate me or even sway me from my path. It takes time to understand and accept values. Too much pressure can have a counterproductive effect on individuals. It helps to make values tangible and tangible instead of just naming them. And finally, values are not a trend; they do not undergo permanent change. Many impulses come from outside, be it from one's own company or from the economy. Nevertheless, I preserve my own values and only adapt their implementation. In addition to external influences, I constantly check internally whether values are being lived. This applies to my employees as well as to me as a manager. For example, when I say that as a manager, I am accessible to everyone, I make sure that I am approachable and present. This means, for example, being on site occasionally in the evening or at night when working a 24-hour shift model. Living your values is not always easy or pleasant, but it's the only way to establish what you believe in the long term and sustainably.

Despite these challenges, or perhaps because of them, a major process of change has taken place in terms of culture and the values attached to it over the last few years that I have been running the department. The change in values in my team has developed slowly but steadily. It has been marked by conflicts and setbacks. Overall, there has been an increase in motivation and cooperation. My team has given me positive feedback on the changes at many points. Even those who initially doubted or had problems adjusting, I was able to convince in many places. I kept my initial values but adjusted in some places in terms of their implementation. Using the example of the Corona crisis, an unpredictable and very special event, I can see that the value framework I have created enables my employees to meet the required dynamics of change of any kind in a stable manner. It is in terms of co-determination and the accompanying acceptance of responsibility that I see the most significant change in the team. The participation of the employees is already internalized in many places and is automatically applied. For example, many people want the team to vote on decision-making processes, and employees like to get involved proactively in issues.

As positive as the changes achieved so far are, they still need more time to turn into stability. Ultimately, I am developing a suitable leadership style myself based on a consistent leadership culture, which I have not yet lived in a continuously stable manner. Many obstacles have not yet been completely cleared out of the way. In a next step, I plan to revise structures and roles according to the values at hand. But at least one thing has already been achieved: my employees no longer leave their heads with the gatekeeper.

Stephanie Bräuer completed a Bachelor's degree in Foreign Trade/International Management at the University of Applied Sciences in Hamburg with a focus on Strategic Management. She then completed her Master's degree in Supply Chain Management at the Rijksuniversiteit Groningen (Netherlands). Stephanie Bräuer has been working at Carl Kühne KG (GmbH & Co.) since 2016. She has been Logistics Manager at the production site in Berlin since 2018.

What Do HR Professionals Do When Value-Based Leadership Is Introduced But Not Lived?

Diana Roth

Abstract

Often, the actual practice experienced differs greatly from the theory. In this chapter, I, as a human resources manager, report on the hurdles that often have to be overcome when introducing value-oriented leadership. I explain which opportunities I have used so that managers not only know and understand value-oriented leadership but also live it in their departments and companies.

1 Now Is the Time! Our Managers Lead in a Value-Oriented Way!

Our CEO loved conventions. Since he was a speaker himself, he always came back to the company afterward with a backpack full of good ideas. In the Monday meeting with all the managers, the sales manager and I as the HR manager usually received not only input but also clear assignments.

On one such Monday in February, he spoke enthusiastically about value-based leadership. His eyes sparkled as he said, "What is crucial for modern companies is how people are treated there. A company like ours has it in its own hands to attract and retain valuable employees. That, dear people, is something you must be aware of!"

The executives present took it calmly. And I suspected what each individual really thought of it – namely, at best, not much.

D. Roth (✉)
Stettlen, Switzerland
e-mail: kontakt@dianarothcoaching.com

J. Lange (ed.), *Value-Oriented Leadership in Theory and Practice*,
https://doi.org/10.1007/978-3-662-65883-3_12

But I was immediately hooked. I had only just read a book on the subject and had already tried to get the CEO excited about this leadership model. However, I still fell on deaf ears.

Sometimes it just takes a push from the outside for new things to happen.

The CEO gave me a clear mandate that day: "Value-based leadership will be implemented – and immediately!"

I was thrilled, bought more books, and immediately started looking for a trainer who was specialized in this very value-based leadership.

2 Introduction of Value-Oriented Leadership

Due to my good HR network, I quickly found what I was looking for. The experienced trainer agreed and worked out a concept on my behalf on how the new leadership culture could be introduced in our company within 1.5 years. He then presented this plan in a Monday meeting of the department heads. There were plenty of discussions and objections, but after 2 h, we had reached an agreement.

This cleared the way for the next step. The training had to be budgeted for. Our finance manager had set aside a small amount for team development for the year. However, this turned out to be too low. So, a re-budget was drafted based on the trainer's quote. The board reluctantly nodded it off.

As so often in SMEs, another 6 months went by, but then we finally took off, full of optimism.

The kick-off would be a 2-day workshop for managers. I carefully prepared this together with the trainer and had the full backing of the CEO. The seminar hotel in the beautiful Bernese Oberland was booked, and the invitations for the first day of training were sent out. I was looking forward to this event like a snow queen because I secretly hoped that this would also have a positive effect on our increasing fluctuation rate.

What I did not suspect at the time was that the project would be a long, grueling, but in the end very rewarding process. In retrospect, many of the stumbling blocks of this SME could have been avoided, and I would have expected more awareness from the trainer in this regard.

But well, these stumbling blocks were on our way, and therefore I would like to mention them here. You learn from experience, and it's nice that I can pass mine on here in this book.

2.1 The First Stumbling Block: The Managers

Leaders can be an enormous hurdle in change processes. I had not been aware of this until then. The introduction of SAP and the new digitalized processes, on the other hand, was like child's play.

Of the 22 managers invited, 17 were registered for the training. Unfortunately, only 14 attended – 1, moreover, with a conspicuous delay and an attitude that clearly showed what he actually thought of the event. Two colleagues had suddenly fallen ill; one had to unexpectedly visit an important customer in Hamburg.

The trainer did his best. He introduced the topic slowly and tried to create a common thematic basis first.

During this introduction, however, he was interrupted several times by the ringing mobile phone of the managing director. He, who had initiated this workshop and wanted to implement the method of value-oriented leadership, left the room several times mumbling an apology. He had to make a quick phone call to London. He was sorry; it was really very important.

The trainer hardly reacted, but then quickly suggested a first break and asked the CEO to talk. He calmly explained how important his attitude was for the managers present. The trainer made it very clear that he, as the managing director, was a role model and that the other managers would orientate themselves by him.

His words showed effect and our boss showed insight. The mobile phone remained silent for the rest of the workshop.

In the course of this first workshop day, we worked out the most important values of our company, as they had already been named in the mission statement. Satisfied with so many good results, we parted late in the evening.

The next workshop day started with a review of the results of the previous day. No sooner had the trainer once again named the values we had formulated and confirmed than a discussion began that was in no way purposeful about the value "clarity," which had still been unanimously accepted the previous day.

It lasted for a solid 2 h, during which I listened and watched in bewilderment.

Around noon, the coach finally stepped in. "Now here's where I make a point!" he interrupted forcefully, waiting until he had the group's undivided attention. He emotionlessly and matter-of-factly reflected his perceptions of the last few hours.

He described the initial delicate beating around the bush as well as the infantile laughter when someone reported a lateral-thinking employee. And he clearly noted a lack of focus on the actual topic of this workshop – namely, the value-based leadership method. At the end, he made his way to the center of the room – time for the Gretchen question, "Do you even want value-based leadership?" His gaze went from one to the other. "Let's stop talking about what you could or couldn't do. Let's talk turkey. There's an elephant in the room here, and I want you to address it."

Briefly, he left the room, returned from the hotel lounge with a red armchair, pushed it into the middle of the seminar room, and asked the CEO to take a seat, "Please!" The trainer made an inviting hand gesture around the room. And as if everyone had been waiting for it, everyone – from the CEO to the executive in the back row – got off their chest what was really on their mind in this context! It was loud, it was intense, but it was good – for everyone!

At the end of this second and last workshop day, the Charter of Values had been signed by everyone, and we knew how we wanted to proceed with its implementation and that there would have to be many more trainings until we would really be ready.

Subsequently, I regularly solicited feedback from participants. Instead of simply handing out a form, I zoomed in with the colleagues or even went over for a short chat. Acceptance of the new leadership method grew among managers with each training session. As the responsible HR manager, I then developed a leadership manual in which the values and the different levels of the leadership model were elaborated. After minor changes in consultation with the managers of our company, the manual was printed and distributed.

Since there had been some changes in the management level during the development phase for value-oriented leadership, the manual was immediately put to use: I was allowed to use it to instruct the new managers in value-oriented leadership.

Now it was time to sensitize the employees to the new management culture as well.

2.2 The Second Stumbling Block: The Employees

One hundred eighty employees were distributed over ten training sessions of just 5 h each. We were not allowed more time. And because managers only want to spare their employees for as long as absolutely necessary, the dates were set for 3 p.m.–8 p.m. with the approval of the CEO.

These were certainly not ideal conditions for winning over employees for such a project. Only grudgingly did the trainer and I go along with it. In order to promote cross-departmental cooperation, we made sure that the groups were made up of a good mix of employees from different departments.

The average age of all employees in the company was 45. So, there were many long-serving employees in the training sessions, and they had all already experienced multiple leadership changes. They then sat in the event with their arms folded and made it clear to the trainer: “I really have better things to do, but I have to …”.

When the trainer explained on the topic of appreciation that one cannot lead in a wrong way, there was not only laughter but also a lot of visible resistance. Even the explanation that value-oriented leadership means, among other things, that the manager leads appropriately to the world in which he lives did not change this. That superiors must not only see people’s differences but also acknowledge them. And that all managers in this company had already been sensitized to this.

It turned out in this training that we had two main types of employees.

Type 1: He values cooperation, dialogue, and collaboration with the other team members. He wants to participate in development and decision-making, because he knows that together we are even more successful.

However, it also became apparent that he tolerates weaknesses only to a limited extent. Despite everything: The working atmosphere is particularly important to him. Also, because he has the ambition to work and appear more productive and positive.

Type 2: Above all, he values an open relationship with the manager, who must necessarily have a high level of professional competence. He likes to work with managers who have goal-oriented guidelines. And he lets the manager know what he really needs to fulfil the job profile.

This insight had a significant influence on the implementation of value-based leadership. The managers received additional coaching to become aware of these two types of employees – represented in every team. We had no doubt: Only with this knowledge and basic information, which showed the demands and needs of all, would the implementation of the new leadership model succeed.

3 Difficulties in Implementation

It became clear relatively early on that although the courses, the manuals, and the checklists were a valuable support, the managers and thus also their teams had incredible implementation difficulties. One major hurdle was the sometimes very different leadership models in the individual departments:

- Leaders with a very authoritarian leadership style clearly emphasized their own understanding of the world and values and were initially unwilling to deviate from this.
- Leaders who wanted to be everyone's darling and never showed dominance and strength gave their employees enormous freedom but no value orientation.
- Managers who took no responsibility for achieving departmental goals and were mostly conspicuous by their absence were not accepted or tolerated.
- Finally, there were the managers who rejected any competitive management style. They were surrounded by employees who expected rewards for their work and dedication.

When the problem was identified, we looked for orientation in the Charter of Values, but as expected, not everyone found it here. The trainer and I often heard words like: "Yes, that's in the Charter of Values, but …."

You can imagine it: Bringing this colorful mixture down to a common denominator was a Herculean task.

It's been a long process. Small advances and major setbacks – just when the CEO quit. The new business manager saw only costs and no benefit in this project. I spoke to him with the tongues of angels and was finally able to convince him not to abandon the processes that were already underway and to stick with the project.

But it still took more than 3 years before I could say to a candidate in job interviews for the first time, "We live and breathe value-based leadership."

4 My Conclusion as a Personnel Manager

1. The introduction of this valuable leadership style must not only be desired by the CEO but explicitly supported at all stages.
2. Value-based leadership is a process that cannot be planned on a board.
3. The hurdles and stumbling blocks during the introduction and implementation in everyday work are part of it. They allow the whole thing to mature.
4. It is imperative that the HR department maintains a close relationship with the trainer to ensure the success of the project.
5. Managers need to be permanently sensitized in order to work out the clear added value for themselves.
6. Employees must be convinced and involved with a great deal of tact – right from the start and not just in a 5-h workshop.
7. It doesn't stop with the successful implementation of value-based leadership. That's where the work really begins. The ethics behind it must flow holistically into all processes.
8. Ideally, the HR manager should address the issue and also be given the competencies to influence all stages of the process.

Value-based leadership – the introduction and implementation are major tasks for any company. But it's worth it – for everyone involved in the process. It is internal and external personnel marketing, which reduces the average sick days, halves the fluctuation rate, allows employee satisfaction to skyrocket, and makes a significant increase in productivity possible. And I think a powerful weapon against the shortage of skilled workers and the war for talent.

Because one thing is certain: it is the companies with value-oriented leadership that will be successful in the coming years.

Diana Roth has been an HR leader, business coach, and speaker since 1984. She also works as an HR lecturer and specialist book author on the subject of HRM in Bern, Basel, and Zurich. With her podcast Abenteuer HRM (iTunes/Spotify), she covers weekly the topics around the topic of HR management and work environments. www.dianarothcoaching.com

MIX
Papier aus verantwortungsvollen Quellen
Paper from responsible sources
FSC® C105338

If you have any concerns about our products,
you can contact us on
ProductSafety@springernature.com

In case Publisher is established outside the EU,
the EU authorized representative is:
Springer Nature Customer Service Center GmbH
Europaplatz 3, 69115 Heidelberg, Germany

Printed by Libri Plureos GmbH
in Hamburg, Germany